THE AUTHOR

Wong Kiew Kit, popularly known as Sifu Wong, is the fo   ... successor of Venerable Jiang Nan from the famous Shaolin Monastery in China and Grandmaster of Shaolin Wahnam Institute of Kungfu and Qigong. He received the "Qigong Master of the Year" Award during the Second World Congress on Qigong held in San Francisco in 1997.

He is an internationally acclaimed author of books on the Shaolin arts and Buddhism including Introduction to Shaolin Kung Fu (1981), The Art of Qigong (1993), The Art of Shaolin Kung Fu (1996), The Complete Book of Tai Chi Chuan (1996), Chi Kung for Health and Vitality (1997), The Complete Book of Zen (1998), The Complete Book of Chinese Medicine (2002), The Complete Book of Shaolin (2002), Sukhavati:The Western Paradise (2002) and The Shaolin Arts (2002).

Since 1987, Sifu Wong has spent more time teaching qigong than kungfu, because he feels that while kungfu serves as an interesting hobby, qigong serves an urgent public need, particularly in overcoming degenerative and psychiatric illnesses.

Sifu Wong is one of the few masters who have generously introduced the once secretive Shaolin Qigong to the public, and has helped many people to obtain relieve or overcome so-called "incurable" diseases like hypertension, asthma, rheumatism, arthritis, diabetes, migraine, gastritis, gall stones, kidney failure, depression, anxiety and even cancer.

He stresses the Shaolin philosophy of sharing goodness with all humanity, and is now dedicated to spreading the wonders and benefits of the Shaolin arts to people all over the world irrespective of race, culture and religion.

THE COMPLETE BOOK OF

SHAOLIN

COMPREHENSIVE PROGRAM FOR PHYSICAL, EMOTIONAL, MENTAL AND SPIRITUAL DEVELOPMENT

WONG KIEW KIT

Author of the bestselling *The Art of Chi Kung*

COSMOS

Published by Cosmos Internet Sdn Bhd
45C (3rd Floor) Jalan Pengkalan
Taman Pekan Baru, 08000
Sungai Petani, Kedah
Malaysia

Disclaimer
We caution all our readers to consult their primary health care provider or professional alternative health care practitioners as this publication should not be considered as medical advice to patients or readers. We encourage all our readers to consult and discuss both the advantages and disadvantages of alternative and complementary medicine, with their primary health care provider or professional alternative health care practitioners. By reading this publication, the reader agrees to the terms of this disclaimer and further waives any rights or claims he or she may have against the Publisher, Author and/or any other parties involved in the publication or the distribution of this publication.

Designed and layout by Saw Seng Aun

Printed in Malaysia by Sun Printers Sdn Bhd

ISBN 983-40879-1-8

CONTENTS

(B) SHAOLIN KUNGFU

INTRODUCTION

If you think this is a book on fighting art, you will be in for some pleasant surprises. Shaolin Kungfu, one of the most beautiful martial arts of the world, is neither the only nor the best of the many Shaolin arts, which range from poetry and medicine to Zen and Mahayana philosophy.

Wong Kiew Kit, a Shaolin grandmaster of over thirty years' experience, gives a fascinating and in-depth explanation of these arts in clear, enjoyable language. Martial artists will find amazing fighting techniques and methods for internal force training. Shaolin Qigong not only promotes health and vitality, but also provides hope to those suffering from "so-call incurable diseases" like hypertension, diabetes, sexual inadequacy and even cancer. Meditation, the supreme Shaolin art, trains the mind for more efficient daily work and play, and, at the highest level, leads to spiritual fulfilment, irrespective of race, culture and religion.

In accordance to Shaolin philosophy, readers are urged not to accept these claims on faith nor reputation, but practice these arts that are systematically explained in the book, and evaluate the claims base on their own experiences. True Shaolin disciples, the author says, do not tell lies.

LIST OF ILLUSTRATIONS

1
A Heavenly Vision
(How Shaolin Monastery Got Its Name)

In heaven above there is Zhulin Monastery; on earth below there is Shaolin Monastery.

The Legend of Shaolin

The Shaolin Monastery. The name itself spells magic to many people. Throughout the ages, it has been romantically linked to numerous sagas and parables involving great kungfu masters, spiritual teachers, generals, emperors as well as ordinary people. Poets sang odes to praise it, famous calligraphers engraved their writings in its many stone tablets, hostile armies razed the monastery to the ground, appreciative governments re-built it to greater glory, martial artists considered its fighting skills the pinnacle of achievements, spiritualists regarded this sacred temple as a fountain of inspiration, while its arts and philosophy have influenced and benefited millions of people in their daily lives.

Yet the Shaolin Monastery existed like a legend in the imagination of the populace — well known, highly esteemed and fascinating, but mysterious and awe-inspiring, because since its founding in the Northern Wei Dynasty in the 6th century, rulers of all succeeding dynasties consecrated the Shaolin Monastery as the temple of imperial worship, making it inaccessible to common people.

In 1928 the monastery suffered its third and most destructive fire in its long history: an angry warlord burnt the monastery for 45 days, resulting in the loss of invaluable treasure and property. This transformed the monastery into folklore. For the greater part of the twentieth century, many people wondered whether the temple was real or just a myth! Only recently, the Chinese government spent much money and effort to restore the monastery following its original model, and classified it as protected historical heritage, thus rekindling the concern for and excitement of the Shaolin tradition.

The Sacred Summit of Songshan

The fabulous Shaolin Monastery is situated at the Central Mountains of Songshan in the Henan Province of China. Songshan consists of two major ranges: the Taishi Mountain in the east, and the Shaoshi Mountain in the west. From afar, Songshan looks like "a pretty damsel having an afternoon nap in spring."

Songshan itself is rich in legends and history. It was the tradition of Chinese emperors, known as Sons of Heaven, to ascend Sacred Summits to pray to Heaven. There are five Sacred Summits in China, located in the five strategic positions: east, west, south, north and central; and Songshan is the Central Sacred Summit.

Ancient China was divided into nine provinces. Songshan is located in the Province of Henan, which was known as the Central Province in ancient times. It was the focus of religious and cultural activities, as well as military and political adventures. The two ancient capitals of China, Sian (later known as Changan) and Loyang, are in this region. The heroic expression, "Rains and winds from eight directions meet at the Central Province", gives us an idea of the romance and excitement of this area.

Taishi and Shaoshi, the two mountain ranges of Songshan, derive their names from an interesting legend. Although the Chinese civilization is not the oldest, it is the longest continuous civilization of the world. All the other great ancient civilizations, like those of the Egyptian, the Mesopotamian, the Mayan and the Indian, mysteriously disappeared from the surface of the earth. Historians have not discovered the cause of their extinction, but many believe that they were wiped off either by a big fire or by a big flood. In Chinese mythology, stories concerning the holocaust are not wide spread, but there are numerous myths about the great deluge. The Chinese civilization is able to survive the big flood because of their wise and dedicated Emperor Xia Yu, who was the ninth generation descendent of the famous Huang Di (or Hwang Ti), the Yellow Emperor, during the legendary period of Chinese prehistory.

Emperor Xia Yu was so busy combating the flood that although he passed his own house on three different occasions, he had no time to enter it. On one occasion his wife was just delivering their baby. Xia Yu could only pause at his door to listen to the infant's cry, then hurried away, not because he did not love the mother and the child, but because his care for his people was greater. This legend of "passing the door thrice without entering it" occurred at Songshan.

Xia Yu had two wives. If you are a supporter of monogamy (like I am), take consolation that having two wives — for an emperor — was an extremely modest gesture, for each Chinese emperor had more than three thousand wives all at the same time! If you know Chinese, you must have come across the character "an" (安), which means "peace". This character is made up of a "lady" (女) under a "roof" (宀), clearly warning that if you wish to have peace in the family, you can have only one wife under one roof. (Even emperors had their many wives under different roofs.) The Chinese characters had not yet been standardized during Xia Yu's time, but the wise emperor must have understood this important principle. So he placed his two wives under separate roofs — his "tai shi" or first wife on the eastern range of Songshan, and his "shao shi" or second wife on the west. That was how the Taishi Mountain and the Shaoshi Mountain derived their names.

By the way, Shaolin monks at the Shaoshi Mountain, were (and still are) not allowed to have any wives — not even first wives. But do not worry if you wish to practice Shaolin arts and still want to keep your wife (wives?); this celibacy rule did not, and does not, apply to secular Shaolin disciples.

Earthly Reflection of Heavenly Monastery

The Shaoshi Mountain with its many pinnacles is one of the most picturesque regions in China. Throughout the ages, poets and scholars have described the spectacular scenes at the Shaoshi Mountain with such beautiful expressions as "blossoming of the lotus flowers", "hundreds of birds fluttering in the wind", "gathering of heroic warriors", and "auspicious dancing of the dragon and the phoenix". Hence, long ago the saying "ascend Shaoshi Mountain, admire spectacular views" was already popular among travellers.

According to a legend, on the sixth day of the sixth month in the 19th year of Tai He of the Northern Wei Dynasty, which corresponds to the year C.E. 495, three travellers climbed the Shaoshi Mountain from different directions to admire the spectacular views. Ascending from the south was a Taoist priest, wearing a long grey gown with the well known yin-yang symbol embroidered in front. From the north was a Buddhist monk, wearing a plain saffron robe; while climbing from the western side was a rich landlord, elaborately dressed in fine silk decked with expensive jewels.

As the three travellers reached the summit, the weather suddenly changed. Clouds from the sky merged with mist rising from the earth, creating a hazy surrounding not unlike the grand void sometimes experienced in deep meditation. But the haze was so thick that the three men were unaware of each other's presence. They sat themselves on a huge, flat rock that shaped like a gigantic drum.

Presently they heard some talking. As they looked up, the haze parted, showing a grandiose view of heaven, with a majestic monastery nine sections deep, glittering in sublime light, and with three bold, golden characters "ZHU LIN SI", meaning "Monastery of the Bamboo Forest", written across the top of the grand entrance.

In front of this heavenly monastery a young novice monk was talking to an old master.

"Sifu," the boy asked, "since Zhulin Monastery has risen to heaven, will there be any monastery on earth?"

"Of course!" the master answered. "In heaven above there is Zhulin Monastery; on earth below there is Shaolin Monastery."

"But where is Shaolin Monastery?"

"Over there!" the old master pointed toward the south east, "at the northern side of the Shaoshi foothill — with the nine-lotus pinnacles in front and the five-bosom peaks behind, and with a majestic waterfall on the west supplying a crystal clear stream flowing towards the east."

This conversation in heaven was clearly heard by the three mortals on earth. They looked towards the direction pointed by the heavenly master. There it was! Amidst the greenery of the Shaoshi forest, they could see a magnificent monastery, in red bricks and jade-coloured tiles, seven sections deep, with three golden characters "SHAO LIN SI" boldly calligraphed on the top across the grand entrance.

The three men could not help uttering a cry of sheer wonder. But as their mundane utterance disturbed the cosmic vibration of the empyrean, the celestial vision blurred away, leaving the three mortals who suddenly realized, rather awkwardly, each other's presence. They hurriedly descended in their separate ways, each carrying some cherished thoughts in their heart.

The landlord said to himself, "If I build a house on this precious spot indicated by the celestial vision, money will flow in like water, and soon I will be the richest man on earth."

The priest, who was also an expert on geomancy, thought to himself, "This precious spot is along the dragon's vein with wonderful energy. If I move my family grave here, my descendants will be assured of power and prosperity, and many of them will become high officials in the imperial service."

The monk reflected pensively, "What a magnificent, sacred spot. If I build a temple here, I can help many people achieve enlightenment." He was so excited that he could not sleep. So in the night, he searched for that precious spot where he had seen the heavenly monastery in celestial light, and he found it between two majestic cypress trees.

"I must put something here as a token of my claim for the land to build a monastery." So the monk, who hardly had any worldly possessions with him, buried one of his tattered shoes between the giant trees.

At dawn the Taoist priest came to the same spot. "Splendid," he said to himself. "Luckily no one has placed any claim on the land." So he staked a pole into the ground to signify his claim.

Soon after sunrise the landlord arrived at the precious spot. He found the pole which the Taoist priest had staked into the ground. "Aha," he said, "this comes in handy for me to hang my hat as a token of my claim to this land."

Three days later the three men met again at the precious spot. Each of them had brought along their own team of workmen to start work on the land they had claimed. They soon quarrelled among themselves on who was the first to lay claim to the land, and none could emerge with a convincing argument.

Just then Emperor Xiao Wen and his imperial retinue passed by on route to admire the spectacular views of Shaoshi Mountain. After listening to their argument and witnessing their tokens of claim, the wise emperor announced,

"The hat is on top of the pole; this shows that the pole was staked earlier than the hat. The shoe is in the ground under the pole; this shows that the shoe was placed there before the pole. Hence this monk has first claim to the land."

The monk was extraordinary. His face was like a red olive fruit, his eyelashes like silkworms, and he had a lion's nose, thick lips and basin-shaped mouth, bushy beard and skin of dark copper hue. His name was Batuo, an Indian monk who had been in China for three years to spread Buddhism.

The Emperor, deeply impressed with Batuo, ordered the Governor of Henan and the local magistrate to aid the Buddhist monk to build the monastery. When Batuo requested the Emperor to name the monastery, His Majesty said,

"This is Shao Shi Mountain; and the two cypress trees form the Chinese character "Lin". The monastery shall be called Shao Lin."

Although the above story is fanciful, it provides some poetic and philosophical background to the founding of Shaolin Monastery. Many readers may find the vision of the heavenly monastery unbelievable or outlandish; but those familiar with the scientifically controlled experiments investigating ESP, or with the new world view inspired by the affinity between modern physics and ancient mysticism may not only find this vision acceptable, but even marvel at how easily yet deeply legends can reflect eastern wisdom on para-psychological and metaphysical matters.

A more factual — but less poetic — account is provided by documents like "Official Records of Dengfeng District", "History of Five Dynasties", and inscriptions on stone tablets at the Shaolin Monastery. These documents recorded that Batuo came from India to China to spread Buddhism. He was well received by Emperor Xiao Wen, who built the Shaolin Monastery for him to translate Sanskrit Buddhist texts into Chinese.

The Shaolin Monastery is therefore not just an ordinary monastery. Its various buildings and their accompanying legends, to be described in the next chapter, are even more extraordinary.

2
The Fabulous
Shaolin Monastery

(Legends and Significance of the Monastery Halls)

Even just judging from the sheer size of the monastery complex and the role it had played in charting Chinese history, it is not surprising why the Shaolin Monastery has been called the foremost monastery beneath heaven.

Foremost Monastery Beneath Heaven

Why is the Shaolin Monastery also called "the foremost monastery beneath heaven"? One of the many reasons is that it was the imperial temple where Chinese emperors prayed to heaven on behalf of the Chinese people, as discussed in the previous chapter. Another reason will become clear when you have read this chapter, and other reasons will reveal themselves as the book unfurls.

Situated at the scenic Central Mountains of Song-shan, about 15 kilometers from the Henan provincial capital of Dengfeng, the extensive monastery complex is actually made up of numerous buildings, namely the Monastery Proper, the Forest of Pagodas, Temple of First Patriarch, Temple of Second Patriarch, Temple of Third Patriarch, and Cave of Bodhidharma.

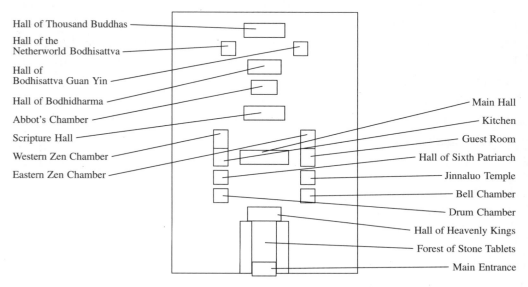

Fig 2.1 The Shaolin Monastery Proper

The Monastery Proper, which is usually called the Shaolin Monastery itself, consists of seven sections, Fig 2.1.   The first section is the Grand Entrance, which is known as "Mountain Gate" in Chinese. At the top of the Grand Entrance in bold, magnificent calligraphy is the name of the Shaolin Monastery in Chinese characters, SHAO LIN SI, which were specially written by the renowned regal calligrapher, the Qing Emperor Kang Xi, and which means the Monastery in the forest of the Shaoshi Mountain.

Inside the building of the Grand Entrance are found some famous Chinese calligraphic works.   One of the most beautiful, in calligraphy as well as in meaning, is a pair of poetic couplets translated below. Though much of its beauty is inevitably lost in the process of translation, there is still enough left behind for our appreciation.   The depth of its philosophy in contrast with the simplicity of its expression is most charming.

This earthly place in heaven, this is the foremost of famous mountains of the four seas.

Transmitted by heart beyond words, this is the primordial of religious teachings of the ten directions.

These poetic expressions, with gentle touches of Chan (Zen), gracefully remind us of the important role Shaolin Monastery played in the Meditation School of Buddhism. You will read an example of transmission by heart beyond words in a later part of this chapter.

Behind the Grand Entrance, on both sides of the central pathway leading to the next building, is found a permanent treasure of Chinese culture — the imposing Forest of Stone Tablets. On these huge stone tablets were engraved precious and lasting examples of famous different styles of Chinese calligraphy by some of the greatest calligraphers of China, such as Wang Zi Jing of the Tang Dynasty, Mi Di of the Song Dynasty, Zhao Mang Fu of the Yuan Dynasty, Dong Qi Zhang of the Ming Dynasty, and Emperor Qian Long of the Qing Dynasty. Many people call this Forest of Stone Tablets, "The Complete Work of Chinese Calligraphy."   There were even inscriptions carved in foreign languages, such as Sanskrit, Japanese and Arabic. It is a rich, rare source for historical studies too, as many of these stone tables also recorded important contemporary events of their times.

The second section of the Monastery Proper was the Hall of Heavenly Kings, which is now in ruin as a result of the 1928 fire. There was once a gigantic bell weighing 11,000 *jin* (Chinese pounds), whose sound when hit could be heard 30 *li* (Chinese miles) away. This unique bell was damaged in the fire, but has been partially restored by the Chinese government.

The next section is the Main Hall, which was also destroyed by the fire, but has been restored partially. On the eastern side of the Main Hall is the Jinnaluo Temple, which houses a statue of Jinnaluo, a legendary figure regarded as the Saint of Shaolin staff techniques. On the western side is the Sixth Patriarch Temple, built in honor of Hui Neng, who was significantly responsible for the transformation of Buddhism from its Indian origin to a distinctively Chinese style.

After the Main Hall is the Scripture Hall where monks listened to sermons, chanted sutras and practiced meditation. It is also called the Library as priceless scriptures, kungfu classics and other invaluable texts were kept here. Some of the earliest Buddhist texts brought over from India by devoted pilgrims, were translated into Chinese at this Library. The Shaolin Monastery also abounded with stories of ambitious martial artists risking their lives trying to steal kungfu secrets from this Library. If you are keen on such secrets, you no longer have to risk your life nowadays to get them. Many of these secrets have been published (mainly in Chinese) and are sold in bookshops! Some of these secrets will be discussed in later chapters.

The Abbot's Chamber is behind the Scripture Hall. The Abbot of Shaolin Monastery is often called "Fang Zhang", which literally means "a square of ten feet", though he is neither a square nor of ten feet. The term was derived from the practice that being the head of a monastery, the abbot was allowed the luxury of more space for his slumber; other monks were provided with planks measuring about two by five feet — hardly enough even for their physical bodies to be stretched. Buddhist monks, therefore, sleep lying sideways, with one arm under their head as a pillow, their legs bent, and the other arm on top of their thigh — hence, the expression "sleep like a bow" in the Shaolin Monastery. This position, which you may find in statues of the reclining Buddha, was the usual position of the Buddha when resting.

Hui Ke Seeking Enlightenment

The next building is known as Bodhidharma Chamber, named after the First Patriarch of the Shaolin arts, namely kungfu, chi kung and Chan (or Zen) Buddhism. It is also known as Standing-in-the-Snow Pavilion, which refers, however, not to the pavilion standing in the snow (though it actually stood there in the open every time it snowed); but it refers to Hui Ke, the Second Patriarch.

Hui Ke, who had been a monk in the Shaolin Monastery for some time, begged Bodhidharma to teach him the way to enlightenment, but he was continuously rejected. One day he stood waiting outside this chamber, while Bodhidharma practiced meditation inside. Heavy snow was falling, but Hui Ke persisted. He waited and waited until the amount of snow fallen on the ground reached his knee. Finally, Bodhidharma emerged from the chamber.

"What are you doing here, Hui Ke?" Bodhidharma asked innocently.

"Sifu, I am waiting for you to teach me the way," Hui Ke answered patiently.

"You can keep standing there, but I am not teaching you the way."

"But, when can you teach me, so that I can be enlightened?"

"Only when the snow turns red," Bodhidharma replied calmly.

Equally calmly, Hui Ke severed his left arm! Blood gushed out and dropped on to the ground, making the snow red. Yet Hui Ke stood upright, and even smiled serenely.
Bodhidharma smiled too. A sense of joyous tranquillity enveloped them.

"What is troubling you?" Bodhidharma asked.

"My mind!"

"Bring out your mind so that I will pacify it."

"It is strange," Hui Ke replied, "now that I search for my mind, I cannot find it."

"You have attained enlightenment. And you are now my successor to spread Buddhism."

This touching story has a deep meaning for me. When I first read it, I was angry at Bodhidharma, and considered Hui Ke foolish. But as I grew in my development, I gradually understood and appreciated its significance, and I would have done the same, had I been Hui Ke or Bodhidharma. This is also an example of "instant" enlightenment, where the final, arcane teaching was transmitted intuitively from master to disciple by way of the heart beyond words.

It is not easy to explain this type of experience intellectually, because it belongs to the realm of intuitive wisdom and not just rational knowledge. Nevertheless it may suffice to mention two significant points.

One, sacrificing an arm is nothing compared to achieving spiritual enlightenment. Again, it is not easy to appreciate this statement unless one has attained certain level of spiritual development. Most people, understandably, will value their arm more than enlightenment.

Two, Bodhidharma was compassionate, not cruel. With his intuitive wisdom, he knew that, that was the best way to help Hui Ke achieve enlightenment. Had he taught his disciple some meditation techniques to practice towards enlightenment, Hui Ke would have just achieved that, i.e. knowing some techniques. At best, Hui Ke would have to practice these techniques for some time before he could one day, hopefully, be enlightened. But now, the enlightenment was instantaneous. What better gift could a master give his disciple?

Meditation, enlightenment and the process of heart to heart transmission will be discussed in some detail in later chapters. Meanwhile, let us examine a more down-to-earth and perhaps better known aspect of the Shaolin arts -- Shaolin Kungfu — as we proceed to the next and last section of the Shaolin Monastery.

The Hall of Lohans

The last section of the main monastery complex is the Hall of Thousand Buddhas, also known as Pilu Hall. Art students who think that Chinese painting is just water color of mountains and streams on paper scrolls, will be in for some surprise as they enter this hall. The hall houses the famous gigantic wall painting covering 300 square meters, depicting 500 Lohans (or Arahants) paying homage to the Pilu Buddha, the Chinese name for Vairocana Buddha. The sheer size of the painting is daunting enough; but that is not its most amazing aspect. The Lohans were not only vividly painted a few hundred years ago, but each of them exhibited a different typical facial expression. This hall, the biggest in the whole monastery complex, is therefore sometimes called the Hall of Lohans. It was here that advanced Shaolin Kungfu was taught.

From the many kungfu students, some good disciples were chosen for further privileged training in this Hall of Lohans, which was out of bound to other ordinary students. From these a very few disciples were further selected, based on their excellent character as well as high kungfu attainment, to receive very special training in the Bodhidharma Chamber, where they are taught top Shaolin secrets. These very special disciples were called "inner-chamber disciples". Hence, nowadays, drawing from the Shaolin tradition, those students in any fields of endeavor, who are favored by their teachers and who have reached a very high level of achievement, are said to have reached the level of "promotion into the hall, entrance into the chamber".

Another remarkable feature that strikes many modern visitors to the Hall of Lohans is the forty eight clearly discernible foot impressions on the floor. These impressions were made by past Shaolin monks while practicing kungfu — by repeating their foot stamping actions millions of times! These foot impressions are a visible reminder of an essential principle of kungfu training which many students neglect to observe: that is, the essence of kungfu training is improving skills and enhancing force (not merely learning elaborate techniques) — the process of which necessitates practicing simple actions over and over again, many, many, many times.

On the western side of the Hall of Lohans is the Hall dedicated to the Bodhisattva of the Netherworld. A Bodhisattva is one who has become a Buddha, the enlightened one who is free from the endless cycles of birth, death and rebirth. But because of his great compassion, a Bodhisattva voluntarily postpones entering Buddhahood so that he can help other beings to achieve enlightenment. This particular Bodhisattva, known as Di Zang Wang in Chinese, or Ksitigarbha in Sanskrit, chooses to go to the Netherworld to help lost souls.

The philosophical concept represented by this Hall of the Netherworld Bodhisattva may brighten the spirit of many people. Some people have a morbid idea of death, especially about the Netherworld. According to Buddhist belief, death is nothing to be afraid of — it is, from another perspective, the birth into another plane of existence. According to Buddhism, life is everywhere, and our world is only one of countless habitable worlds in countless galaxies where there are also countless heavens. Even in our own world system, there are more than twenty realms of heavens, compared to only one realm each of humans, demi-gods, spirits and hells. Even those who go to the Netherworld need not despair. Di Zang Wang and other compassionate teachers will be there to help whoever desire help, irrespective of the religion these lost souls believe in.

We will now enter another very different world —the world of martial art. The hall on the eastern side is of particular interest to martial artists all over the world. This is the White Robe Hall dedicated to the Great Compassionate Guan Yin Bodhisattva, who is often translated into English as the Goddess of Mercy, although in Buddhist thought, a Bodhisattva is many levels higher than a god or goddess. This hall is therefore also known as the Hall of Guan Yin.

Guan Yin Bodhisattva, known as Kannon in Japanese, Chen-re-zig in Tibetan and Avalokitesvara in Sanskrit, is extremely popular among Mahayana Buddhists. She is a Bodhisattva of boundless compassion who will see and listen to all sufferings, and will give assistance to whoever asks for it. "Seek and you will be given" is a saying taught in Buddhist as well as other religious philosophies. Most people may think this is just too good to be true, but its great philosophical truth can be explained by such Buddhist wisdom like karma being generated by thought, and the phenomenal world being a creation of mind.

In this hall are found some splendid wall paintings of martial art. If you wonder at the seemingly incongruence of finding rich martial art material in a hall dedicated to the embodiment of mercy, you will be pleasantly surprised at the depth of Shaolin philosophy. Shaolin teachings have always stressed the love of humanity, and Shaolin Kungfu, being the most wide-spread expression of the Shaolin teachings, is built upon and manifests this principle of compassion. This principle will become obvious in later chapters.

One of the famous paintings in this hall is the fresco showing "Thirteen Shaolin Monks Rescuing the Tang Emperor", which recorded the great contribution of Shaolin in the establishment of the Tang Dynasty. The modern popular international movie on the Shaolin Monastery, the first of its kind in Shaolin's history, was based on this painting.

The most fascinating paintings for martial artists are two huge frescoes on the southern and the northern walls of this hall, respectively depicting Shaolin monks in various unarmed kungfu patterns, and Shaolin monks practicing with a great variety of weapons. These pictures are a permanent, genuine record of the way Shaolin Kungfu was actually performed during the Ming Dynasty, the time these frescoes were painted; and hence they can serve as a reliable yardstick to judge how valid some modern martial arts are in claiming to be Shaolin styles. This hall, therefore, is aptly called the Hall of Shaolin Kungfu.

We have just examined the various main buildings of the Monastery Proper, some relevant stories and related aspects of Shaolin philosophy. Do not worry if you feel a bit dazzled by the abundant material; anyone would, when faced with the space of probably the world's largest monastery, and the time of over a thousand and fifty years compressed into a chapter. We may have a better perspective if we list out these buildings, from front to back, and their related concepts:

1. Grand Entrance — a touch of Zen.
   Forest of Stone Tablets — The Complete Work of Chinese Calligraphy.
2. Hall of Heavenly Kings — in ruins.
3. Main Hall — in ruins.
   Jinnaluo Temple — Shaolin staff techniques.
   Six Patriarch Temple — Chinese Buddhism.
4. Scripture Hall — Buddhist and kungfu texts.
5. Abbot's Chamber — sleeping like a bow.
6. Bodhidharma Chamber — transmission by heart.
7. Hall of Thousand Buddhas — foot impressions.
   Bodhisattva of Netherworld — compassion.
   White Robe Hall — mercy and Shaolin Kungfu.

Pagodas, Temples and the Shadow-Rock

Besides the Monastery Proper, there are many other auxiliary buildings spread all over the very extensive Shaolin Monastery complex.

About 300 meters towards the west of the Monastery Proper is the Forest of Pagodas, one of the most important historical relics in China. This is different from the Forest of Stone Tablets situated behind the Main Entrance of the Monastery Proper.

From the layman's viewpoint, this Forest of Pagodas is the final resting ground of great Shaolin monks, though from a higher spiritual viewpoint (like that of the Mahayana Buddhist), the consciousness or mind of these monks or of anybody, does not die.

But what was buried were not their bodies. According to traditional Buddhist rites, the physical remains were cremated, and inside the bodies of great monks were often found "crystals". These crystals, which are often called relics, resulted from the crystallization of chi or energy. They are probably the products of energy centers or chakras. This is an area of knowledge still generally unknown in the west. These crystals (real solid material that you can see and feel) were regarded as treasure, and were kept inside the pagodas. This Forest has a rich collection of about 220 pagodas of every dynasty since the Northern Wei, but the majority were of the Ming period, including those of Ming princes and princesses who had renounced their luxurious palace lives to seek spiritual fulfillment.

There are three temples in the Shaolin complex dedicated to the first three Patriarchs of Zen Buddhism. It is of interest to note that although Batuo is the founder of the Shaolin Monastery, Bodhidharma is honored as the First Patriarch. This is because the type of Buddhism preached by Batuo was Hinayana Buddhism, which emphasized personal enlightenment; whereas the type preached by Bodhidharma was Mahayana Buddhism, which included helping others to attainment enlightenment. It was Mahayana Buddhism that became established in the Shaolin Monastery, as well as in the whole of China. As Bodhidharma was the founder of Chan (or Zen) Buddhism, a major school of Mahayana Buddhism, he is venerated as the First Patriarch. Zen Buddhism is at the same time the easiest and hardest type of Buddhism. You will understand why, when you read about Zen Buddhism in a later chapter.

The Temple of the First Patriarch is an architectural wonder. It was almost exclusively built using wood, yet its moon-shaped beams and other supports have remained intact for nearly a thousand years. The Temple of the Second Patriarch is dedicated to Hui Ke, Bodhidharma's successor; and the Temple of the Third Patriarch is dedicated to Seng Can, the successor of Hui Ke.

There is no Temple of the Fourth Patriarch at the Shaolin complex because Seng Can's successor, Dao Xin, moved to Dongshan Temple in Huangmei District of Hubei Province, where the Fifth Patriarch, Hong Jen, also taught. Hong Jen's successor, Hui Neng the Sixth Patriach, moved further south, to Baolin Temple in Cao Xi District of Guangdong Province. Hui Neng did not appoint a sole successor as the Seventh Patriarch, because he wanted many of his disciples to spread Zen Buddhism. Hence, historically there were altogether six patriarchs in Chan or Zen Buddhism, and three of them taught Zen Buddhism at the Shaolin Monastery, illustrating how important Shaolin is in Zen — a fact many people, including Zen enthusiasts themselves, may not be aware!

Behind the Monastery Proper at one of the five bosom peaks, is the Cave of Bodhidharma. This was where Bodhidharma meditated for nine years facing a cave wall, so intensely that the rock surface was imprinted with his image! This rock, known as the Rock with Bodhidharma's Shadow, is now exhibited in the Hall of Thousand Buddhas. A noted scholar, Xiao Yuan Ji, inscribed on a stone tablet the following lines with a touch of Zen about this rock:

There is a rock in Shaolin, which is a person.
It is clearly a person; and it is clearly a rock.
What kind of rock? A face-person rock.
What kind of person? A face-rock person.
He is a face-rock Buddha,
A prince, meditating for nine years,
He becomes a Buddha
Becoming a Buddha, his body becomes void,
And his body enters the spirit of the rock,
And the rock resembles his body,
And all schools are united by Shaolin.

The Defender of Righteousness

The Shaolin Monastery complex, which covers almost the whole of Shaoshi Mountain, is probably the biggest in the world. The numerous buildings, including those in the Monastery Proper, were not built all at the same time, but were added on during different dynasties. At its height, there were two thousand monks staying in the Shaolin Monastery. The monks were classified into four types: administrative monks, research monks, service monks and martial art monks.

While the long history of the Shaolin Monastery was glorious, with many emperors bestowing it with honors and gifts, there were also painful periods. In the year 574, Emperor Zhou Wu Di blamed the economic unproductivity of Buddhist monks and Taoist priests for the country's depression, and decreed that all temples in the empire be closed. However his successor, Emperor Jing Di, reopened the temples six years later, and Shaolin Monastery was renamed "Zhi Hu Monastery", meaning "Climbing-up-a-Mountain Monastery". This new name was unpopular, and the next year when Northern Zhou Dynasty was replaced by Sui Dynasty, Shaolin Monastery resumed its original name as well as received new land from the new emperor.

The Shaolin Monastery suffered three disastrous fires. The first fire was towards the end of the Sui Dynasty about the year 618, when rebels attacked the Monastery. The second fire was caused by the revolutionary "Red Band Army" about the year 1368 at the end of the Yuan Dynasty, whose emperors also bestowed many favors to Shaolin. The third fire was caused by war-lords in 1928 during the republican period.

There were also subsidiary temples under the Shaolin Monastery. Some of these are extensive and famous in their own right, such as Longtan Temple (meaning the Temple of Dragons' Lake) in Shandong Province, and Sichan Temple (the Western Temple of Zen) in Guangdong Province.

You may be surprised to know that there were two Shaolin Monasteries in China. Besides the one situated at Songshan in the north, the other Shaolin Monastery was built in Quanzhou in Fujian Province in south China by the Ming Dynasty. Though it was smaller than the Songshan Shaolin Monastery, the Fujian Shaolin Monastery played a very important role in the teaching and spread of Shaolin Kungfu in the south.

During the succeeding Qing Dynasty, this Fujian Shaolin Monastery became a center for revolutionaries loyal to the former Ming Dynasty. Hence the Qing army, with the help of mercenary martial art experts from Tibet, surprised and razed the Monastery to the ground. Some Shaolin masters escaped and spread the Shaolin arts and philosophy in south China and overseas. One of them was the Venerable Jiang Nan, who passed on the Shaolin arts through three generations to me. Most Shaolin schools in various parts of the world today owe their lineage from this southern Shaolin Monastery.

The Shaolin values of righteousness and perseverance ultimately prevailed. Shaolin disciples descendent from this southern Monastery later helped Dr Sun Yat Sen to overthrow the decadent Qing Dynasty and establish the first Chinese republic. The present Chinese government has erected a stone tablet at the site of this former Fujian Shaolin Monastery.

At the present time, some people have the mistaken impression that Shaolin disciples are revolutionary by nature, or are frequently engaged in secret society activities. This is because of the closeness in time to the patriotic and sacrificial involvement of Shaolin disciples in Dr Sun Yat Sen's secret societies in overthrowing the unpopular Qing Dynasty. If we examine the history of Shaolin in its proper perspective, we can clearly see that Shaolin disciples were always supportive of good governments, and had often helped to overcome internal oppression and foreign aggression, such as helping the Tang Emperor to subdue oppressive rebels, and helping the Ming Emperor to repulse Japanese naval attacks. This is in line with the Shaolin philosophy of upholding righteousness.

Even just judging from the sheer size of the monastery complex and the role it had played in charting Chinese history, it is not surprising why the Shaolin Monastery has been called "the foremost monastery beneath heaven." There are, of course, other reasons for its importance and greatness, and in the next chapter we shall examine generally the various Shaolin arts that have influenced and benefited both eastern and western societies for many centuries.

3
Fit For Emperors And Generals

(Precious Arts of Shaolin)

Even if you can master only one of the three Shaolin treasures, you will have achieved, in the words of a popular saying, a precious art that is more valuable than even the art of changing stones to gold by touch!

The Three Living Treasures

Of the numerous living treasures derived from the Shaolin Monastery, three stand out prominently. They are chi kung, kungfu and meditation. In the past these Shaolin treasures were kept within the monastery walls, taught only to privileged disciples who had proven themselves worthy of these fascinating arts. Now you do not have to become a Shaolin monk to learn them; they are available to you in this book. Nevertheless, merely reading about them is not enough, though it will give you interesting knowledge and reading pleasure; you need to invest some time and effort to practice these fascinating arts, and if you wish to get the best benefits you have to learn from a genuine master. What benefits can we get from these Shaolin arts? Very briefly, chi kung gives us health and longevity; kungfu provides vitality and enables us to defend ourselves when needed; and meditation brings us to our highest and greatest achievements!

Health is not merely being free from illness; but includes enjoying our food, sleeping soundly, being amiable to all beings around us even though some of them may get on our nerves, having mental freshness and experiencing inner peace. Longevity, to be desirable, is not merely enduring old age; but a continuation of youthfulness into our mellow years approximating our potential life span.

Shaolin Chi Kung provides some excellent ways to achieve health and longevity. It may surprise some readers to find out that many of the Shaolin methods to achieve excellent health are performed in elegant, gentle manners, quite unlike the vigorous, demanding activities of typical physical exercises like gymnastics, body building and aerobics.

Moreover, unlike many sports and games where your performance starts to go downhill after your peak at twenty five or thirty, the health and other benefits of Shaolin Chi Kung increases with age! You will find, for example, that at fifty you are less likely to fall sick, sleep and eat better, and produce more satisfactory work than you were at twenty five. Why is this so? Because Shaolin Chi Kung develops you internally as well as externally, so that all your body systems, mental as well as physical, continues to function naturally at their optimum.

In this way — maintaining and promoting all the natural functions of our body (the psyche and physique as one unity) — Shaolin Chi Kung enables us to live as fully as possible our potential life span, which most scientists agree to be at least 120 years. Hence, if you practice Shaolin Chi Kung conscientiously (which, incidentally, is an enjoyable experience), you can expect to live to a ripe old age, still with your body systems functioning properly.

Beauty in Poetic Motion

Aiming for excellence is a cardinal aspect of Shaolin philosophy. Shaolin disciples aim more than just living a healthy long life; they want their life to be meaningful and rewarding for themselves as well as for others.

In order to lead a more meaningful and rewarding life, besides having health and longevity, we need vitality — the energy and zest that enable us to get the best from our work and play every day of our life. Practicing Shaolin Kungfu will give us this vitality. Even more, Shaolin Kungfu enables us to defend ourselves or our loved ones if the need unexpectedly arises, hence giving us tremendous confidence and security that come from the awareness that we can handle any eventualities.

Shaolin Kungfu is the best and most beautiful martial art in the world (please see Chapter 14 for justification of this claim). It is not only very effective for self-defense, but it also provides an excellent system for developing such qualities like perseverance, tolerance, courage, discipline and the ability to make fast, sound decisions — qualities which, in our modern law-abiding society, are probably more useful than mere fighting skills.

Seeing a performance of good Shaolin Kungfu is seeing beauty in poetic motion. It is a poetry of artistic forms, courage, strength, agility, precision and gracefulness in rhythmic combination. Shaolin Kungfu force is bewildering. How and why, for example, can Shaolin masters be so powerful yet so calm and gentle, or can spar for hours yet do not feel tired? Shaolin Kungfu principles often reveal some profound wisdom. What would you do, for example, when your arm is held by an opponent twice your size, or when you are attacked by numerous aggressors at the same time? Such abilities and knowledge, which were once employed for effective fighting, can now be fruitfully transferred to our work, play and daily peaceful living.

Enjoying good health is the basis of Shaolin philosophy, and being able to look after ourselves no matter what happens, is an important aim of the Shaolin arts. These accomplishments symbolize two fundamental stages in life's journey to attain the ultimate goal. The first stage of good health lays the foundation; the second stage of courage and perseverance resembles the intermediate growth. What, then, is the ultimate goal? It is none other than the supreme achievement of every person — unconscious to him (or her) if he is not ready, but inevitable when he is sufficiently developed to transcend the physical.

A Way to Enlightenment

The ultimate goal is spiritual fulfillment, irrespective of whichever religion the seeker professes, or claims not to profess. The highest of the Shaolin arts is to show *a* way to enlightenment by practicing meditation. Shaolin meditation is not ritualistic nor religious; but it is spiritual, it transcends the physical self.

Nevertheless, if you are not ready for this transcendental stage, then please ignore it, and you can still enjoy the other benefits perfectly. You may approach this spiritual aspect of the Shaolin arts when you are ready, and only if you desire it. Freedom of choice, and a deep respect for others' preferences are important aspects of the Shaolin philosophy. But if you wish to experience the richest fruit of the Shaolin arts, the beautiful, blissful state of mind enjoyed by masters and laymen alike, the later chapters of this book will show the Shaolin way to enlightenment, which, it must be stressed, does not insist on any particular concepts nor infringe on any religious beliefs. And the enlightenment is based on experience, not just faith. In other words, one becomes enlightened because he experiences enlightenment, not because he reads about it or believes in certain doctrines.

These three Shaolin arts — chi kung, kungfu and meditation — are the living treasures of Shaolin. Even if you can master only one of them, you will have achieved, in the words of a popular saying, a precious art that is more valuable than even the art of changing stones to gold by touch! To many of us, especially those who are more materialistic, this saying certainly sounds exaggerated, even ridiculous; but to others who value other things besides money, there is much truth in the saying.

Aspects of this truth will become obvious when we study these arts in greater detail in later parts of this book. And you are invited, as you read the book, not merely to judge the saying in the light of new information revealed in these chapters, but also to share the fascinating but real experiences that many uninitiated readers previously might not have dreamt to be possible. These Shaolin arts were once taught to emperors and generals. It may be inspiring for those intending to embark on these arts, to know that many princes (and a few princesses), especially during the Ming Dynasty, were ready to sacrifice their luxurious lifestyles to enter the Shaolin Monastery to seek spiritual fulfillment.

The Practical and the Spiritual

It is a mistake if you imagine that the Shaolin arts are concerned with things or ideas far out of this world. In fact, the Shaolin arts, including the very advanced ones, are practical. Much of these arts teach us how to live better and more meaningful lives here and now.

Actually the materialistically inclined can benefit tremendously from the Shaolin arts. For example, Shaolin Chi Kung enables them to he healthy and energetic so that they can work harder and longer to acquire more material wealth, if they prefer so. Shaolin Kungfu gives them the courage and the endurance to persevere and to rise up after every fall. Shaolin meditation provides them with a freshness of mind and a clarity of thought that they can see and grasp opportunities when they arise, or even to create them if the opportunities are not presently available.

Yet, in practice, most of the greatest Shaolin masters never exploit their powers to amass material riches. They lead, in the eyes of common people, a very simple life — not because they are incapable of earning much money nor enjoying worldly pleasures, but because they prefer the bliss of simplicity. These masters find that the independent, carefree interaction with sincere friends or with nature, is far more rewarding than the stressful competition with, or even the ultimate victory over, business or political rivals. At a much higher plane, the masters discover that the deep contemplation on intuitive wisdom, and the realization of one's mind merging with the universe, are far more blissful than all the worldly pleasures can offer.

Of course, only the masters can attain such high levels. Even among Shaolin disciples, the majority of them are concerned with the benefits of the more physical levels, like good health, stress-free living, abundant energy and a wholesome attitude towards life. Yet, the masters' examples can provide us with much inspiration, especially at times of economic or emotional depression.

Even when we are down, if we know that great masters have voluntarily forgone the very same possessions or reputations that we have so vainly fought to have, it can suddenly dawn on us that these possessions or reputations are not so important after all. If we already possess them, it is not the end of the world if they are suddenly lost; or if we have not acquired them but we wish to, it is also not the end of the world if we fail in our endeavor. It is note-worthy to mention that the Venerable Bodhidharma, the First Patriarch of the Shaolin arts, was a prince, yet, like the historical Buddha before him, he chose to give up the grandeur and luxury of the palace to lead, and help others to lead, a richer life at the Shaolin Monastery.

It is a great mistake to think that Shaolin philosophy is fatalistic or nihilistic. In fact, it is the contrary. The purpose of the Shaolin arts is to help us actualize our aims, worldly or otherwise. And a fundamental Shaolin principle is that we have to put in a lot of effort if we want success. If a Shaolin disciple, for example, wishes to earn a lot of money — a worldly aim which the Shaolin philosophy has nothing against — the Shaolin arts provide much help in the form of good health, energy and clear thinking in his process of money earning. But he has to work hard to achieve success. It is an inevitable truth cherished in Shaolin philosophy that nothing worthwhile can be obtained without perseverance. Shaolin philosophy also demands that his means must be honorable, and when he succeeds in making much money, he should use it wisely.

Inter-Relationship of Kungfu, Chi Kung and Meditation

One wonderful feature of these three most important Shaolin arts is that while they are closely inter-related to form a continuous development, each can be followed independently with tremendous benefits. A brief introduction to how these arts developed, will give some insight into their inter-relationship as well as their separate functions.

In CE 527, the great Buddhist monk from India, Bodhidharma, arrived at the famous Shaolin Monastery in China to teach Buddhism. He found that most of the monks at the monastery were so weak that they often dozed off to sleep during meditation. Bodhidharma believed that physical and emotional health are essential to mental health, and all three are essential to spiritual development. A physically or emotionally unhealthy person will lack the freshness and calmness of mind to endure long hours of meditation, and meditation is the essential path to enlightenment.

This concept of the unity of mind and body was particularly significant at this point of history in the development of Buddhism. Many Buddhist masters neglected their physical body and emphasized only the mind. They went to the extent of regarding their body as a "smelly skin receptacle", and were glad to dispose off this smelly prison so that the real You — the You before you were born — could be liberated. But Bodhidharma taught that as long as You still live in your body, your body is important, though he also regarded the mind as supreme.

So Bodhidharma taught the Shaolin monks a series of physical exercise called the Eighteen Lohan Hands. The original purpose was to strengthen the monks, and to enable them to stretch themselves and relax their muscles after sitting motionlessly for long hours in meditation. Bodhidharma also taught them a series of internal exercise known as Sinew Metamorphosis. The aim here was to strengthen the monks internally, changing even their sinews and tendons, so that they could have the energy as well as tranquility to meditate for long hours.

Later, however, the Eighteen Lohan Hands developed into Shaolin Kungfu, while Sinew Metamorphosis became the basis of Shaolin Chi Kung. The growth and spread of Shaolin Kungfu was phenomenal, affecting almost every type of martial arts in China, and greatly influenced martial arts of other countries, such as Japanese karate, Korean taekwondo, Siamese boxing and Malay silat.

Shaolin Chi Kung, on the other hand, was taught exclusively to selected disciples. Hence not many Shaolin disciples knew Shaolin Chi Kung, which was guarded as a top secret. However, the situation now has changed. Shaolin Chi Kung masters are sincere in wanting to spread this wonderful art to other people for the benefit of humanity. Indeed, Shaolin Chi Kung has much to offer modern societies, irrespective of race, religion and culture. Numerous patients suffering from so-called incurable diseases, for instance, have had their sickness relieved after practicing Shaolin Chi Kung from me.

Actually, from the historical perspective, both Shaolin Kungfu and Shaolin Chi Kung were originally not ends themselves, but were means to an important purpose. Many people, including kungfu and chi kung masters, may be surprised at this statement, and may vehemently dispute it. But it cannot be denied that when Bodhidharma first initiated kungfu and chi kung (or what later turned out to be kungfu and chi kung) he did not intend them to be used for fighting nor curing illnesses; rather he devised them as aids to the all important meditation, so that the monks could easier attain enlightenment.

It was much later that both Shaolin Kungfu and Shaolin Chi Kung developed into virtually independent arts, often losing touch with their original purpose at their inception. Hence, it is not uncommon nowadays that most students of Shaolin Kungfu and Shaolin Chi Kung, especially those at the elementary level, are not familiar with each others' arts, and both groups know little about Shaolin meditation.

This also explains that Shaolin Kungfu, Chi Kung and meditation or Zen can be practiced separately and exclusively. Indeed, many people are doing this, and have achieved very high standards, since the three Shaolin arts are by themselves very advance arts in their own right. Yet, understanding their inter-relationship will be of tremendous advantage even if we choose to practice only one of the arts independently.

Qualities of a Good Teacher

It is obvious that merely reading about the Shaolin arts, will not give you the fantastic benefits mentioned above. If you want the benefits you must put in time and effort to get them. This is a timeless, universal truth. You cannot buy them like one buys modern technology or a corrupt office, no matter how much you are ready to pay. You may buy advice, instruction or knowledge on how best to practice the arts to get the benefits, but you yourself must work for them.

This book will offer you some very good advice and methods. If you are already familiar with these Shaolin arts, you will find this book exceedingly useful; but if you are a beginner you may have difficulty following the teaching materials, though some of the materials are actually written for beginners. It is highly recommended that students should learn from a master, or at least a qualified instructor.

Getting a good Shaolin master or instructor is not easy. As in many other disciplines, unsuspecting students often waste much time learning superficially from mediocre instructors, or worse still, learning something else that bogus instructors pass off as Shaolin arts.

What, then, are the qualities students should look for, when seeking a good teacher? The following are some helpful guidelines.

A good teacher must have attained a reasonably high standard in the Shaolin art he teaches. The cynical saying that "those who know, do; those who do not, teach" certainly does not apply here. A kungfu master may not win every match he fights in, but he must be able to put up some reasonable defense even if he loses. Nowadays, many so-called kungfu instructors, including some well-known ones, actually do not know how to fight!

Of course, intending students should not challenge the teacher to test if he could fight. Although challenges were not uncommon in the past, such actions are unbecoming and extremely rude nowadays. Nevertheless, intending students can have a good idea by observing whether sparring and force training are systematically taught.

Secondly, a good teacher should also have some sound theoretical knowledge on his discipline, and he should not mind if we ask him relevant questions politely. But if he starts giving excuses like the answers are too complicated for us to comprehend, or he would not tell because they are secrets, then we have good reasons to suspect.

However, there may be masters who have attained a very high level in their art, but who have little or no theoretical knowledge. In fact there are numerous stories about meditation teachers who insisted that their students follow their instructions without questions. Bodhidharma himself is reputed to have asked his students to burn their books, for enlightenment is an intuitive, not an intellectual, attainment. These rare, great masters are an exception; and if we ever have the honor to meet them, it is not difficult to recognize them because they radiate an invisible but perceptible field of greatness.

Thirdly, a good teacher should be able to prescribe remedial treatment if his students unwittingly hurt themselves. Sustaining physical injuries is a common occurrence in Shaolin Kungfu training, but it does not cause any problem because the master can overcome this with kungfu medicine or remedial exercises.

Advanced chi kung training can cause serious internal injuries if it is not practiced properly. A good master, besides warning his students beforehand the pitfalls to avoid, must also be able to provide remedy. In advanced meditation, injury to the psyche may occur if it is not practiced correctly. Hence a good master with knowledge of remedy is necessary.

The fourth quality of a good teacher is that he must be systematic, generous and inspiring in his teaching. An expert may be very deep in his art, but if is unwilling to impart knowledge or haphazard in his teaching, students are not likely to learn much from him. Someone mentioned that mediocre teachers instruct, good teachers teach, but great teachers inspire. An inspiring teacher not only makes learning an enjoyable experience, but motivates us unobtrusively so that we are spurred to soar the heights.

But the most important quality of a good teacher, the hallmark of a great master, is that he must hold and practice in his daily living high moral values. Without this quality, no matter how competent he is in his art, or how effective in his teaching, he forfeits the honor to be called a great master, and remains a mere expert or instructor. Understandably, great masters are rare gems; if you find one, treasure him dearly.

Breaking the Patient's Arm to Cure It

Shaolin also excels in other fields. Besides kungfu and chi kung which have greatly enriched Chinese medical philosophy and practice, Shaolin's contribution to Chinese medicine in the field of traumatology is remarkable. More will be said about Shaolin traumatology later; here it suffices to give a brief introduction.

Traumatology is a unique branch of Chinese medicine, with no equivalent in the west. Known colloquially as "die-ta" (pronounced "th'iet ta) in Romanized Chinese, or "tit-ta" in Cantonese, which literally means "falls and hits", this major branch of Chinese medicine specially deals with injuries caused by incision, contusion, dislocation, fracture, and violent blows resulting in internal damage. It is extremely popular among the lower income groups where injuries sustained through falls and hits are common.

As kungfu practice and actual fighting often cause these types of injuries, traumatology or *tit-ta* is closely associated with Chinese martial arts. Traditionally, almost every kungfu master is also a *tit-ta* therapist. All my four kungfu masters, for instance, are *tit-ta* experts.

For lack of a better term, traumatology or *tit-ta* may be called "kungfu medicine". Indeed this important aspect of Chinese medicine frequently operates outside the mainstream of Chinese medical practice, with the interesting result that many orthodox Chinese medical practitioners know little about *tit-ta*, and many *tit-ta* specialists know little Chinese medical theory.

But the practical knowledge and skills of these *tit-ta* specialists are superb. Many people prefer *tit-ta* specialists to osteopathic surgeons. A few of these *tit-ta* specialists are so skillful and confident that when patients consult them because their fractured limbs have been poorly set by conventional treatment, these masters break the patients' limbs so as to set them properly again! One such specialist happens to be my close friend, Sifu Chow, who is also a master of Shaolin "Iron Palm". He will re-fracture his patients' limbs with a quick, sharp strike with his own arm.

Poetry and Other Arts

As Shaolin Kungfu, Chi Kung and meditation or Zen are so famous, they tend to overshadow other Shaolin arts, though these other arts by themselves are highly commendable. This is no surprise because many of the monks of the Shaolin Monastery were no ordinary people seeking refuge from the hustle of society, but distinguished poets, scholars, artists, philosophers, scientists and other men of learning, who wished to lead a higher spiritual life at the temple. Besides meditation and temple duties, they had much time to pursue their interests or hobbies. Some examples of these extraordinary Shaolin monks included the world renowned Chinese astronomer, Yi Xing; the famous pilgrim and translator, Xuan Zang (Hsuan Tsang); the eminent painter of plum flowers, Bie Shan; and the "wondrous" physician, Zhan Zhi.

Poetry was a popular pastime at the monastery. Much of the principles and philosophy of Shaolin Kungfu, for instance, is written in poetry. Not only the monks were remarkable poets, other people outside the monastery, including emperors, empresses and some of China's greatest poets, wrote beautiful poetry to praise Shaolin. The following poem suggesting the coming of Bodhidharma and the Shaolin mystical arts was written by the famous romantic poet, Li Po.

Seeker of Elixir at Song Shan

The sage's face is like an ancient crop
His ears to his shoulders firmly drop
Meets Wu of Han in his regal dream
The saint speaks with a glorious gleam
Seeking elixir to here I strive
To attain the joy of eternal life
Truth and fancy in a mystic twist
His shadow merges gently into the mist
The Emperor having enlightenment found
Rests at last in the Maoling ground

It is indeed an amazing, yet inspiring, result of modern development in communication and other fields, that these Shaolin arts, which were once practiced and developed by people of extremely high physical, emotional, mental and spiritual attainments, are now made available in this book to be shared with you. As we proceed to study these arts in detail, we can draw much inspiration from the fact that these arts which were fit for emperors and generals, were once taught exclusively to very special people.

4
Movements Of Health, Vitality And Longevity

(The Shaolin Way to Physical and Spiritual Health)

We cannot call a person healthy if, even when he is not clinically ill, he is easily prone to anger or nervousness, has poor memory or dullness of thought, and beset with vice and wickedness.

Various Concepts of Health

Although most people agree, at least on their lips, that health is better than wealth, not many really take some time and trouble to keep themselves healthy! Most people actually pay more attention to medicine than to health: they are quite contented going through life taking little or no notice of health, until sickness occurs when they will resort to medicine. Hence, to many people, health becomes synonymous with being free from disease.

What health is, has been debated by different peoples at various times. The great statesman of ancient Greece, Pericles, defined health as "that state of moral, mental and physical well-being which enables a man to face any crisis in life with the utmost facility and grace." Christopher Magarey, from whom the above quotation is taken, suggests that we should add "humor" to the list.

All known ancient peoples of the world's greatest civilizations, like the ancient Egyptians, Mesopotamians, Mexicans and Indians, referred to health holistically, taking care of man's spiritual as well as his physical well-being. It is no historical coincidence that ancient physicians were also usually priests. The failure to understand or appreciate this physical-spiritual unity of man, probably more than any other factor, has led many scholars to comment that the medical practices of these great ancient peoples were predominantly superstitious.

This holistic view is still prevalent today. For example, Dr. Vasant Lad says that Indian medicine "views health and disease in holistic terms, taking into consideration the inherent relationship between individual and cosmic spirit, individual and cosmic consciousness, energy and matter." Shaykh Hakim Moinuddin Chishti, a modern Muslim healer, says that "there must be a knowledge and consideration of the physical, mental and spiritual planes of existence for there to be true health." This wholesome attitude towards health is also shared by the World Health Organization, though it understandably leaves out the spiritual aspect, defining health as "a state of complete physical, mental and social well-being and not merely the absence of disease or infirmity."

The Chinese have always viewed health holistically. Even in medicine, which the Chinese have traditionally given less prominence than health, and where shamanism has never been a practice in its long medical history, prevention is always regarded as superior to cure. To be healthy, besides being free from illnesses, one must also be emotionally stable, mentally fresh, morally upright and experience a sense of inner peace. We cannot call a person healthy if, even when he is not clinically ill, he is easily prone to anger or nervousness, has poor memory or dullness of thought, and beset with vice and wickedness.

Physical as well as Spiritual Health

Yet, to have health is not difficult, if we are prepared to spend about fifteen minutes a day to practice some Shaolin Chi Kung exercises, two of which are described below. These exercises are time-tested, and they not only give you physical, emotional, mental and spiritual health, but also promote your vitality and longevity!

It is understandable if some readers find this claim unbelievable. What! Just do these simple exercises fifteen minutes a day, and you will get health, vitality and longevity? Yes, but in accordance with Shaolin philosophy, you are asked not to believe this and other claims basing on faith alone, but try the exercises, only then give your comments. In fact, the methods to develop many fantastic Shaolin feats, like Iron Palm and Golden Bell, where the adept can break bricks and take punches without sustaining any injuries respectively, are quite simple — if we know how. The greatest difficulty is to practice — not just off and on, but every day for at least a few months before you see any result, and then continuously as your daily program as long as you value physical and spiritual health more than you value laziness.

What is spiritual health? Spiritual is not the same as religious. In fact the Chinese, in my opinion, are not a religious people, though they are spiritual!

The concept of religion as the west knows it, is quite foreign to the Chinese. Hence it is no coincidence that if you ask a Chinese coming from a typically Chinese environment like in China, Taiwan, Hong Kong, Singapore or Malaysia, which religion he professes, the chances are seven out of ten times that he has difficulties answering you. The Chinese generally do not limit their respect to one particular religion only, because they believe that Truth or Reality can be realized by different people in different ways. That explains why many Chinese can be Buddhist, Taoist and Confucianist at the same time.

Chinese are generally spiritual; they believe in the existence of spirit or soul. Spirit is closely related but not necessarily similar to mind, though because of linguistic and cultural differences between English and Chinese, the terms "spirit" and "mind" may sometimes be used interchangeably.

Spiritual health means the well-being of the spirit, and is independent of the specific religion, or lack of it, the person professes. More will be discussed about spiritual development in later chapters; meanwhile it suffices to note that morality is the basis of spirituality. Furthermore, a person who appeases ghosts or demons is spiritually unhealthy, and one who lacks any cosmic awareness is spiritually undeveloped. Chi kung can give you both physical and spiritual health.

Various Arts of Energy

Chi kung, spelt as "qigong" in Romanized Chinese, is the umbrella term the Chinese uses to refer to various arts of developing energy — the energy that keeps you, me and all other beings alive. We normally derive this vital energy, or life force, from the air we breath and the food we eat. Outside our bodies, this energy is generally referred to as cosmic energy. Besides enhancing this life-sustaining function of energy, chi kung also methodically uses energy for promoting health, vitality and longevity, as well as for generating internal strength, mind training and spiritual development. Spiritual health will be discussed in more detail in later chapters.

Vital or cosmic energy has been developed and used since ancient times by various peoples from different great civilizations throughout history. These arts of energy have been known by various names. The ancient Egyptians, Indians and Tibetans called their arcane arts the mystery art, yoga and the art of wisdom respectively; while more recently peoples have called their application of vital or cosmic energy, or aspects of it, by a variety of names, such as calisthenics, Taijiquan (Tai Chi Chuan), channelling, radonics, bio-feedback, para-psychology and various studies of psi. Although the objectives and the methods of these disciplines may be vastly different, the fundamental common factor among them is energy, which the Chinese call chi (qi).

There are many types of chi kung: some are elementary, dealing with healing and general well-being; while others are esoteric, concerning psychic training and mystic experience. Shaolin Chi Kung is one of the most comprehensive and advanced, ranging from health and martial arts to mind expansion and spiritual fulfillment. The following two chi kung exercises are comparatively basic amongst the Shaolin arts, and are designed for health, vitality and longevity.

Lifting Sky and Levelling Earth

The first exercise is called "Lifting the Sky", which is one of the best exercises for health. Stand upright but relaxed, with feet fairly close together. Straighten your arms and hold your palms facing downwards in front near your groin so that they are about right angles to the arm, with fingers pointing each other, Fig 4.1 (a).

Bring your straight arms forward and upward in a continu‹ palms face the sky. Simultaneously breathe in gently and visualiz energy flowing into you. Hold both the palms and the breath, and p‹ the sky, Fig 4.1 (b).

Then bring the hands down from the sides, simultaneously breat‹ and visualize all negative energy flowing out with your breath, ‹‹ ‹ ‹.1 (c). Negative energy represents negative thoughts and emotions, any illness you may have, and any rubbish in your body detrimental to your health. Repeat the process about ten to twenty times. Then stand still, relax, close your eyes and enjoy the flow of vital energy in your body for a few minutes.

This Lifting the Sky exercise is one of the best exercises in chi kung. If you practice it every day, in six months time you will probably have some idea why it is so highly valued. You will find that this exercise is a basic requirement for many other advanced Shaolin arts described in later chapters.

(a)   (b)   (c)

Fig 4.1 Lifting the Sky

The second exercise is called "Three Levels to the Earth". Stand relaxed with your feet about shoulder's width apart. Hold your straight arms with palms facing downwards at your sides at shoulder's level, Fig 4.2 (a).

Squat down fully and simultaneously breathe out, Fig 4.2 (b), gently visualizing vital energy flowing up your spine. It is important not to raise your heels; your feet are fully on the ground throughout the exercise.

Then gradually stand up, and breathe in simultaneously, visualizing cosmic energy flowing into you and down the front part of your body into your abdomen. Your straight arms are at shoulder's height all this time. Repeat about ten to twenty times. Then drop your arms and bring your feet together. Close your eyes, stand still for a few minutes and enjoy the flow of vital energy down your arms and legs.

(a)   (b)

Fig 4.2 Three Levels to the Earth

You are grossly mistaken if you think this "Three Levels to the Earth" is merely to loosen the leg muscles. Among many benefits, it will strengthen your heart. Indeed it has helped many of my students who have heart problems to recover. Nevertheless, those with heart problems must practice this exercise cautiously; they must not feel giddy, tired or be panting for breath after the exercise.

You may perform "Lifting the Sky" and "Three Levels to the Earth" separately, or one set after another. It is important that you should not be disturbed while standing still in a meditative state. Should there be any sudden loud noise or disturbance, assure yourself that that interference cannot harm you in any way; and think of your spirit and your vital energy being intact. This is an utmost important precaution against any unfavorable side-effects should you be unwittingly disturbed.

The essence of these two and other chi kung exercises is not the physical movements, but the energy flow and heightened state of consciousness brought about by correct breathing and meditative visualization. It is the realization of this essential point that makes the crucial difference between a set of simple physical exercises and an esoteric art. In other words, if you merely perform the physical movements, even perfectly, but miss out the energy flow and meditative visualization, you are not likely to get extraordinary results. The breathing and the visualization *must* be done gently; they must never be forced. If you find it hard to visualize, then just a gentle relevant thought is sufficient.

Chi Kung for Health, Vitality and Longevity.

How do these Shaolin Chi Kung exercises give health, vitality and longevity? The answer is: by cleansing meridians and harmonizing yin-yang.

Chinese medical philosophy states that if you "cleanse your meridians and harmonize yin-yang, hundreds of illnesses will be eliminated." Those not familiar with Chinese medical thought, and seeing it from the western medical perspective, may think the statement ridiculous. But actually it is a very concise statement of a great medical truth, and will be explained in some detail in Chapter 19.

Briefly, it means that when the meridians — or pathways of energy flow — are clear, our vital energy can flow harmoniously. Our vital energy not only brings nutrient to, and toxic waste from, every cell in our body, but also stabilizes our emotions, strengthens the mind and nourishes the spirit. When yin and yang are in harmony, all our life sustaining systems, like feed-back, self-resistance, self-curing and regeneration, will function optimally. In this way, good physical, emotional, mental and spiritual health is maintained.

After attaining good health, the next logical stage is increasing vitality. There are some differences between health and vitality, though the difference is one of degree rather than kind. A person may be free from clinical diseases, emotionally stable, mentally fresh and spiritually sound, but he may still lack the energy to play a few rounds of squash, think creatively over a demanding problem, take the family out after a hard day's work, or continue to savour the pleasures of a healthy sex life (if he or she wants) when most of his (her) colleagues are complaining of chronic back pains.

The chi kung exercises promote your vitality in the following ways. First, by paying attention to your breathing, you gradually increase your lung capacity for a more efficient exchange of your stale air for fresh air. More importantly, you learn to tap cosmic energy, and with your cleansed meridians and heightened state of mind, you can more efficiently transport this energy to the relevant parts of your body for better work and play. The waste products produced by your brain and body cells in the processes of increased activities are also more efficiently disposed off. Hence, not only your muscles are less fatigued, but your mind is also more alert.

The bafflingly simple Shaolin Chi Kung exercises also promote your longevity. We have a potential life span of at least 120 years. Why many people cannot last even half that time? There are two principal reasons — accidents and illnesses, which may take away life immediately, or reduce its quality so much that its potential length is ultimately shortened.

Accidents — at work. play or home — are likely to happen to two extreme groups of people: those who are very quick tempered, and those who are very slow in their reaction. By promoting emotional stability (which will be discussed in Chapter 19), Shaolin Chi Kung makes its practitioners calm and relaxed even in trying situations. Chi kung cleanses the meridians, promoting better flow of electric impulses to and from all parts of our body, hence improving reflexes and reaction. In this way, Shaolin Chi Kung minimizes the two principal causes, thus greatly reducing the possibilities of accidents.

Shaolin Chi Kung not only cures illnesses, but more importantly, it prevents illnesses from happening. It increases our self-resistance, and expands our mental and spiritual capacities, hence preventing contagious and psychosomatic diseases. As soon as there is wear and tear, stress and blockages, harmonious energy flow inside our body immediately repairs or cleanses them, thereby preventing organic diseases and enabling all our cells, tissues and organs to approximate their potential life spans. It is no surprise that chi kung adepts live to a ripe old age, yet look, feel and act young.

In the Shaolin Monastery in the past — and also in today's kungfu schools that value and follow Shaolin traditions — only when a disciple is healthy, he is allowed to practice Shaolin Kungfu. Though it is not the best gift the Shaolin Monastery has offered to humanity, Shaolin Kungfu is certainly the most famous and most widely practiced of all the Shaolin arts. In the next chapter, you will find out that its greatness lies not so much in its remarkable effectiveness as a fighting art, but in other worthy qualities.

<u>5</u>
Poetry Of Strength And Courage

(The Philosophy and Dimension of Shaolin Kungfu)

Yet, the best application of kungfu is not just to fight. The qualities of a good fighter that we develop in kungfu training — like courage, calmness, sound judgement, fluidity of movements, and mental freshness — can be applied to make life more rewarding and meaningful for ourselves and for other people.

The Fascination of Kungfu

Would you like to have good health, excellent self-defense, speed and agility, freshness of mind, internal strength, courage and confidence, as well as the ability to perform beautiful, poetic movements which represents the crystallization of years of study and experiment by great past masters? These and other benefits will be yours if you conscientiously practice genuine Shaolin Kungfu.

Just like in any worthy project, you must be prepared to pay the price, which is hard, regular work. You may become knowledgeable in it by *learning* from a master or a good book, but you will never be a master yourself unless you have put in years of consistent *practice*. One does not merely learn Shaolin Kungfu — which is comparatively easy; one has to practice, practice and practice to become proficient — and this can be extremely exacting. Moreover, you need to learn and practice genuine Shaolin Kungfu from a good, generous master; if you learn a debased, albeit pretty, form that pretends to be Shaolin, you are likely to waste your time.

One sure way of knowing genuine Shaolin Kungfu from the debased or pretentious stuff is to have a sound understanding of what actually Shaolin Kungfu is.

Kungfu means Chinese martial art. This term is popularly used in English, and colloquially among overseas Chinese; though the present official term is "wushu". Throughout its long history, many Chinese terms were used to refer to martial art, and some of the more common ones included "jiaoli", "xiangbo", "quanfa" and "wuyi".

Shaolin Kungfu refers to the style of martial art that originated from the Shaolin Monastery, and is the most widely practiced kungfu style today by peoples of different religions, cultures and nationalities, so that when the term "kungfu" is used unqualified, it generally refers to Shaolin Kungfu. The other very famous style of kungfu practiced by many peoples all over the world is Taiji Kungfu, commonly called Taiji-quan (T'ai Chi Chuan), which is a short form of Taiji Quanfa.

Historical Development

Kungfu has been practiced since prehistoric time, but the first time it was institutionalized was at the Shaolin Monastery in CE 527, when the Venerable Bodhidharma taught the monks "Eighteen Lohan Hands" and "Sinew Metamorphosis". Before that, kungfu was practiced individually, not as an institution. This institutionalization of kungfu was of tremendous historic significance, because it enabled kungfu to be studied and developed as an art, not just for fighting as was previously done; and to be accumulated, classified and transmitted as a legacy, not merely used for ad hoc, personal needs. Later, Shaolin monks spread Shaolin Kungfu to secular disciples beyond the temple walls.

By the time of the Tang Dynasty (7-10th centuries), Shaolin Kungfu had far surpassed other styles, so much so that the saying "Shaolin Kungfu is the best in the world" was popular. During the Song Dynasty (10-13th centuries), a famous general, Yue Fei, taught Shaolin Kungfu to the armies, from which Xingyi (Hsing Yi) Kungfu and Eagle Claw Kungfu were derived. Xingyi Kungfu, meaning "martial art of form and meaning", uses twelve animal forms (dragon, tiger, monkey, horse, tortoise, cockerel, kite, swift, snake, hawk, eagle, bear) and five elemental processes (metal, water, wood, fire, earth). Eagle Claw Kungfu is noted for the use of its powerful finger-grip on an opponent's tendons and energy points, effectively numbing or paralyzing him — a specialized art known as "qin-na" in Chinese. Fig 5.1 and 5.2 show a typical pattern from Xingyi and Eagle Claw Kungfu.

Fig 5.1 Xingyi Kungfu

Fig 5.2 Eagle Claw Kungfu

Towards the end of the Song Dynasty, a Taoist master, Zhang San Feng, modified Shaolin Kungfu into Wudang (Wu Tang) Kungfu, which later developed into Taijiquan, Fig 5.3. The hallmark of Taijiquan when a Taiji set is performed, is its gentle, graceful movements which some people may mistake as Chinese ballet. But do not be misled; these graceful, gentle Taijiquan movements are actually deadly fighting patterns.

Fig 5.3 A Pattern from Taijiquan

In the Yuan Dynasty (13-14th centuries), a kungfu genius, Bai Yi Feng, invited numerous Shaolin masters from all over the country back to Shaolin Monastery for demonstration. The masters of the following five styles were most prominent: Emperor's style, Bodhidharma's, Lohan's, Crane and Monkey. These masters combined their arts into a single style called Wuzu Kungfu, which means "martial art of five ancestors." This style emphasizes chi training, internal force and narrow stances, Fig 5.4.

Fig 5.4 Kungfu of Five Ancestors

In the Ming Dynasty (14-17th centuries), a secular disciple at the Shaolin Monastery, Wang Lang, found that by using suitable techniques a praying mantis could defeat a larger-sized cicada. With the help of his master he invented Praying Mantis Kungfu. Later he travelled all over the country to incorporate other effective fighting techniques into his style. Praying Mantis Kungfu, Fig 5.5, which is a crystallization of eighteen styles, is well known for its kicking techniques.

Fig 5.5 A Kick of the Praying Mantis

Yet, the great derivation of parental Shaolin Kungfu into numerous branches was still to come. In the Qing Dynasty (17-20th centuries) the imperial army razed the southern Shaolin Monastery at Fujian as it had become a center for revolutionaries. Shaolin masters escaped underground to various parts of China, and to avoid the Qing armies, Shaolin Kungfu was called by various names, usually after the surnames of the masters or after the most significant features of Shaolin Kungfu the particular masters emphasized. Some of these popular derivative Shaolin styles are Hoong Ka (Hongjia) Choy-Li-Fatt (Chai-li-fo), Wing Choon (Yong-chun), White Crane, Black Tiger, Dragon style, and Monkey style.

Hoong Ka Kungfu is famous for its solid stances; Choy-Li-Fatt for long range fighting; Wing Chun Kungfu for economy of movements; White Crane for long-reaching arms; Black Tiger for its tiger claw; Dragon style for graceful body-work; and Monkey style for deceptive agility. Fig 5.5 to 5.11 show a typical pattern from these styles.

Fig 5.6 Solid Stance of Hoong Ka Kungfu

Fig 5.7 Long Range of Choy-Li-Fatt

Fig 5.8 Short Movements of Wing Chun

Fig 5.9 Long-Reaching Arms of White Crane

Fig 5.10 Tiger Claw of Black Tiger

Fig 5.11 Gracefulness of Dragon Style

Fig 5.12 Agility of the Monkey

The Four Dimensions of Kungfu

There are four aspects or dimensions in kungfu, namely form, force, application and theory.

Form is the visible aspect; it refers to all the kungfu patterns and sets that a beginner normally learns when he starts practicing kungfu. Through the learning of kungfu form, the student is exposed to the techniques that he can use for combat. As kungfu techniques are vastly different from ordinary daily movements, he has to put in sufficient practice so that these previously unfamiliar stances and movements become familiar to him, so that when he has to use them in combat situations, he can do so spontaneously and accurately.

But form is only one aspect of kungfu. In many ways, it is the least important aspect, though for a beginner it is essential that he knows some kungfu form. Obviously if he learns only kungfu form, and does not progress to other dimensions of kungfu, he will not achieve much even though he may have practiced for a long time. This, unfortunately, is the case with many students nowadays. They may perform kungfu form beautifully, even win titles in kungfu demonstrations, but they cannot fight, for the simple reason that they have never learnt to fight.

But before we can fight well, we must develop the necessary force to fight. "Force", here, is a poor equivalent of the Chinese term "gong" (pronounced as "kung"), which also includes skills. Force is an invisible aspect. Perhaps this is one significant reason why many students neglect force training. Kungfu masters have always advised that "if you only practice kungfu form, but never develop force, your training will be futile even if you practice a life time."

Force is not just brutal strength. In fact, brutal strength is strongly discouraged in kungfu training. Force, or more appropriately "gong", refers to how powerfully, accurately and fast you execute techniques in combat, and also in our daily work and play. For convenience, force may be classified into external and internal, and into basic and specialized. For example, appropriate breathing methods to enhance energy level and flow, is internal and basic force training; while developing Iron Palm to achieve a powerful strike, is external and specialized.

The third dimension of kungfu is application, which is the functional aspect. Though actual fighting is not common in our law-abiding society today, an ability to defend ourselves is certainly an invaluable asset. Perhaps more meaningfully is the feeling of courage and confidence that this self-defense ability provides, and which can be rewardingly manifested in our daily life.

Kungfu application for combat has to be learnt and practiced. It is both unreasonable and unrealistic to expect students to be able to defend themselves just by performing kungfu form or even training kungfu force. You may have an Iron Palm, but if you can only use it to break bricks, then your specialized force is not very practical. And just giving students pairs of gloves to spar, without providing proper methods to initiate them from prearranged sparring to simulated fighting, is a sure way of making them a laughing stock when they fight like small children during competitions. Students need to be taught how to fight well, and there are excellent methods in Shaolin Kungfu to do so, which we shall study in Chapters 7 to 9.

Yet, the best application of kungfu is not just to fight. The qualities of a good fighter that we develop in kungfu training — like courage, calmness, sound judgement, fluidity of movements, and mental freshness — can be applied to make life more rewarding and meaningful for ourselves for and other people.

The fourth dimension of kungfu is theory — the philosophical aspect. This includes all the written and unwritten records of the histories, traditions, principles, methods, techniques and philosophy of kungfu. Some of this material is written or passed down in poetry. The histories and traditions of various kungfu schools and masters provide the student with much inspiration and moral guidance. By studying the vast amount of literature on kungfu principles, methods and techniques, we obtain access to and greatly enrich ourselves with the results and discoveries of past masters in their studies and experiments. We can benefit with the effort of a few days, what it took masters years to discover.

The philosophy of kungfu involves not just fighting and health. Some of the material is amazingly profound, and concerns man and the cosmos, sometimes preceding modern science in wisdom. Shaolin masters had profound knowledge of cosmic and vital energy long before modern physicists and medical scientists used similar concepts in their studies of the subatomic particle and the interrelationship of our body systems. The masters deliberated on various concepts of mind long before our modern psychologists realize that there are different levels of consciousness. An understanding of such philosophy not only enhances our kungfu, but also serves as a gateway to the profundity of eastern wisdom.

General Aims of Kungfu

Why do we practice kungfu? Surprisingly, many people practice kungfu without being aware of its aims. Even if they do, they seldom assess the progress of their kungfu training in relation to these aims, with the unfortunate result that they achieve very little benefits from their undirected and purposeless training.

There are three main aims in practicing Shaolin Kungfu, namely effective fighting, excellent health and personal growth. These aims also apply to all styles of kungfu.

The first and primary aim of kungfu is for effective fighting, without which kungfu (any kungfu, including the deceptively gentle Taijiquan) becomes meaningless as a martial art. Yet, many instructors stress that their kungfu is not for fighting, and they would reprimand students who suggest incorporating combative skills into their practice! Except for specific, valid reasons — such as being modest, avoiding unnecessary challenges, or preventing aggressive students from abusing their art — these instructors do not know what they are saying or do not mean what they say. It is such mediocre instructors, who themselves do not know how to apply kungfu for fighting, that contribute to the present rapid degradation of kungfu into what masters have always warned against, namely "flowery fists and embroidery kicks", that is, a debase kungfu form that is nice to look at but utterly useless for combat.

Of course, to be able to fight well is different from being aggressive or brutal; nor does it imply a desire to fight to prove one's ability. But any person who has practiced kungfu for some time, must be able to fight, otherwise he has failed to realize the fundamental function of kungfu.

However, we must also guard against the other extreme: actively encouraging kungfu students to fight, and even taking sadistic pride in brutal combat efficiency. Although a Shaolin master is an excellent fighter, he does not like to fight if he can help it; and if he has to fight, because he is so masterful, he can show his superior fighting skills without unnecessarily hurting his opponent. Should he have to kill, as in the past, he would try his best to do so quickly, painlessly and mercifully. A Shaolin master will not torture his opponent, even if the latter is a most-wanted criminal or an arch enemy.

The second aim of kungfu is health — physical, emotional, mental and spiritual. It is interesting to note that although kungfu is an excellent system for promoting health, the health benefits are an incidental, not a primary, function of kung fu. In other words, a student derives health benefits from practicing kungfu, not because kungfu is specially designed to promote health, but because these benefits are an incidental bonus! Yet these health benefits are excellent, even better than what he would get from health promotion exercises! How does this paradox come about?

This is because of two reasons: the basic prerequisite for kungfu training is good health; and the requirement for efficient fighting is excellent health. Before any person even thinks of starting Shaolin Kungfu, he should first of all be healthy. If not, he has to strengthen himself first, like practicing those chi kung exercises shown in the previous chapter.

Next, being merely healthy like ordinary healthy people is not enough. An efficient Shaolin fighter, besides other things, must have enough stamina to spar for an hour or two without feeling tired, enough power to strike down an opponent who may be twice his size, enough endurance to withstand a few punches and kicks that he may fail to defend, speed and agility so that he can execute reflexive actions, and calmness and clarity of mind that he can make correct split-second decisions. Not many, if any, health exercises develop these kinds of abilities as

Shaolin Kungfu does. And of course when we have developed these abilities through Shaolin Kungfu training, we do not have to waste them on petty fighting; they can be better employed in our daily work and play.

Hence, with this understanding, we can better appreciate that instructors who say "My kungfu is only for health" (usually followed by "and not for fighting") are not likely to give us the best benefits for health, even if we ignore the combative aspect of kungfu. It is the training to become a good fighter that these qualities — like stamina, endurance, emotional stability and mental freshness, which are so invaluable to health — are nurtured as second nature to the Shaolin Kungfu disciple.

Further more, the health benefits that you get from Shaolin Kungfu are superior to those you get from ordinary physical exercises like jogging, swimming, games and aerobics. The reason is simple. The benefits you derive from physical exercises will deteriorate once you have passed your peak; whereas those from genuine Shaolin Kungfu will be enhanced even when you age! Why? And how? Because in Shaolin Kungfu, the training is not just external, which has physical limits, but internal, which transcends the physical as it trains energy and mind.

The third aim of kungfu, which elevates Shaolin Kungfu from being an excellent martial art to even greater heights, is personal growth. Shaolin Kungfu training itself is an intrinsic process of character development. A student develops spiritually not just because of his teachers' constant advice and the strict Shaolin moral code, but more significantly because of the various developmental stages he has to go through in his long demanding journey to become a master.

A genuine Shaolin disciple has discipline and perseverance not because he has been told by his teachers that these qualities are necessary for kungfu training, but because he experiences and develops these qualities himself as he, for example, wakes up daily at five in the morning, despite the luxury of cozy sleep, to repeat and repeat thousands of times some monotonous techniques not for a few days or months, but for years.

At an advanced stage, he becomes calm and compassionate, not only because of the nurturing influence of the monastic environment and his caring seniors, but also because that his harmonious energy flow from constant chi kung practice has flushed out all negative emotions, and his mental expansion from meditation enables him to open himself and share cosmic love. And when he has become a master, he feels spiritual bliss not because the scriptures mention that it is so, but because through his practice he actually experiences the boundless joy of his spirit in unity with the whole cosmos.

6
Form And Function In Motion

(The Fundamentals of Shaolin Kungfu)

All patterns of all styles of kungfu (including Taijiquan) exist because of their combative functions: these patterns, no matter how flowery they may appear to the uninitiated, are not put there to please spectators.

Gateway to Shaolin Force Training

Nowadays when a student learns kungfu, he usually starts with kungfu forms, which consists of patterns and sets, and is the visible aspect of kungfu. The other three aspects or dimensions of kungfu are force, application and theory.

In the past, masters normally start with force training, and students had to spend months repeating monotonous exercises to develop force or "gong" before they were taught any fighting techniques. If you are game enough to try some force or "gong" training, the horse-riding stance shown in Fig 6.1 and summarily described below is a good gateway to Shaolin Kungfu.

Fig 6.1 The Horse-Riding Stance

For a beginner, it is best to learn the stances from a qualified instructor. The description below only mentions some salient points. In the horse-riding stance, your body should be upright, and your thigh almost parallel to the ground. Relax, empty your mind of all thoughts and breathe naturally. Remain at this stance for as long as you can, making sure that you do not raise higher as you become tired. Most beginners may last less than a minute, but persist until you can stand (or "sit") at the stance for at least five minutes. This will probably take you a few months of daily practice.

Fig 6.2 Bow-Arrow Stance

Fig 6.3 False-Leg Stance

Fig 6.4 Unicorn Step

Fig 6.5 Single-Leg Stance

Practice the other stances: bow-arrow, false-leg, unicorn, and single-leg. See Fig 6.2 to 6.5 for details. The following are some crucial points.

In the bow-arrow stance, the body weight is distributed equally between both legs. Both feet (especially take note of the back foot) are firmly on the ground. The bend of the front knee is forward rather than side-way; the back knee is straight. Both the front foot and the back foot should "hook" inward, i.e. if you turn from the horse-riding stance to the right to form the right bow-arrow stance, turn your right foot about forty five degrees to the right, and your left foot about sixty degrees to the right. Your body should face squarely in front in the direction of your eyes.

In the false-leg stance, it is very important *not* to support any body weight on your front "false" leg. The toes of your front leg just touch the ground, with less than ten percent of the body weight. Both knees are bent. Make sure that you do not bend your body backward. Adjust yourself so that you feel your center of gravity is at your "dan tian", i.e. about three inches below your navel.

The unicorn stance, sometimes called the unicorn step, is quite difficult for beginners. Guard against the common mistake of throwing your body forward, with much of the body weight on the front leg. One bent knee should be placed in the notch at the back of the other bent knee. This can be more readily achieved if your feet are wide enough apart, your back heel raised, and you sit "backward" onto the stance rather than bending forward over your front leg. Your center of gravity should be located between your feet (not directly above the front foot which is a common mistake among beginners), about a third or half-way from the front foot.

Your body should be fairly straight when you stand at the single-leg stance. Your standing leg may be straight or slightly bent at the knee. The raised leg should be fully bent with the toes pointing downwards (not in front) to protect your groin. Maintain your balance.

Make sure that you can perform these stances well for they form the basic footwork of Shaolin Kungfu, and the horse-riding stance is the foundation of most force training methods.

After the stances, it is important to practice any suitable leg stretching exercises to prevent your leg muscles from becoming stiff, so that you will not only have solid stances, but your legs are also supple. Fig 6.6 shows some examples of leg stretching exercises which you may use.

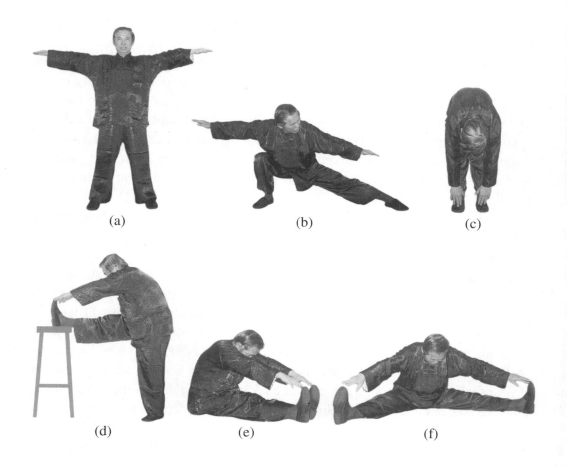

(a)   (b)   (c)

(d)   (e)   (f)

Fig 6.6 Some Leg Stretching Exercises

When you can stand at the horse-riding stance comfortably for at least five minutes, you may proceed to train the "Art of One-Finger Shooting Zen", which is the fundamental (meaning very important) method of developing internal force in our Shaolin Wahnam School, and is briefly described below.

The whole training is performed on the horse-riding stance. Hold one hand in the typical Shaolin One-Finger Zen form at breast level, Fig 6.7 (a). Move the One-Finger Zen form slowly forward, simultaneously breathing out with a "shss..." sound coming from your kidneys, Fig 6.7 (b). Bring the One-Finger Zen form back to the breast level, breathing in gently, Fig 6.7 (c). Repeat twice, then shoot out the One-Finger Zen, breathing out explosively with a "her-it" sound coming from your abdomen, Fig 16.7 (d). Make a small circle in front of you with a "tiger-claw", Fig 16.7 (e), then bring the tiger-claw downwards to below your knee with a "yaa..." sound vibrating at your lungs, Fig 16.7 (f). Breathe out with a "ha..." sound, relaxing your whole body. Repeat with the other hand. Then repeat the whole process many times.

When you are familiar with the mechanics of the exercise, channel internal force to your finger with the relevant movement. This aspect of internal force channelling, as well as how to make the appropriate sounds from the respective organs, have to be personally taught by a master or qualified instructor.

The term "kungfu" is actually derived from the process of force training; learning techniques is better expressed by the term "quanfa", which means techniques of the fist. Force training is extremely demanding, with the result that students lacking self-discipline, and most beginners lack self-discipline, drop off easily.

In the past, masters were generally not worried if students dropped off, as they did not depend on their students for their livelihood. But the situation is quite different nowadays when instructors live on students' fees. Probably because of this, modern instructors are not as demanding, and many of them even have done away with initial force training, starting off their students with kungfu patterns right at the beginning, a practice which can make kungfu practice easier but which is not necessary good for genuine kungfu training.

(a) (b) (c)

(d) (e) (f)

Fig 6.7 One-Finger Shooting Zen

Black Tiger and Drunken Man

A kungfu pattern is a kungfu movement, or a series of movements. If you stand at a left bow-arrow stance and strike out a straight right punch at heart level, Fig 6.8, this is a pattern; and this pattern is very common in many styles of martial art. In Shaolin Kungfu, every pattern has a name, which is often meaningful and poetic. This particular pattern is called "Black Tiger Steals Heart".

Fig 6.8 Black Tiger Steals Heart

A particular pattern provides a student with some of the best ways to achieve certain combative purposes. There are of course countless ways a person can strike his opponent with a straight punch. He may, for instance, stand with both feet fairly close together instead of wide apart as in the bow-arrow stance, or he may launch his body forward to give extra weight instead of holding it upright as in the stance above.

It was probable that early fighters punched in this way as this is more "natural" than the Black Tiger pattern. But gradually fighters discover from their experiences that this "natural" way had numerous set-backs, and other "learnt" ways might give certain advantages. For example, if they stood naturally with feet fairly close together, they only had a short reach; and if they launched their body forward, they would lose their balance more easily. Hence, the more enterprising fighters might experiment with placing one leg forward as they struck, and keeping an upright posture to have better control of balance.

Through years of trial and error, past masters improved their fighting techniques. It was a long, tedious process, but gradually they discovered that attacking and defending in certain special ways gave certain advantages for specific purposes, and they stylized these movements into kungfu patterns. "Black Tiger Steals Heart" represents a crystallization of many years of such experimentation: by using this pattern when making a straight attack, the attacker can have many technical advantages in most situations.

However, in more complex situations — like when you have to deflect a high attack from one opponent, avoid a low attack from a second opponent, and strike a third opponent all at the same time — another pattern, like the one shown in Fig 6.9 and is known as "Drunken Man Offers Wine", may give better advantages. Why, then, do we bother to learn simple patterns like the Black Tiger when we could start with complex patterns straight away, even though we may take a longer time to learn these complex patterns? Would it not be logical to learn only the best patterns?

Fig 6.9 Drunken Man Offers Wine

When we learn a kungfu set, we are actually learning the best patterns with reference to some special objectives. A kungfu set is a collection of kungfu patterns linked together in some meaningful ways.

While the Drunken Man in the above example is preferred to the Black Tiger in certain situations, in other situations the Black Tiger can serve our purposes better. For example, it requires good balance to execute the Drunken Man well, and unless the exponent has developed internal force, the Drunken Man's strike, even if it hits, may not be decisive. Hence, for a beginner who is not likely to meet complex situations often, the simpler Black Tiger is a better pattern.

Combative Functions of Flowery Patterns

Many students, and some instructors, say that most Shaolin Kungfu patterns are too flowery to be practical for combat, thinking that the most effective techniques are fast, simple punches and kicks. This misconception is the result of insufficient understanding of the profundity of Shaolin Kungfu. All patterns of all styles of kungfu (including Taijiquan) exist because of their combative functions: these patterns, no matter how flowery they may appear to the uninitiated, are not put there to please spectators. If they are beautiful to watch (in fact they are), that is a happy coincidence.

Fast, simple punches and kicks are useful for simple situations. But if a situation becomes more complex, like when an opponent has grasped your punch or kick, and has pinned you to the ground with your arm or leg entangled, you need a more complex pattern to overcome this situation. In Shaolin Kungfu, there are techniques to overcome virtually any situation. It is naive to suggest that your opponent is not fast enough to catch your arm or leg. If he is a master, he will not only be fast enough, he will also create opportunities where catching your arm or leg becomes a certainty.

Most students do not know enough kungfu principles and techniques to be able to choose from the vast kungfu repertoire, the appropriate patterns for practice and use. Beginners do not even know how to stand and strike or defend in particular ways so as to gain technical advantages. A master overcomes these problems for his students by teaching them appropriate kungfu sets. A kungfu set represents a meaningful selection of the best kungfu movements for some well defined objectives, evolved by past masters over hundreds of years. When you learn a Shaolin Kungfu set, for instance, you are not just learning some personal actions of your instructor, you are inheriting a legacy of fighting techniques of an established institution.

Most Shaolin Kungfu sets are comparatively short, consisting of about 36 patterns; others are intermediate, about 72 patterns; while some are long, about 108 patterns. Kungfu sets are usually given meaningful and sometimes poetic names. Some examples of Shaolin sets are "Cross-Roads at the Four Gates", "Tiger and Crane", "Plum Flowers", "Seven Stars", and "Dragon's Strength".

Formation and Structure of Kungfu Sets

What are the important principles underlying the formation and structure of kungfu sets? The various patterns in a set are linked together for one, some or all of the following reasons.

A master discovered some favorite patterns which he found useful for combat. In order to facilitate his practice, he linked them into a sequence, so that he might not have to scratch his head trying to recall which patterns he had missed. These useful patterns, which might have taken the master years to develop, now come to us in a kungfu set.

From their experience in actual fighting or during sparring practice, past masters discovered that particular attacking patterns were likely to be followed by certain preferred patterns, because these preferred patterns were best suited to meet these attacks. For example, if you give your opponent a straight punch — unless he is a master who may respond in an extraordinary manner, or a fresh beginner who may just be stunned — most probably your opponent would block or dodge your attack, and the way he blocks and dodges generally falls within a small range of a few alternative movements. The masters, therefore, could anticipate the likely counters their opponents would make. In this way they devised short sequences of continuous patterns, and linked these sequences into a set. Hence, when you learn a good kungfu set, you are not just learning the physical form, but also all the strategies and principles underlying the arrangement of the constituent patterns.

Selecting the appropriate patterns to teach his students is an important function of a master. From his reservoir of countless patterns he would choose those that suit the level of his students (elementary, intermediate or advanced), and the objectives of the training (specializing on throws, meeting a bigger-sized opponent, countering kicks, etc.). Then he links these appropriate patterns, preferably in appropriate sequences, into a set. This task is made so much easier if past masters have done it for him, as in the Shaolin tradition where there are so many sets to choose from.

Advanced students often specialize in special kinds of kungfu force like Iron Palm, Tiger Claw, or No-Shadow Kicks. Obviously, if a student has spent three years every day striking his palm into some iron filing to develop his Iron Palm, it would be unwise of him to practice patterns that involve a lot of rolling on the floor or jumping in the air — patterns that are suitable for those who specialize on the Monkey and the Eagle styles. His master, or the advanced student himself, would select patterns that make full use of the palms, and link them into a set consisting of techniques that can best implement his specialized force.

Special sets are not for advanced students only. Many beginners, because of their different nature or different needs, may require special sets. For example, it is both impractical and unprofessional for an instructor to teach high kicking techniques to young girls who love wearing tight skirts; or to tell them to harden their arms against rough poles so that they could block with equal force a powerful attack from a brute. A knowledgeable master would construct suitable patterns into a special set that can enable the girls to make good use of their natural conditions, such as low kicking techniques to the opponent's shin (whereby their tight skirts become an advantage in bracing their thighs so that the kicking momentum snaps from their knees); and deflecting (instead of blocking) the opponent's attack so that brutal force can be neutralized with minimum strength. Shaolin Kungfu is rich in such sets.

Some sets are devised for force training, not for fighting techniques. Often the patterns in these sets are performed with the student remaining stationary on a horse-riding stance or a goat-stance (which is higher and narrower than a horse-riding stance). Sometimes the patterns are performed slowly, or as if without using any strength. So if you have laughed at Shaolin students performing kungfu patterns on a horse-riding stance, saying that in actual fighting you do not remain stationary like that, or the wide stance would expose your groin to the opponent's kick, you probably have an answer now. Shaolin students also normally do not fight in that manner; these horse-riding patterns are meant to develop kungfu force as a preparation for fighting, not meant as fighting techniques themselves. And if a master exposes his groin during fighting, beware! It is likely to be a trap.

Do not be Deceived by Slow, Graceful Motion.

It is a mistake to think that if an exponent performs his patterns slowly or apparently without strength when he practices his kungfu set, he will be equally slow or lacking in force during combat. I made that mistake when I learnt Wuzu Kungfu in my younger days. With my earlier experience in Hoong Ka Kungfu where my master always asked me to use strength during training, I was greatly puzzled when my Wuzu instructor constantly reminded me not to use strength when practicing my San-zhan set. The San-zhan, meaning "Three Battles", is a fundamental Wuzu Kungfu set to train internal force. But although I had practiced the San-zhan for more than a year, I did not have any internal force.

Looking back with hindsight, I now realize that the fault was not with the set, but with me: I did not understand the inner aspect of the set sufficiently to derive the best benefit from my practice. I began to have doubt. I asked myself, "How could someone ever fight effectively if he did not use strength?" But when I sparred with my seniors, who did not use strength, they were so powerful that my arms were often swollen. There was no doubt that my seniors had internal force. "How come your arms are so powerful?" I asked. "Practice Sanzhan," they answered.

It was many years later that I had some glimpses of this intriguing question. My Shaolin master, Sifu Ho Fatt Nam, returning from the palace, told me that he just taught the Sultan the Shaolin Pakua Set. This Pakua Set happens to be one of my favorite sets, and is performed fast and vigorously.

"Wouldn't this Pakua Set be too vigorous for His Highness?" I asked. "No, if it is practiced slowly and gracefully; and with proper breath coordination, it is excellent for His Highness' health."

And my master explained some very significant points. "For us, we perform the Pakua Set with speed and power to benefit from its excellent combat aspect, for that is what we need. We are not worried about its health aspect, because we are already very healthy and fit. His Highness does not need the combat aspect, but the health aspect serves him very well."

My master opened for me a fascinating new dimension of Shaolin Kungfu hitherto unknown to me when he showed me how the Shaolin Pakua Set could be performed slowly to generate internal energy flow. He continued, "Most

people think that Shaolin Kungfu is hard. That is only the elementary stage.
All good martial art has hard and soft aspects. Any martial art that has only one
aspect is not complete, and hence inadequate. Shaolin proceeds from hard to
soft, while Taijiquan proceeds from soft to hard. Advanced Shaolin can be very
soft."

I later discovered that in many advanced kungfu sets, the patterns are
performed slowly because, in conjunction with a meditative state of mind, this is
a good way to induce internal energy flow. When energy is flowing smoothly,
the movements, which are first initiated slowly, can be exceedingly fast, so fast
that an on-looker can hardly see the movements. Many spectators were surprised
when I employed this principle to demonstrate the Dragon's Strength Set as a
guest-artiste in a public performance organized by the Science University of
Malaysia Kungfu Club some years ago. This was what great masters in the past
meant when they said, "Let mind lead energy, and let energy lead form." This is
also what many Taiji masters regard as the pinnacle of achievement in Taijiquan.

Cross-Roads at Four Gates.

Using mind and internal energy to perform a kungfu set is of course an
advanced stage; at the initial stage, muscles and mechanical strength are used in
a kungfu set performance. The first kungfu set taught to the monks at the southern
Shaolin Monastery in China, was called the "Cross-Roads at the Four Gates", or
"Shi Zi Si Men Quan" in Chinese. I am very fortunate that this historic set has
been transmitted down my Shaolin lineage and was taught to me by my master,
Sifu Ho Fatt Nam. The thirty six patterns of the complete set are shown in
diagrams in the chart in Fig 6.10, and the directions of movements in Fig 6.11.
Understandably, it is difficult, especially for beginners, to learn from diagrams.

(1)   (2)   (3)   (4)

(5)   (6)   (7)   (8)   (9)

(10)   (11)   (12)   (13)   (14)

(15)   (16)   (17)   (18)

Fig 6.10 Cross-Roads at Four Gates

Fig 6.10 Cross-Roads at Four Gates

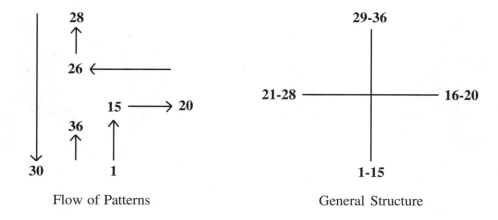

Flow of Patterns   General Structure

Fig 6.11 Directions of Movements of Four Gates

The names of the thirty six patterns are listed below:

1. Dragon and Tiger Appear.
2. Double Stars Onto the Earth.
3. Thrice Threading of Bridge.
4. Amitabha Palm.
5. Flower Hidden in Sleeves.
6. Poisonous Snake Emerges from Pit.
7. Single Dragon Emerges from Sea.
8. Block the Big Boss.
9. Carrying the Insignia.
10. Horse-riding Punch.
11. Single Tiger Claw.
12. Phoenix Flaps Wing.
13. Beauty Looks at Mirror.
14. Tiger-Tail Hand-Sweep.
15. Black Tiger Steals Heart.
16. Flower Hidden in Sleeves.
17. Poisonous Snake Emerges from Pit.
18. Single Dragon Emerges from Sea.
19. Threading the Bridge at Bow-Arrow.
20. Black Tiger Steals Heart.
21. Single Whip Saves Emperor.
22. Flower Hidden in Sleeves.
23. Poisonous Snake Emerges from Pit.
24. Single Dragon Emerges from Sea.
25. Threading the Bridge at Bow-Arrow.
26. Black Tiger Steals Heart.

27. Sharp Knife Trims Bamboo.
28. Lohan Hits Gong.
29. Catch Tiger in Mountains (right).
30. Catch Tiger in Mountains (left).
31. Cannon from Ground.
32. Organ-Seeking Kick.
33. Black Tiger Steals Heart.
34. White Crane Flaps Wings.
35. Dragon and Tiger Meet Together.
36. Hiding Two Tigers.

Because of linguistic and cultural differences, the translated names of some patterns may appear ridiculous, though in Chinese they are meaningful as well as poetic. For example, the literal translation of Pattern 25 is "Midnight Noon Thread Bridge", which is nonsensical if we do not understand the Chinese language. "Midnight Noon" is the short form of "midnight noon stance", which is another name for the bow-arrow stance. "Thread" refers to a particular kungfu technique whereby the exponent can use minimal force to deflect a powerful attack. "Bridge" is a kungfu term for the forearm. Hence, in more comprehensible but lengthy language, this pattern can be named "Standing at the bow-arrow stance to use a deflecting technique with minimal force at the opponent's forearm to neutralize his attack"!

The salient points of kungfu sets are frequently summarized by past masters in the form of poetry, often with deep, hidden meanings comprehensible only to the initiated. The following poem veils some interesting secrets of the Four Gates Set.

> Shaolin Four Gates trains bridges and stances
> Secrets are found in flowers in the sleeves
> Block the Boss and Carry Insignia with punches
> Phoenix Flap its Wings to rustle leaves
> To Hit the Gong in unexpected slanting motion
> To Seek the Organ, show the shadow hand
> The marvel of Catching Tigers in the Mountains
> Only from the master can students understand

Although this Cross-Roads at Four Gates is a basic set taught to beginning Shaolin students, it can be appreciated at many levels. At the elementary level, the set is simple, with the main objective of training fundamental arm movements and footwork. A kungfu principle advises that for most ordinary combat situations, if your "bridges" are powerful and stances solid, you have won thirty percent even before fighting begins.

At the intermediate level, the combative application of its patterns is fascinating. It is amazing that these seemingly simple techniques can be so artistically and beautifully used to neutralize many complicated attacks. For example, presume that as you strike with a Black Tiger, a very common attack, your opponent grips your wrist, trips your front leg, and presses down at your elbow with his other hand, threatening to break or dislocate your elbow joint, while you sprawl forward with your other hand barely preventing your face smashing on to the ground, Fig 6.12. Or presume that your opponent grips both your wrists, and executes a thrust kick at your chest, Fig 6.13. How would you counter such attacks?

Fig 6.12 Lohan Tames a Tiger

Fig 6.13 White Horse Presents Hoof

If you think that such attacks do not occur in a real fight because they are too complicated to execute, you are mistaken. When I was training under Sifu Ho, even senior students could often use such attacks on me. For a Shaolin master, applying these "complicated" attacks is quite easy. Read the next chapter and treat yourself to the fascination of Shaolin application.

7
Fighting In Beautiful Movements

(Kungfu Application for Combat)

A kungfu exponent moves the way he moves, not because he wants to please spectators, but because that way gives him the best technical advantages in specific combat situations. His kungfu form is the result of, and practiced for, effective fighting; not devised for attractive demonstration, though to the uninitiated many kungfu patterns may appear flowery.

The Combative Function of Kungfu

The primary function of kungfu, any type of kungfu, is for fighting, though in our present law abiding society this may not be its most important benefit. This combative function of kungfu can never be over-emphasized, for without it kungfu as a martial art loses its meaning.

Yet, it is simply shocking that nowadays so many people learn or teach kungfu without ever touching on this combative function. Of the thousands of kungfu students I have met, more than eighty percent have never ever sparred, even amongst their classmates! With the present world situation where most kungfu competitions today are based on demonstration rather than sparring, this unfortunate trend is likely to continue. This brings forth a pitiful sense of waste, for kungfu is actually a wonderful fighting art — if we know its combative application.

Of course, stressing the combative function of kungfu does not necessarily imply encouraging kungfu students to fight. In fact I am of the opinion that some kungfu students and instructors become aggressive because of their conscious or unconscious attempt to cover up their combat inefficiency. In my experience, kungfu masters who can fight well are generally humble and peaceful people, far more serene and tolerant than masters of most other martial systems, probably because they are so confident of their fighting abilities that they feel no need to fight or spar for confirmation.

According to legend, a disciple from the southern Shaolin Monastery had to fight his way through a hundred and eight wooden robots before he could graduate. These wooden robots were so ingeniously constructed that they executed some tricky and advanced attacking techniques besides all the common fighting movements. So a Shaolin graduate who successfully passed through this famous "Lane of 108 Wooden Robots" was necessarily a formidable fighter.

Patterns, Variations and Sequences

Of the many excellent methods to teach fighting skills in Shaolin Kungfu, a basic approach is to explain and demonstrate to students the combative functions of every pattern of a kungfu set that they have competently learnt. In my teaching, I often ask my students what they thought were the applications of their kungfu patterns, before I explained to them. In this way I set them thinking, laying a helpful foundation whereby they could later discover the uses of other patterns themselves.

Knowing the uses is only the beginning; students must practice using these patterns in combat. In other words, it is not enough just to know that this pattern can be used to dodge a kick, and that pattern to lock an opponent's arm; students must actually practice dodging kicks and locking arms, not just once or twice, but hundreds of times.

When an opponent kicks you, or when you try to lock his arm — unless he is incompetent — he is not going to remain still to let you complete your moves uninterruptedly, as is often shown in martial art magazines or even live demonstrations. In theory his next moves are limitless; but in practice, they fall within a range of possibilities that can often be anticipated by an experienced master.

So, the next stage is to learn and practice the "variations" of the kungfu patterns. The term "variations" as used here is translated from Chinese, and refers not to the various ways a particular pattern can be performed, but the various likely follow-up patterns a kungfu exponent would use immediately after he has executed a particular pattern.

For example, after I dodge an opponent's kick, a likely pattern he would use is to follow up with a straight punch. Hence my variation is a pattern called "Lohan Hitting a Gong", moving forward diagonally to meet and push away his punching arm, and striking him at the same time. It is likely for him to "float" my arm and strike my side ribs which are (purposely) exposed. I follow up with "Save the Emperor with a Single Whip", striking his elbow or extended arm. He is likely to move away his arm and strike my face (which is probably the best part of my body for him to attack in this situation) with his other hand. Accordingly I follow up with "Hiding Flowers in the Sleeves" and "Single Dragon" in one smooth continuous movement, blocking his attack and then striking him. Please see Fig 7.1 to 7.7.

(7.1) (7.2)

(7.3) (7.4) (7.5)

(7.6) (7.7)

Fig 7.1-7 A Variation from Hitting Gong

The short sequence of patterns mentioned above is a variation of my dodging a kick. All these patterns are found in the Shaolin set, "Cross Roads at Four Gates". Notice that in this variation, I use only my right hand throughout, which is one of the fundamental principles of arm use in this basic set. In this example, I can effectively use only one arm to counter the opponent's use of both hands and a kick.

Of course, in a real fight, the opponent may not react in the way anticipated above, though that way is one of the most logical if he is to exploit technical advantages of the existing situations. The opponent, for example, may follow with a second kick, instead of a punch; or he may just move back after the first kick. Irrespective of the method he chooses, I can still follow up with "Lohan Hitting a Gong".

He may dodge my Lohan fist, or block it with force instead of "floating" it up. I still can continue with "Single Whip", in this case, hitting his ribs instead of his elbow, and moving my body slightly forward instead of back as in the previous case. The opponent may block my arm, or grip it with one or both hands; and yet I can carry on with "Hiding Flowers" and "Single Dragon". Hence, if the kungfu exponent is expedient, he can use the same variation even if the opponent reacts differently. Please see Fig 7.8 to 7.14.

(7.8)   (7.9)

(7.10)   (7.11)   (7.12)

(7.13)   (7.14)

Fig 7.8-14 Another Application of Hitting Gong

Nevertheless, if the opponent's responses are vastly different, such as after the initial kick, he jumps to attack my head, or squats down to grasp my leg, then I have to employ another variation. Generally if a kungfu exponent is familiar with some variations, it is often adequate to handle most common combat situations that issue from that particular pattern. To simplify matters for students, past masters have arranged these variations into appropriate short sequences consisting of a few likely patterns.

One interesting question is whether kungfu exponents must fight in stylistic form. Can they fight "naturally", without going into such elaborate stances and patterns? It must be emphasized again that in a fight, or even in routine form practice, a kungfu exponent moves the way he moves, not because he wants to please spectators, but because that way gives him the best technical advantages in specific combat situations. His kungfu form is the result of, and practiced for, effective fighting; not devised for attractive demonstration, though to the uninitiated many kungfu patterns may appear flowery.

These combative kungfu patterns have been developed through the ages, and are usually not spontaneous to those who have not practiced them.

In other words, for those people who have never practiced kungfu, it is "unnatural" for them to fight the way a kungfu master would fight. Hence, unless you have practiced these kungfu movements well for combat, you will find yourself very clumsy, sometimes comical, when you try to use them in a fight, even if you theoretically know their combat application. My master advised me "not to learn kungfu but you practice it."

Some Amazing Applications

Let us examine some of the combat applications of the kungfu patterns found in the basic Shaolin set, "Cross Roads at the Four Gates". There is at least one useful function for every kungfu pattern; otherwise that pattern would have been eliminated. Usually there are many functions for one pattern, but in the description below, space permits that only the main points of one or two applications are mentioned.

Shaolin disciples are very courteous; even in a fight they need not have to be impolite. "Dragon and Tiger Appear" is a Shaolin greeting, even to the opponent. But if your opponent tries to hold your two arms, you can use this pattern to release his hold, and at the same time jab into his neck with your left palm, punch his jaw with your right fist, and strike his groin with your left knee.

If the opponent grabs you from your back, surrounding your body with his two arms, you can release the hold with "Double Stars to the Earth", followed by "Thrice Threading of Bridge" to separate his hands.

The "Amitabha Palm" is an effective way to release a grip on your wrist. You can effect the release "from inside" or "from outside", Fig 7.15. Follow up with a strike at his chest or face, pushing away his arm outwardly or inwardly respectively as you strike out. So, it is not easy for anyone to hold you, if you know Shaolin Kungfu application. Philosophically, this symbolizes that the Shaolin arts can help you to free yourself from any constraining situations in life.

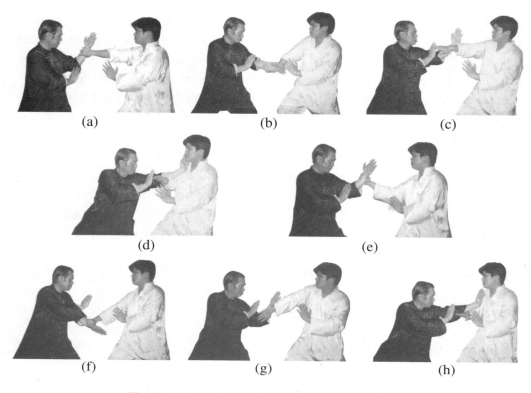

Fig 7.15 Releasing a Grip with Amitabha Palm

Just like many things in life can be very profound though they appear simple on the surface, many deceptively simple looking Shaolin patterns are amazing in their uses. "Flowers Hidden in Sleeves" is an example. Let us look at two interesting applications. Suppose someone grips your neck from behind with both hands. Turn about, swing your arm round, and lock both his arms with "Flowers Hidden in the Sleeves", Fig 7.16 to 7.18. You see, it is not easy to strangle a Shaolin disciple, even from behind.

Fig 7.16-18 Flowers in the Sleeves

Your opponent has gripped your right wrist with his right hand, and tripped your front leg, sending you sprawling forward. When he hits down hard at your left elbow with his left palm, he may dislocate or break it. But do not worry — if you know Shaolin kungfu application. Move your left foot slightly forward to regain balance, and "Hide Flowers in your Sleeves". Notice how easily this simple movement neutralizes his seemingly intractable attack. By moving your left foot slightly, you have changed the fulcrum of attack on your right elbow, so that when he presses it with his left hand to dislocate it, it turns out that he is actually helping you to execute your pattern, and if he is not careful, now it becomes his turn to lose balance! As you jerk down your elbow and turn your arm in the "Hiding Flowers" pattern, your opponent has to release his hold on your right wrist, or else *his* wrist will be dislocated or suffers extricating pain. Present him a "Single Dragon" (i.e a punch) to his face. Please see 7.19 to 7.22.

(7.19) (7.20)

(7.21) (7.22)

Fig 7.19-22 Neutralizing an "Intractable" Attack.

"Poisonous Snake Emerges from Pit" and "Single Dragon Emerges from Sea" are simple attacking patterns with the palm and the fist. But a master can use these simple patterns in some amazing ways. For example, a novice swings a round-house kick at a master. Instead of blocking or dodging, the master just swiftly moves in with a "Single Dragon", striking the novice's abdomen. The round-house kick, which is actually a clumsy attack, especially by a novice, will not hit the master, because before it has travelled half its distance, the master's thrust punch will have sent the novice tumbling backward.

"Block the Big Boss" is a useful technique to use to deflect an opponent's frontal attack, especially when your arm is already extended forward. It is also an amazingly simple technique to counter seemingly unmanageable attacks, like when your opponent, holding your arms apart, give you a right thrust kick to your chest. Turn your body to sit at the sideway horse-riding stance, jerking your elbow down so that your forearm deflects your opponent's right thigh. The turning of your arms as you lower yourself into your sideway horse-riding stance will release your opponent's hold on your arms. As he kicks, you punch. His kick will not reach you because you have deflected his thigh, and also you have turned your body sideways. You can easily hit his genitals, but for compassionate reasons, strike his abdomen instead, Fig 7.23-25.

(7.23)   (7.24)   (7.25)

Fig 7.23-25 Hitting Your Opponent as He Attacks

Catching Tigers in Mountains

When you attack with a "Horse-Riding Punch", you opponent may counter with a low attack to your exposed side ribs. Bring your elbow back with "Carrying the Insignia" to block his attack, turning your body slightly for better effect, without moving your legs. If someone is close behind you, after making sure he is an enemy and not a loved one, you can use this pattern as an elbow strike.

"Single Tiger Claw" is used to grip the opponent's wrist, and applied by a master with internal force, he can numb or paralyse the opponent's arm. "Phoenix Flaps Wing" is a close-body elbow attack.

A simple way to block a frontal strike is to use "Beauty Looks at Mirror". If the opponent withdraws his attacking hand, you can follow through with "Tiger-Tail Hand-Sweep" to strike him. Complete the coup de grace with a simple but powerful "Black Tiger Steals Heart".

Although it looks simple, "Threading the Bridge at Bow-Arrow" can be a deadly pattern. After "threading", or deflecting, an opponent's attack, follow through with a strike at a vital point near his arm pit while his arm is still extended forward.

When your opponent executes a thrust kick, step backward slightly to avoid his kick but not too far that you lose contact, and strike his shin with a "Single Whip". "Sharp Knife Trims Bamboo" is a useful double palm attack to the opponent's side. In "Lohan Hits Gong", the gong is your opponent's head.

"Catch Tiger in Mountains" is one of the most beautiful patterns in Shaolin Kungfu, and its beauty lies not so much in its appearance but in its combat functions. Years ago, a fifth dan karate master from Japan specially paid a visit to my master, Sifu Ho Fatt Nam, to test his Shaolin Kungfu. With a thundering shout and in lightning speed, the Japanese expert executed a double flying kick at my master, who responded with "Catch Tiger in Mountains". The Japanese flew over the head of the Chinese. There was no contact between the masters. After he had steadily landed, the Japanese master turned round, gallantly bowed, thanked my master, and said the match was over. Spectators, who had come to see an exciting match, were very disappointed, as they did not understand what actually had transpired.

Later, over tea, the Japanese expert told my master that in his travels round the world, so far no one had successfully met his lightning flying attacks. Most people, taken by surprise, would retreat; but they would still be hit, because he simply flew into and kicked them. Some would move aside to the left or right, but the karate master was so agile that he could twist his body in the air accordingly to the directions his opponents had dodged, and kicked at his surprised opponents. Only my master, he said, could successfully neutralize his hitherto ever victorious attack with a movement that he had never seen or imagined before.

My master confided in me that no one else, except the two of them, knew that he had beaten the Japanese master with that "Catch a Tiger" pattern, and he told why. In line with the poem describing the salient points of the "Four Gates" set, I will leave you with the excitement of discovering from a Shaolin master the marvels of this "Catch tiger in mountains" pattern, and why or how my master had defeated that Japanese expert.

Do not Blow Off his Genitals!

"Cannon from Ground" is a deadly, effective technique Shaolin disciples would not use unless necessary, for this cannon would blow off the opponent's genitals. Instead of using the fist, Shaolin disciples may use their legs in "Organ-Seeking kick" at the opponent's reproductive organs. Even when the opponent is an arch enemy, Shaolin disciples usually find it not necessary to blow off his genitals; so they hit or kick the thigh or abdomen instead.

"White Crane Flaps Wings" is as elegant in its appearance as in application. There are many ways this pattern can be used in combat, though many beginners will find it hard to imagine how this seemingly demonstrative movement can be effective in fighting. One way is when two opponents just begin to hold your wrists at both sides. If you flap your wings, moving your palms fast against their wrists, they will have to let go off your wrists to avoid the extricating pain your palms cause against their twisted wrists. In another application, this "White Crane" pattern is a devastating Organ-Seeking Kick, with the flapping wings as distraction.

"Dragon and Tiger Meet Together" is similar to "Dragon and Tiger Appear". Possibly the dragon and the tiger were good friends of Shaolin monks in the past; together with the snake, the crane and the leopard, as they often appear in Shaolin Kungfu. After setting two tigers (two fists) to roam about, Shaolin monks hide them at the end of a kungfu set. The circular way the fists are turned in "Hiding Two Tigers" is effective in releasing wrist holds.

Flowery Movements and Kungfu Tradition

Even a brief description of the combat application of these comparatively simple Shaolin Kungfu patterns reveals the rich range of Shaolin self-defense techniques. One should note that the applications explained above are only the basics; due to space constrain, other applications of the same techniques are not mentioned.

Some time ago when the popularity of Japanese karate and Korean taekwondo took the world by storm, many kungfu practitioners including some old teachers who were mistaken to be masters due to their age rather than their kungfu attainment, were rudely awakened to their combative inadequacy when compared to the combat effectiveness and directness of karate and taekwondo. These kungfu practitioners expounded that kungfu was not as effective as karate or taekwondo for combat because kungfu patterns were too elaborated and flowery. They suggested trimming the elaborate movements of kungfu, leaving behind only obvious fighting patterns like punches, blocks and kicks. In other words they suggested changing kungfu into karate or taekwondo. (This is the reverse of opportunist instructors who are basically trained in karate or taekwondo, but, because of the magical attraction of the word "kungfu", add a few kungfu moves into their martial art and claim to teach kungfu.) Some teachers even renamed their schools such and such "do", and adopted the color-belt graduation system.

Apparently, these practitioners were unaware of the depth and tradition of Chinese kungfu. There are no extraneous movements in kungfu; every move has a purpose, and this purpose is almost always martial in nature. If any kungfu movement appears extraneous or flowery to an observer, it is because he fails to understand its deeper martial significance; simplifying the movement would spoil the very purpose for which it is designed. For example, in the pattern "Flowers Hidden in the Sleeves", turning the wrist in a small circle, keeping the elbow sharply bent and placing the upper arm close to the body, may appear extraneous; someone admiring the straight-forward movements of karate and taekwondo may suggest trimming those elaborate movements into a simple block. The crucial point is that this pattern is not merely a simple block, and the trimming will eliminate many subtle applications, some of which have been described earlier in this chapter.

Suffixing "do", such as judo, kendo, karate-do, hapkido, huarongdo and taekwondo, is a typically Japanese or Korean, but not a Chinese, tradition. "Do", which is "tao" (spelt as "dao" in Romanized Chinese), means "the way".

In the Japanese context, this suffixing of "do" represents a transformation of the deadly martial arts of the classical warriors (often denoted by the term "jitsu") to the recreational "martial sports" of our modern times. For example, the deadly techniques of jujitsu and kenjitsu, upon which ninjas and samurais owed their life and death, are replaced by safer techniques of judo and kendo for modern sport.

The term "do", or "tao", is comparatively insignificant in the Chinese tradition, because throughout Chinese history, kungfu has always been used for fighting, and seldom as a sport, though Shaolin Kungfu was also used for spiritual development. (Interestingly the most commonly used term for kungfu in the Chinese language today is "wushu", which inclines towards sport rather than combat, although the term means "martial art".) Hence, as a rough guide, if you come across any type of kungfu which carries the suffix "do", it often suggests that the instructor is much influenced by the Japanese or Korean tradition.

In genuine kungfu tradition, belt grading is absent; there may be grading, but the level of attainment is not usually shown by colored belts. Traditionally, the belt or sash of a kungfu practitioner, which is very different in look from that found in karate or taekwondo, and irrespective of whether the practitioner is a novice or a master, is usually black in color, and is meant to hold his trousers, not to indicate his attainment level.

Hence, it actually does not make much sense if someone tells you he is a kungfu black-belt. And if an instructor advertises himself as a kungfu red belt 8th dan, my first impression is that he is probably unfamiliar with kungfu tradition.

There is, of course, no implication that belt grading in not useful. It has been useful in many martial arts like judo, karate and taekwondo, and some genuine kungfu instructors have adopted it; but the point is that belt grading, at least at present, is not a kungfu tradition.

8
From Kungfu Form To Combat Application
(Specific Techniques to Handle Various Situations)

Remember that the one practicing with you is your partner, not your enemy. Your aim therefore is to help each other to improve your combat efficiency, and not to hit each other.

Getting Ready for Combat

Have you ever wondered how kungfu students could fight by just learning routine sets? They could not, no matter how many sets or how long they might have learnt those sets. Learning routine sets is just the preparation — to equip students with the necessary kungfu patterns. If they want to apply these patterns to fight well, they have to undergo different types of training. Shaolin Kungfu is rich in such training methods, though many students may not know them!

Some instructors provide their students with pairs of gloves to spar on their own. This is unmethodical, and usually in such spontaneous situations the students would be unable to apply what they have earlier learnt in their set practice. There are actually a number of steps between set practice and free sparring, and the students should approach these steps methodically.

There are two principal approaches in learning kungfu application. One approach is to proceed from patterns to situations: for each kungfu pattern, we find out what it is used for in combat situations. The other approach is from situations to patterns: for each typical combat situation, we find out what patterns can be suitably employed to overcome that situation.

For example, we have learnt a pattern, "Beauty Looks at Mirror". We find out that in fighting, we can used it to block a palm strike to our eyes, or a punch to our heart. It can also be used as a diagonal slashing attack against an opponent's throat. This approach is from a pattern to situations.

Alternatively, we can think of some possible ways an opponent may attack us. A very common attack is a straight punch to our chest. We examine the various kungfu patterns we have learnt and select those that can effectively counter this type of attack. From our "Four Gates" we can use patterns like "Beauty Looks at Mirror", "Flowers Hidden in the Sleeves" and "Block the Big Boss" to meet this straight punch. This approach is from a combat situation to kungfu patterns.

Kungfu masters go further than this stage. For example, in the patterns-to-situations approach, they ask themselves, if the attack to the eyes is a powerful kick instead of a vicious palm strike, can they counter the attack as effectively with "Beauty Looks at Mirror"? Probably not, because a blocking forearm is generally not as powerful as a kicking leg. In the same way they reason that even if the attack is a palm strike, but if the attacker is a massive brute and the defender a small-sized lady, the beauty may not be effective with her "Mirror Hand".

So the masters have to think of other ways to counter such a combat situation. The beauty may, for example, step slightly aside to avoid the brutal force of the massive attack, spread her arms so that her front palm strikes at the attacking forearm, and simultaneously kicks at the attacker's genitals as in the pattern "White Crane Spreads Wings". No matter how massive or brutal the attacker may be, if his genitals are being kicked, even by a small-sized lady, he will be put out of action long enough for the harassed victim to run away.

The example starts with patterns-to-situations but concludes with the situations-to-patterns, illustrating that the classification into the two approaches is arbitrary and for convenience of study. Such study was common at the Shaolin Monastery where masters and monks had much time and opportunity to discuss and experiment with various combat situations and a wide range of kungfu techniques. We benefit from their invaluable effort as we learn and practice the Shaolin arts.

In the previous chapter we use the patterns-to-situations approach to learn some applications of the patterns in the basic Shaolin "Four Gates" set. Here we select some common combat situations and learn the specific techniques to counter them.

Shaolin Specific Techniques

For convenience, all attacks can be classified into four main categories, namely hitting, kicking, felling and gripping. Let us examine some specific techniques and their underlying principles in dealing with the common attacks of all the four categories.

Suppose an opponent pierces at your eyes or throat with his fingers, in a pattern known as "Poisonous Snake Shoots out Venom". Step back into the bow-arrow stance and block his attack with "Beauty Looks at Mirror", Figure 8.1. Notice that because you have moved back a step, even if you failed to block his vicious attack, it will still not reach you. This illustrates an important philosophical principle of life. Even if you are faced with a very threatening situation, if you are ready to retreat just one step, you can frequently defuse the situation without having to fight ferociously.

Fig 8.1 Beauty Looks at Mirror

Probably the most frequently used attacking pattern in most styles of martial art is the straight middle punch, like "Black Tiger Steals Heart" in Shaolin Kungfu. Besides using the "Mirror Hand" as in the previous example, you can counter with "Single Tiger Emerges from Cave", which is accomplished by moving half a step backward into the false-leg stance and blocking his attack with a circular movement of your hand held in a tiger-claw formation, Figure 8.2. This type of blocking, which uses minimal force against maximal force, is known as "leaning" in Shaolin Kungfu: you "lean" your arm against his attack. You may, if you are competent, follow up with a tiger-claw grip at the opponent's arm.

Fig 8.2 Single Tiger Emerges from Cave

Now your opponent attacks you with a low "Horse-Riding Punch". You move back into a sideway false-leg stance, and hence away from his attacking area, and chop your palm into his attacking forearm or elbow, in a pattern called "False-Leg Hand-Sweep", Figure 8.3.

Please note that you are not blocking, but attacking him instead. This seemingly simple pattern demonstrates an advanced level of countering an attack. Countering can be classified into three types: first defend then counter; defense cum counter; and no-block direct counter. This "no-block direct counter" not only avoids his attack, but strikes the opponent at the time when his attack is fully spent.

Fig 8.3 False-Leg Hand-Sweep

In the next attack, your opponent attempts to slap your face, in an interesting sounding pattern called "Devil King Waves Fan". This time you move slightly forward into the bow-arrow stance, block his sideway-circular attack with one arm, and strike him with your other fist, in an equally charming pattern named "Old Elephant Drops Tusk", Figure 8.4. A friend looking at you now may imagine you to be an elephant, with your attacking arm as the elephant's trunk, and your defending arm as the remaining tusk! This is an example of "defense cum counter".

Fig 8.4 Old Elephant Drops Tusk

Hitting attacks can be generalized into four kinds: high, middle, low and sideways. We have just learnt how to counter them. And if you know how to counter one typical example of one kind, you can usually counter other examples of the same kind. For example, if you can apply "Beauty Looks at Mirror" to counter "Poisonous Snake Shoots out Venom", you can usually apply the same specific technique against similar high hitting attacks, irrespective of whether they are palm, fist, knuckle or finger strikes to your throat, eyes, mouth or nose.

Countering Various Kicks

Some people mistakenly think that kicks are superior to hitting attacks because they are more destructive and more difficult to defend against. If this were true, then most if not all of the hitting attacks in Shaolin Kungfu would have been replaced. In fact, it is generally easier to defend against kicks than against hits, because a hand attack is more versatile and tricky than a kick. A hand attack by an exponent with internal powerful is more deadly than a kicking attack too. Let us now learn some efficient ways to counter high, middle, low and sideway kicking attacks.

An opponent gives you a high kick, a technique that is usually discouraged in Shaolin Kungfu unless the situation warrants its application. High kicks bare the vital reproductive organs, making it easy for the opponent to strike them. To think that the opponent is not knowledgeable nor fast enough to exploit this weakness, is a sign of shallow learning. Never underestimate your opponent: it is a fundamental Shaolin principle that we always regard the opponent to be as good as if not better than ourselves. That is why practically every Shaolin attacking movement takes into account of the possibility of the opponent's sudden counter attack. Moreover, high kicks make balancing awkward, as well as limit the full use of the other three limbs.

Actually it is easy to counter high kicks. Just move your body slantingly back, without even moving your legs, and without doing anything else, except, perhaps, watching his unsightly view. We could move in for the coup de grace, but we do not, because since we never underestimate our opponent, we must be careful that this tempting exposure may be a trap. Another important Shaolin principle advises that it is better to miss an opening than to risk rushing into a snare. The attacking pattern here is known as "Kicking the Sky", which can often be interpreted as kicking wildly; and the defense pattern is "Taming a Tiger with a String of Beads", Figure 8.5.

Fig 8.5 Taming a Tiger with a String of Beads

The next kicking attack, a middle side kick, has better aim; it is targeted at the heart or the liver. Despite its destructive objective, this pattern has a gentle, even poetic name, "Happy Bird Hops up a Branch". Sit back on your sideway horse-riding stance — this movement will move your body away from his attack — and simultaneously, just as he has kicked his full extent, lock his leg with your two tiger claws, with one arm supporting his extended leg and the other hand gripping his foot, as shown in Figure 8.6. This pattern is called "Two Tigers Subdue a Dragon".

Now you have a few alternatives. If you twist his foot, you could dislocate his ankle. Or you could, still holding his leg, move in and kick the shin or knee of his other leg. This is an example of "first defend then counter".

Fig 8.6 Two Tigers Subdue a Dragon

What would you do if your opponent kicks your shin or knee, as in the pattern called "Yellow Oriole Tests Water"? Just skip back gently, sit on your low sideway horse-riding stance, and "hang" your fist (i.e. hit with your back knuckles) onto his attacking foot. This "no-block direct counter" pattern is called "Heavenly Priest Stamps Insignia", Figure 8.7.

It is important that you should be looking at your opponent's face, and not at his foot as many students would do, and be ready for his likely follow up attack on your face.

Fig 8.7 Heavenly Priest Stamps Insignia

The opponent executes a whirlwind kick, which may look similar to, but in some ways different from the round-house kick of other martial arts. The Shaolin whirlwind kick is performed with the body comparatively vertical, unlike the more horizontally inclined body position of the round-house kick.

Moreover the whirlwind kick is executed more from the knee, unlike the round-house kick where the whole leg is involved. To counter this whirlwind kick, slant your body backwards and "thread" away the opponent's leg with your hand following the direction and momentum of the kick. This "thread" is a typical Shaolin technique where gentle movement is used against a powerful attack.

It is executed as follows: move your hand in a small circular and forward manner as if you are sewing with a needle and thread, except that instead of holding your thumb and index finger together like when you are holding a needle, you point your thumb and index finger forward. This defense pattern is called "Thread the Clouds to See the Sun", Figure 8.8.

Fig 8.8 Thread the Clouds to See the Sun

Gripping and Felling Attacks

One expression of the beauty and richness of Shaolin Kungfu is its wide range of attack and defend techniques. If you want to subdue your opponent but do not wish to hurt him badly by punching or kicking him, you will be fascinated with the gripping techniques of Shaolin Kungfu. But first, let us learn how to get yourselves out of the opponent's grips.

The opponent grips your forearm with a tiger-claw technique. Relax and swing your arm in a circle, completing your swing with the back of your fist "hanging" (i.e. hitting with the back knuckles) onto your opponent's face. The swing of your arm will twist his wrist in such a way that he has to release his grip. This pattern is called "Rolling Thunder", and is an example of "defense cum counter", Figure 8.9.

It also illustrates the principle of "soft against hard", where you use a graceful swing instead of brutal strength to release yourself from the grip.

(a)   (b)

Fig 8.9 Rolling Thunder

Now your opponent grips your hair from your front, in a pattern with an unlikely name, "Saint Pulling Hair". Prevent him from pulling by holding his hand with your one or two hands. Then, still holding his hand to your head, bend slightly and turn your head a complete round, twisting his hand in the process, in a pattern called "Lion Turning Head", Figure 8.10.

(a)   (b)

Fig 8.10 Lion Turning Head

There are some weak points in this pattern that you must take care. The movement is relatively long, and in the process of turning your head, your opponent may attack you with his other hand. It is actually not a good pattern to use in actual combat (unless your opponent is slow or unskilled), but a good pattern for practice because it illustrates the principle of releasing his grip by turning his wrist.

When you are familiar with the philosophy of this principle, you can use other less lengthy and more elegant techniques to implement the same principle.

Figure 8.11 shows an example. You hold his hand as before, but instead of bending his wrist by turning your head a complete round, you bend his wrist by a sharp jerk of your head downward and slightly forward, with your hands pressing hard at his palm against your head so that his wrist bend backward unnaturally.

As he releases his grip (he has to, or else his wrist will be dislocated), while still holding his hand with your two hands, turn his arm sharply to one side so that his palm face upward, getting him under your control.

You must be very careful when you practice this technique with a partner so as not to dislocate his wrist. This pattern is called "Two Dragons Subdue a Serpent". Figure 8.12 shows the close-ups of the wrist-bending technique.

Fig 8.11 Two Dragons Subdue a Serpent

Fig 8.12 Close-Ups of the Wrist-Bending Technique

Beside hitting, kicking or gripping, an opponent may attack you by felling you to the ground. There are many felling techniques in Shaolin Kungfu, including some where there is no need to use the hands. The opponent uses two felling techniques against you, a sweep and a push. The examples show how to counter them.

In the "Frontal Leg Sweep", the opponent tries to fell you by pulling you forward and simultaneously uses his leg to sweep your leg in front. Lift your attacked leg and place it behind his sweeping leg. Stretch back and straighten this leg of yours, bend the other leg to form a bow-arrow stance, and simultaneously turn your waist sharply while your hands sweep at your opponent's chest; with your straightened leg acting as fulcrum, you fell your opponent backward. This pattern is known as "Fisherman Casts Net". Notice that you return his leg sweep with your hand sweep.

(a) (b) (c)

(d) (e)

Fig 8.13 Fisherman Casts Net

Now your opponent tries to fell you backward, using a pattern called "Uprooting a Tree". He places one leg behind you, sits low on his Horse-Riding stance, and push at your shoulders.

Following the direction of his push, turn your waist and body so as to form the unicorn stance, and brush off his pushing hands. Then swiftly turn your Unicorn stance into a Bow-Arrow stance, by reversing the turning of your body and widening your legs. Strike your opponent with "Double Butterfly Palms", Figure 8.14.

Alternatively, if you do not wish to hurt him with a strike, just push him away. Here, although you return a push with a push, you are not responding tooth for tooth, because while your push is comparatively harmless, his push, if the victim is unskillful or unfortunate enough to land on the back of his head, may be fatal!

(a)   (b)

(c)

Fig 8.14 Double Butterfly Palms

Methodology of Practice

Practicing specific techniques against particular combat situations is a good introduction to kungfu application. Your result will be multiplied if you follow some sound methodology of practice. The following are some good suggestions.

First of all, remember that the one practicing with you is your partner, not your enemy. Your aim therefore is to help each other to improve your combat efficiency, and not to hit each other. So you must control your attacks so that even if your partner fails to defend them, you will stop your attacks a few inches from his body. Even if you accidentally hit him, your strikes merely touch him, without causing him much pain.

On the other hand, if you are accidentally hit by your partner, your reaction should *never* be: "That bastard hit me; I will get even with him!. You just wait and see, bastard!" Instead, you should say to yourself, or to him: "Thank you for demonstrating my weakness in a most practical way. Luckily it is from a partner; if it were from an enemy it could be serious. Benefiting from this lesson, I will not let that happen again."

Do not make the gross mistake of thinking that such an attitude is trite or naive; it makes the difference between taking your martial art as a training for violence, or as a path for spiritual development.

If you are too good for your partner, for your as well as his benefit, you have to adjust yourself to his level. This means that you may have to purposely slow down your movements or use less force so that he has a chance to match you. If you frustrate his movements every time, it means that both of you can practice up to this stage only, with no opportunity to go beyond.

You can benefit a great deal by practicing with someone below your standard. Because you are superior to him in techniques or force, you need not have to worry, for example, about which kungfu patterns you should use next, or whether your block is powerful enough to stop his attack.

This means you can focus on other important factors like timing and spacing, or in more advanced levels, on implementing certain principles or strategies. If you are sparring with someone equal to or above your level, you are usually too busy worrying about immediate techniques to think of such invisible factors that often decide the outcome of the combat.

With this philosophy in mind that the sparring practice should benefit both mutually, and not an occasion to boast off one's superior skills, let us look at the practical aspect of the training. Initially, practice with a partner only one preselected situation many, many times until your movements are smooth and spontaneous.

Then reverse roles so that you can have some idea of how your opponent would feel and move. Resist the temptation of proceeding to new techniques before you are competent in the present ones. Remember that the onus of the training is to improve skills rather than to learn more and more techniques.

Only when you and your partner are familiar with a few specific techniques and their combat situations, one will attack the other without prearranged selection. Initially limit the range to only two or three combat situations, then gradually widen the range as you progress.

If you are a beginner you will find it very difficult, but not impossible, to practice kungfu techniques from a book, because the successful implementing of a technique often depends on finer points like the best position to place your legs and the right time to execute your move — points that are best learnt from a master personally.

Even if you cannot find a master, at least learn from a qualified instructor. If you do not have the advantage of learning from a master or an instructor, do not feel discouraged if you do not attain the results described in the book. It is likely that you have not performed the form properly even though you think you have followed the description correctly.

In your practice, especially at the beginning stage, your partner acting as your opponent merely initiates the combat situations, then allows you to implement the relevant specific techniques without attempting to frustrate your actions.

It is important to bear in mind that these simulated situations are different from real fighting situations, where your opponent is not likely to be so passive. But the simulated situations with cooperative partners constitute a useful practicing procedure.

Later, if you are expert enough, real combat situations may actually resemble simulated situations, not that your real opponent does not want to frustrate you, but that you are so well practiced that he simply has no chance to intercept your movements. But if your opponent is well practiced too, then he will be able to make appropriate changes while you try to overcome him, or even before you start your counter techniques. This, of course, leads to a sequence of attack and defense, with some probable variations.

The next logical step in the application of kungfu for combat is to learn and practice short attack and defense sequences. This is explained in the next chapter.

9
From Arranged To
Free Sparring
(Practicing Variation in Combat Sequences)

*Since life, as many philosophically inclined have suggested, is
often a struggle, many of these principles can be fruitfully
applied to our daily living.*

Various Factors of Combat

It is indeed amazing that nowadays the majority of people who practice
kungfu, including Taijiquan, do not know how to apply it for combat although
they call it a martial art. Because of inadequate understanding, many kungfu
practitioners jump straight into free sparring immediately after learning kungfu
sets. The result is both shameful and comical.

If they have to fight, their effort is like children's fighting, without any
semblance of kungfu form at all, even though they may have learnt kungfu for
many years!

Of course it is not because kungfu is ineffective, but because they have
never really practiced kungfu; they have merely learnt what past masters called
"flowery fists and embroidery kicks", a form of kungfu movements that are
pleasant to look at but useless for fighting.

This comment about flowery fist may make some people angry, but as a
Shaolin disciple, I choose to say the truth and am prepared to defend my statement.
Some people may challenge me, not to a debate on this view, but to a fight,
which I believe is irrelevant because if they beat me it just shows that they are
better fighters but does not necessarily disprove the validity of my statement.

It is more rewarding for kungfu enthusiasts, whether they practice genuine
kungfu or flowery fists, to examine effective principles and methods of combat
application and help to restore the glory of kungfu, whatever its styles, as a
reputable *living* martial art.

I am very privileged to have access to the knowledge and practice of combat
methods passed down from the Shaolin Monastery, and they are shared in this
book. Judging from the number of championships that many of my students
have won, it can be reasonably said that these methods are effective.

It must be stressed again that articulating the martial aspect of kungfu is very different from suggesting violence or brutality. Indeed, among different types of martial artists, a kungfu fighter is best known for his graciousness and calmness in dealing with opponents. It should also be remembered that effective fighting is only one of the many useful functions of kungfu.

Below are the basic steps a student in our Shaolin tradition will go through from kungfu form to free sparring.

1. Learning and practicing kungfu patterns and sets.
   This is what most kungfu practitioners do, but unfortunately the majority of them remain only at this level.

2. Understanding and practicing the combat application of kungfu patterns individually.
   Here we study and practice each of the kungfu patterns in a kungfu set with reference to combat, as explained in Chapter 7.

3. Applying specific patterns to counter particular combat situations.
   We examine the range of common attack patterns, and practice the relevant counters against them. For example, from observation we know that most people commonly attack by punching and kicking, and some by felling and gripping; we equip ourselves with counters against these typical attacks, as explained in Chapter 8.

4. Linking individual combat situations into a combat sequence.
   In an actual fight, combatants normally do not stop at just one or two patterns, but engage in a short sequence of numerous patterns. The patterns in a sequence usually follow a logical order. This will be presently explained in this chapter.

5. Practicing variations of combat sequences.
   The student must familiarize himself with numerous variations so that he can change from one sequence to another spontaneously. This will also be explained in this chapter.

6. Practicing prearranged sparring sets.
   The movements are prearranged, thus freeing the practitioners from thinking about what patterns to use next so that they can concentrate on other invisible factors of combat like correctness of form, spacing, timing, fluidity of movements, and balance. This will be discussed in the next chapter.

7. Free sparring.

If the students have practiced the above stages well, he will graduate into free sparring methodically, and be able to apply kungfu techniques spontaneously.

Each step above may be divided into a few sub-steps for specific purposes. For example in Step 5 above, students may practice different sets of variations for surprise counters or feign moves.

All the steps mentioned above are concerned mainly with only one factor in combat, i.e. techniques. Other important factors include skill or force, and tactics or strategies.

You may be very knowledgeable in techniques, but if you cannot execute the techniques skillfully or with sufficient force, you are not likely to beat your opponent.

Force training will be explained in other chapters. You may be forceful and know many techniques, but if you do not understand tactics and strategies, you are unlikely to make the best use of your ability and knowledge.

While techniques are applicable to individual movements during the combat, tactics and strategies refer to overall situations. For example, if you meet a Western boxer who is very fast with his punches, you may adopt an overall tactic of avoiding his punches and concentrating on attacking his legs; you would also implement a strategy whereby he will move forward to attack you thus exposing his legs for your surprise counter attack. The Song of Attack and Defense below, besides other things, provides some useful tactics and strategies; more will be explained in Chapter 11.

Shaolin Principles of Attack and Defense

Before we practice combat sequences, it is helpful to examine some relevant principles on attack and defense. Since life, as many philosophically inclined have suggested, is often a struggle, many of these principles can be fruitfully applied to our daily living. You will marvel at the richness of such Shaolin principles. I have gathered some of these principles into a Chinese poem for use in my kungfu school, Shaolin Wahnam Kungfu Institute. The following is the English translation.

Shaolin Song of Attack and Defense

The Shaolin principles of attack and defense
Have been passed down to the Wahnam School
Four steps are needed before you attack
Evaluate, ready, exploit then strike the fool

Against a massive opponent, strike his sides
If weak, attack the front like smashing bricks
Never charge in recklessly like a bull
It's unwise to start combat with flying kicks
Reckless charging gives your body away
High kicks leave your organs exposed and frail
As you attack it's necessary to ask the way
Distract him with false moves as well as real

"Three reaches" are essential in attack
Your movements be as fast as wind
The opponent's strong points you avoid
And aim for his weakness in a wink

In attacking you must be able to defend
Opportunities you must exploit or make
With mind and energy be fully prepared
Both "hard" and "soft" you can give and take

The heart is calm and clear like water still
Don't ever be angry for that affects your skill

Not only be skillful in attacks
But also defend well in any fight
Tell whether his attacks are feigned or real
Notice whether his movements are heavy or light

Neither be worried by powerful moves
Nor off-guarded if attacks are soft and slow
Be not anxious if opponent's fierce and fast
Respond with appropriate speed and blow

Counter high attacks with "threads" and "lifts"
"Flick" away or "lean" against middle strikes
"Chop" or "slash" against low attacks
For side attacks, "block" or "intercept" with might

If an attacker rushes in like a horse
Dodge to let him through with gee
Even if he has strength of a thousand pounds
Once he misses futile his strength will be

Defense must always incorporate attack
Timing and spacing must be right
When the opponent's move and strength are spent
That's the golden time to counter strike

Wonderful results these principles will bring
If you keep practicing from spring to spring

Some Marvelous Advice for Combat

Much of the above poem is self evident, though there may be secrets hidden behind surface meanings, and some concepts go much deeper than simple explanation. In the paragraphs below, only the more puzzling points are explained.

I call my kungfu and chi kung school Shaolin Wahnam, after the names of my masters, Sifu Lai Chin Wah and Sifu Ho Fatt Nam, as my respect and appreciation for their kindness and generosity in teaching me.

Four steps are necessary before we make any moves in combat. We evaluate the strong and the weak points of our opponent. At the same time, we must always be ready for his sudden attack, or to initiate attack ourselves. So, we seek or create opportunities. When opportunities occur, we exploit them and strike so fast and decisively that the opponent, despite being skillful and knowledgeable, is made to be a fool.

It is interesting to note that the same principle of four essential steps is useful in everyday living, like when we apply for a new job or start our own business. We evaluate the current situations; prepare ourselves adequately; seek or create opportunities; and exploit opportunities when they occur.

At the time we charge in to attack our opponent, he may strike us suddenly, and such a strike is not easy to defend if we only concentrate on attacking. To avoid this weakness, as we move in speedily we place one hand (usually our left hand) in front to guard against his possible attack, or to push aside his raised defensive hand or hands.

This is known as "asking the way". Besides the above two functions, this "opening" hand also serves to test the opponent's strength, and to distract the opponent. As a distraction, the left hand is a false move, but if the opponent does not respond to this "opening" hand, it may be changed into a real attack.

The "three reaches" refer to reaching with the heart, reaching with the feet, and reaching with the hands. Before we make any move, we must be clear of where we want to attack and what attacking patterns to use. For example, after assessing the opponent, we decide to attack his abdomen, but we wish to distract him first with a false attack to his throat, and we also plan that should he successfully defend himself against these two moves, we will send a "black tiger" to his solar plexus. This is reaching with the heart. (See Sequence Two in the Combat Sequences below.)

In other words, we have a clear purpose and direction of movement, even before we make the first move. This plan, of course, is a guideline, so that we will not be undecided nor hesitant when we have moved within the combative sphere of the opponent. If the situation warrants it, we may have to make expedient changes.

When we move in as the opportunity offers itself, our false attack must target at his throat, not at his nose nor mouth nor aimlessly in the air — because our heart has reached the decision to attack his throat. Our feet must be placed in such a way that we can effectively strike him — not that we would miss him by inches even if he does not move. (In practice, however, we purposely miss by inches.) This is reaching with the feet.

If he moves back (as in Sequence Two), we must move forward accordingly if we wish to strike him, otherwise we would not reach with our feet. Our hands (or any parts of our attacking body) must be able to strike him effectively — without having to stretch our limbs unnaturally, twist our body uncomfortably, or sacrifice our balance. This is reaching with our hands.

These "three reaches" will be useful in life. We need to be clear of our purpose and direction if we wish to make our lives more meaningful and rewarding for ourselves and for others — reaching of the heart. We must place ourselves favorably at the sphere of action — reaching of the feet. Mere wishful thinking is not enough; we must put in effect what we plan to do — reaching of the hands.

In any attacking move, we must always be ready for the opponent's surprised counter attack. Hence, in Shaolin Kungfu, we always "cover" our vital parts even in the midst of a fervent attack, and leave room for our own retreat should the need arises.

Therefore, high kicks where the vital organs are exposed and where we stand gingerly on one leg, are almost never used in Shaolin Kungfu. It is difficult, though not impossible, to retreat if an opponent strikes at the vital organs at the same time we lift our leg to kick at the sky. If a Shaolin disciple wishes to kick at the opponent's head, for example, he would do so while jumping high so that the other non-attacking leg will protect his own vital organs.

We can transfer this combat principle to our daily life. Whether in work or play, it is unwise to be so wrapped up in attack that we expose our vital weakness. If the opponent strikes at this vital weakness, he will reverse all the advantages we may have previously gained.

Any efficient defense must include attack. If we only defend, whether in kungfu sparring or in ordinary life, at the best we achieve a draw. If we never counter attack, we may be forced into to a continual passive, receiving position. One of the best moment to counter attack is when the opponent has just completed one move and before he recovers himself for the next move. In an argument, for example, if your opponent is attacking you with a string of demanding questions, you can easily reverse the situation by applying this Shaolin principle: as soon as he has completed a question, ask him whether he realizes that his question is misleading or irrelevant, followed by your string of factual or rhetoric questions.

Combat Sequences

"A picture is worth a thousand words," says a Chinese proverb. The pictures in Fig 9.1 to Fig 9.12 illustrate twelve basic Shaolin Combat Sequences. Understandably, finer points are difficult to be shown.

A combat sequence is a short series of attack and defense patterns, to prepare students for free sparring and actual fighting. The patterns are selected and arranged according to some specific purposes and principles. Besides practicing the form, spacing and timing, students should also emphasize fluidity of movements, and spontaneity of response.

The following is only a very brief description of these sequences. Please refer to the accompanying illustrations.

1. **Triple Punches — Beauty Looks at Mirror.**
   The attacker initiates three straight punches continuously. Notice that in the second punch, the attacker must move a small step forward with his left leg so as to "reach with his feet".

(a)   (b)

(c)   (d)

Fig 9.1 Triple Punches — Beauty Looks at Mirror

2. Three-Level Punches — Low Horse-Riding Punch.

The attacks are aimed at the top, bottom and middle levels. The attacker must move a step forward for the second and third attack.

(a)   (b)

(c)   (d)

Fig 9.2 Three-Level Punches — Low Horse-Riding Punch

3. Whirlwind Kick — Block the Big Boss.

The leg attack is aimed at the defender's ribs. The defender applies a "hard" counter, and his horse-riding stance must be firm. He blocks the attacking leg at the thigh or knee (the opponent's weak point), and not at the lower leg (his strong point in this situation).

(a)   (b)

(c)   (d)

Fig 9.3 Whirlwind Kick — Block the Big Boss

4. Flowers in the Sleeves — False-Leg Hand-Sweep.

As the attacker strikes with a low horse-riding punch, the defender grips his wrist, and strikes at his elbow, dislocating or breaking it. The attacker neutralizes this by moving his left leg diagonally forward, with "Hiding Flowers in the Sleeves", and countering with another low Horse-Riding punch.

Fig 9.4 Flowers in the Sleeves — False-Leg Hand-Sweep

5. White Crane Flaps Wings — Tiger-Tail Hand-Sweep.

After the defender has swept at the attacker's arm as the latter attacks with a low punch (and then withdraws to avoid the sweep), the defender follows up with a left palm chop at the attacker's temple. The attacker withdraws into a False-Leg stance and "threads" away the chop, followed by an organ-seeking kick.

Fig 9.5 White Crane Flaps Wings — Tiger-Tail Hand-Sweep

(a)   (b)

(c)   (d)

Fig 9.6 White Horse Presents Hoof — Single Whip

(a)   (b)   (c)

(d)   (e)

(f)   (g)   (h)

Fig 9.7 Felling Tree with Roots — Slash the Bamboo

6. **White Horse Presents Hoof — Single Whip.**
   Four vigorous attacks in one continuous movement. The "Single Whip" is used to strike at the kicking leg.

7. **Felling Tree with Roots — Slash the Bamboo.**
   The defender uses unicorn step and butterfly palms to neutralize the attacker's felling techniques. The attacker counters with organ kick, then poisonous snake. The defender grips the attacking arm, presses at the attacker's elbow, and trips the latter onto the ground. The attacker steps his back leg diagonally forward and neutralizes with "Flowers in the Sleeves".

8. **Push Mountains — White Horse Presents Hoof.**
   The defender counters the attacker's "Push Mountain" with a thrust kick. The attacker retreats into a Unicorn Step, and counters with "Dark Dragon Wags Tail".

(a)   (b)   (c)

(d)   (e)   (f)

Fig 9.8 Push Mountains — White Horse Presents Hoof

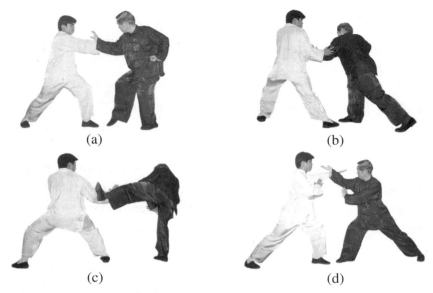

(a)

(b)

(c)

(d)

Fig 9.9 Lead Horses to Stable — Happy Bird on Branch

(a)

(b)

(c)

(d)

(e)

(f)

Fig 9.10 Eagle Claw Technique — Butterfly Palms

9. **Lead Horses to Stable — Happy Bird on Branch.**

   To neutralize the attacker's pull, the defender moves forward with the pulling momentum, and executes a side kick at the attacker.

10. **Eagle Claw Technique — Butterfly Palms.**

    The attacker uses two Eagle Claws to grip the defender's arm. The defender counters with "Butterfly Palms". The circular movement of the defender's arm releases the attacker's grip.

11. **Tames a Tiger — Golden Cockerel Grips Throat.**

    If someone trips you onto the ground and presses your elbow, one way to counter this attack is "Flowers in the Sleeves", as in Sequence Seven. Another "softer" way is "Golden Cockerel Grips Throat", as in this sequence.

(a)   (b)

(c)   (d)

(e)   (f)

Fig 9.11 Tames a Tiger — Golden Cockerel Grips Throat

12. Basking in Mist — Bending Willow.

What would you do if someone grip your palm and bend it backward. Response with "Poisonous Snake Basking in the Mist".

(a)   (b)

(c)   (d)

(e)   (f)

Fig 9.12 Basking in Mist — Bending Willow

The specific techniques described in the previous chapter, and the combat sequences summarily mentioned above provide a good introduction to Shaolin application for combat. When such information is conveniently presented in a book, it is easy for many martial art students to make the common mistake of merely reading it or going over the movements superficially.

If you want to be proficient in kungfu fighting, you must practice these (or other) combative techniques devotedly until they have become second nature to you. As a rough guide, you should practice these techniques and their various developmental stages as explained below, for *at least* one year so that you become familiar with them.

Developmental Stages in Combat Application

The following is a helpful program for practicing combat sequence in stages. In the description below, the one who starts the sequence, and who is usually the attacker, is called the initiator; and the one who responds to the initiator's first move, and who is usually the defender, is called the responder.

1. At the first stage known as "Pre-Choice", both the initiator and the responder have decided before hand which sequence will be used for practice. Be familiar with one sequence before progressing to another sequence. The initiator and the responder should change role so that both have the experience of what an opponent would feel and do in such combat situations.

2. In the second stage known as "Self-Choice", the initiator chooses the sequence he wishes to start with, *without* the responder knowing before hand. Initially they should limit themselves to only two choices, then gradually increase the range of choices. Remember the purpose of the training here is not to surprise your partner with a tricky choice or a cunning move, but to provide him with the opportunity to respond correctly, and later spontaneously, to your moves. You may, therefore, have to purposely slow down your movements to help him, if he is not as skillful as you.

3. The next stage is called "Surprised Counter". Instead of responding to the initiator's first move according to the prearranged sequence, the responder surprises the initiator with a counter-attack. The initiator, therefore, has to ward off this surprised counter before continuing with his planned attack. Such surprised counters should not be too often; they should be employed when the initiator does not expect them.

4. The fourth stage is called "Continuation", whereby instead of completing a sequence, any practitioner continues logically into another sequence without any break in between. Hence the last move of the first sequence becomes the first move of the second sequence with the two sequences linking into one continuous sequence.

5. In the next stage, instead of following the prearranged patterns of a certain sequence to its completion, either practitioner may branch out from that sequence into another sequence. This stage, known as "External Change", is similar to "Continuation" except that the linking into another sequence is not *at* the end of the first sequence, but somewhere *between* the middle and the end of the first sequence. Sometimes, a modification or change of pattern may be necessary at the point of transition.

6. When the practitioners are familiar with the "External Change" stage, which is a change of one sequence into another, they may proceed to the "Internal Change" stage, which is a change within the sequence. In other words, at any point of the first sequence, any practitioner may use a different pattern instead of the prearranged pattern in that sequence, thus leading to a change of the sequence itself. This stage is similar to "External Change" except that the change is made in the earlier part of the sequence, without waiting for the sequence to run even half its prearranged patterns.

7. When the "Internal Change" stage is used frequently, it becomes free sparring. In the stages described above, the practitioners, if they are ready, may continue into other stages, or combine appropriate sequences. For example, in the "Continuation" stage, the practitioner may continue to three or more sequences, and they may make appropriate external or internal changes in each of the sequences. As they introduce changes or modifications to their movements, they also use other patterns not found in these twelve sequences. In this way, they are able to spar freely without being particularly conscious of the developmental processes involved.

10
Further Training For Effective Fighting

(Developing Fundamental Sparring Skills)

The decisive factor in combat is often not the extent of patterns or techniques the combatants know, but the depth of skill (including force and speed) in their command.

Variation in Combat Sequence Training

An effective way to learn kungfu application for actual fighting is through combat sequence training, as explained in the previous chapter. Another effective way is through practicing prearranged sparring sets. A sparring set is a routine of prearranged kungfu patterns where two, and sometimes more, practitioners engage in simulated fighting. It is like a long collection of extended combat sequences.

Although both practicing combat sequences and practicing sparring sets contribute to proficiency in free sparring, there are some fine differences between these two types of kungfu training.

As combat sequences are short, each comprising of only a few patterns, they are more easily managed by practitioners, and hence provide a useful vehicle for the practitioners in learning how to make appropriate technical changes from the prearranged sequences to suit the current combative situations, and to link suitable sequences together wherever necessary.

Sparring sets, on the other hand, are long, each usually comprising more than thirty patterns, and are thus not so suitable for the purposes which combat sequences excellently provide, but sparring sets are very useful for developing fundamental skills like correctness of form, spacing, timing, fluidity of movement, and balance which are essential for effective combat.

Before we examine how a sparring set can help us to develop these fundamental skills, let us briefly study how to make appropriate changes or linkage with combat sequences.

Let us look at Sequence 1 as shown in the previous chapter, and represent the attacking patterns as A, B, A, C, which are a right punch, a left punch, a right punch again, and a leaning-block against the opponent's punch. After completing these four patterns, instead of withdrawing to end the sequence, the initiator (or attacker) can continue with Sequence 3, represented as A, D, F, G, which are a right punch, a threading-block against the opponent's counter, a right whirlwind kick, and a vertical-arm-block (Block the Big Boss) against the opponent's horizontal hand sweep.

In this linkage of the two sequences which are performed continuously as if they are one sequence, the last "A" of Sequence 1 becomes the first "A" of Sequence 3, and the leaning-block (represented as "C") is modified to become the threading-block ("D"), so that the whole continuous sequence now become A, B, A, D, F, G. This variation of the combat sequence practice is called "Continuation", which is the fourth step in the Developmental Stages mentioned in the previous chapter.

This variation of the initiator in the combat sequence will offer the responder the opportunity in learning how to make appropriate changes to meet changing situations. If the attacks are made in two separate sequences, the separate responses will be as follows.

Against A, B, A, C in Sequence 1, the response will be M, N, G, O, which represent a right mirror-hand block, a left mirror-hand block, a vertical-arm-block, and a low punch. Against A, D, F, G in Sequence 3, the response will be M, P, G, Q, which are a right mirror-hand block, a right dragon-punch (after "threading" with the left hand), a vertical-arm-block, and a horizontal hand sweep.

If the two attacking sequences are combined as A, B, A, D, F, G, then the combined response will be M, N, G, O, G, Q, performed as one continuous sequence, where the low punch ("O") in the response of Sequence 1 replaces the dragon-punch ("P") of Sequence 3.

The description of the above variation may look complicating, but the actual performance is quite simple. Symbolically the variation can be represented as follows:

Initiator: A B A C + A D F G -> A B A D F G
Responder: M N G O + M P G Q -> M N G O G Q

Suppose you initiate A, B, A, C (Sequence 1), and your partner responds with M, N, G, 0. But as soon as he performs "G", and before he can continue with "O", you swiftly intercept him with a felling technique.

Such a felling technique is found in Sequence 7, which we can represent by A, H, I, J, K, P, where "H" is the felling technique. (To avoid complexity, here we need not worry about what other patterns are represented by the letters.) Hence your combined sequence, without any break in between, is A, B, A, H, I, J, K, P, where your second "A" in Sequence 1 becomes the first "A" in Sequence 7. Quite spontaneously your partner will respond with M, N, G, R, S, T, U, V. This is the developmental stage of "External Change", and can be symbolized as:

A B A C + A H I J K P -> A B A H I J K P
M N G O + M R S T U V -> M N G R S T U V

If your partner is off-balanced the first time he blocks your punch, you need not continue with the intended Sequence 1, but change immediately to Sequence 7 to exploit his weakness. The first "A" in your intended sequence becomes the first "A" of your changed sequence. In other words instead of performing A B A C as planned, you immediately change to A H I J K P.

This developmental stage is known as "Internal Change". Similarly, at any point in your changed sequence, you may make further changes if suitable.

Hence, because of their manageable lengths, combat sequences are very useful for practicing variation of techniques in combat application. However, knowing the techniques and their variation in combat sequences is not sufficient. The decisive factor in combat is often not the extent of patterns or techniques the combatants know, but the depth of skill (including force and speed) in their command.

Four Gates Sparring Set

Because of its substantial length, a sparring set, which is a long prearranged routine of simulated combat, is a good vehicle for developing combative skills, as the engaging exponents are relieved of the mental burden of deciding what patterns or techniques to use next, so that they can concentrate on skills.

The Four Gates Sparring Set, which is derived from the Cross-Roads at Four Gates Set is illustrated in four sections. It is difficult enough to show the patterns; to show detailed or subtle movements, or skills like spacing and timing is out of question. Therefore, readers who wish to have a deeper appreciation of this beautiful sparring set would have to consult a master. Nevertheless, the illustrations, despite their limitations, give some idea of Shaolin Kungfu application in action.

Fig 10.1 Four Gates Sparring Set — Section A

Fig 10.2 Four Gates Sparring Set — Section B

(1)

(2)

(3)

(4)

(5)

(6)

(7)

(8)

Fig 10.3 Four Gates Sparring Set — Section C

(9)

(10)

(11)

(12)

(13)

(14)

Fig 10.3 Four Gates Sparring Set — Section C

(1)

(2)

(3)

(4)

(5)

(6)

(7)

(8)

Fig 10.4 Four Gates Sparring Set — Section D

(9)   (10)

(11)   (12)   (13)

(14)   (15)

(16)   (17)

Fig 10.4 Four Gates Sparring Set — Section D

The names of the patterns of the Sparring Set are given below. The two practitioners engaged in the sparring are conveniently termed A and B; dashes indicate that A and B assess each other before making any moves; arrows show the flow of action. For example in Patterns 4 and 5, A executes a Single Dragon Punch and B responds with Block the Big Box. Immediately, B counters with a Horse-Riding Punch and A responds with Block the Big Boss.

Section A:
1. Amitabha Palm — Amitabha Palm.
2. Low Horse-Riding Punch -> Mirror Hand (right).
3. Snake Emerges from Pit -> Mirror Hand (left).
4. Single Dragon -> Block the Big Boss.
5. Block the Big Boss <- Horse-Riding Punch.
6. Carry the Insignia <- Black Tiger (left).
7. Horse-Riding Punch -> Single Tiger Claw.
8. Phoenix Flaps Wings -> Tiger Tail Kick.
9. Single Whip -> Rolling Gourd.

Section B:
10. Butterflies Flying — Bow-Arrow Amitabha Palm .
11. Mirror Hand <- Black Tiger.
12. Hand Sweep <- Horse-Riding Punch (left).
13. Chop Mountain (left) -> Thread, Whirlwind Kick.
14. Block, Horse-Riding Punch -> Snake on Ground.
15. Flowers in Sleeves -> Mirror Hand.
16. Phoenix Flap Wings -> Oriole Shows Toes.
17. Single Whip -> Tiger Crosses Hill.
18. Trim Bamboo -> Trim Bamboo.
19. Lohan Hits Gong -> Lohan Hits Gong.

Section C:
20. Amitabha Palm — Amitabha Palm.
21. Block the Big Boss <- Whirlwind Kick (right).
22. Block the Big Boss <- Whirlwind Kick (left).
23. Horse-Riding Punch -> Mirror Hand (right).
24. Black Tiger -> Mirror Hand (left).
25. Snake Emerges from Pit -> Tiger Claw (right).
26. Flowers in Sleeves -> Tiger Claw (left).
27. Snake Emerges from Pit -> Snake Basking in Mist.
28. Single Tiger (left) -> Hitting Vital Point.
29. Hand Sweep, Punch (left) -> Tiger Crosses Hill.
30. Tiger Crosses Hill <- Trim Bamboo.

31. Single Whip <- Horse Presents Hoof (left).
32. Catch Tiger in Mountain <- Whirlwind Kick.
33. Cannon from Ground -> Rolling Gourd.

Section D:
34. Butterflies Flying — Amitabha Palm.
35. Mirror Hand (left) <- Black Tiger.
36. Flowers in Sleeves <- Dragon Punch (left).
37. Flowers in Sleeves (cont) -> Block Big Boss.
38. Shift, Horse-Riding Punch -> Hand Sweep.
39. Golden Dragon <- Chop the Mountain (left).
40. White Crane -> Bow-Arrow Hand Sweep.
41. Tame the Tiger <- Pierce Punch on Ground.
42. Golden Dragon <- Hanging of Lotus.
43. Thread, Single Dragon -> Kick Shuttle.
44. Catch Tiger in Mountain -> Golden Cockerel.
45. Cannon from Ground -> Standing Crane.
46. Kick, Punch -> Tiger Claw.
47. White Crane — White Crane.
48. Greeting — Greeting.

Fundamental Skills in Combat

To secure victory in combat, we must pay attention to the following three areas:

1. To ensure that our techniques are appropriate and flawless so that the opponent cannot derive any technical advantage over us;
2. To seek weaknesses in the opponent's techniques so as to exploit them to defeat him;
3. To create opportunities to enhance our own advantages and expose the opponent's weaknesses to ensure victory.

Practicing a sparring set, like the Four Gates Sparring Set described above, is a useful way to acquire the knowledge and ability needed for the first two areas. The third area concerns tactics and strategy, and will be discussed in the next chapter.

Acquiring flawless techniques in ourselves and seeking weaknesses in our opponents can be realized through the development of fundamental combative skills like correctness of form, right spacing, correct timing, fluidity of movements and good balance.

Correctness of form is the most basic of the fundamental combative skills. If the form of our techniques or patterns is faulty, not only we forfeit the advantages that these patterns specially provide for the particular combative situations, but also our opponents may exploit the faults to defeat us.

Although correctness of form is emphasized in solo set practice, it is in sparring sets that this fundamental skill is put to an acid test. For example in Pattern 2 of the Four Gates Sparring Set, if the opponent moves his blocking arm too far out, Fig 10.5, I exploit his faulty form by "slipping" my hand round his arm and strike his face with a "hanging fist", Fig 10.6.

Fig 10.5 Faulty Form of Mirror Hand

Fig 10.6 Slipping Round with Hanging Fist

Poor spacing is a common weakness among many combatants. For example when the opponent attacks me in Pattern 11, I move back a step while blocking his attack with my Mirror Hand. Thus he has to move forward to bridge the gap if he wants to attack me again.

In Pattern 12 he moves his *front* leg a step forward as he inflict his low Horse-Riding Punch. If he does not move forward, i.e. if his spacing is faulty, I need not bother to defend against this attack because it will not reach me even if I do nothing, Fig 10.7.

So, if I am well trained to exploit his weakness in spacing, I shall strike him the spilt second he has started to strike me, such as chopping his head as in Fig 10.8. In this way, as soon as his non-effective attack is spent, my chop is already at his head.

I must, however, not neglect the following two points: bridge the gap to improve my spacing, and guard his attacking hand even though at this situation his attack is non-effective for it may be a feint move to tempt me.

Fig 10.7 Non-Reaching Attack due to Bad Spacing

Fig 10.8 Exploiting Weakness of Non-Reaching Attack

Timing is one of the most difficult combative skills to learn. It is obvious that even if your defense pattern is correct, but if you are slow, you will still be hit. But if you are too quick, it may also be a weakness! For example, in the Sparring Set, I inflict a right Whirlwind Kick at my partner, and he defends with Block the Big Boss, as in Pattern 20, as illustrated in Fig 10.9. Then he jumps round to perform the second Block the Big Boss *before* I execute the second Whirlwind Kick. He has committed the error of blindly following the prearranged sequence, instead of responding to my initiative.

Exploiting his weakness of wrong timing, I change my intended whirlwind kick into a side kick, thus hitting him, Fig 10.10. He is hit not because he does not know how to defend, but because of incorrect timing, which is a common occurrence among many combatants.

Fig 10.9 Blocking a Whirlwind Kick

Fig 10.10 Exploiting Weakness of Poor Timing

One sure way to tell a novice from a master is to observe the manner they move. The movements of a novice are staccato and clumsy, whereas those of a master are fluid and elegant, with related patterns flowing from one into another in continuous harmony — in sole practice as well as in sparring. The harmonious flow of a master concerns not only his own patterns, but also incorporates and overwhelms those of his inferior opponent.

In other words, the master adjusts the momentum of his movements according to that of his opponent so as to control him.   For example when an opponent executes a left Dragon Punch at me, as in Pattern 35, I block and instantaneously counter with Flowers in the Sleeves, Figures 10.11 and 10.12.

There are two movements — block and counter-punch — but they flow together as one pattern. If this is performed skillfully, and if the opponent is hesitant, he will be hit the moment his dragon-punch attack is just over. However, if the opponent is also fluid, he follows my attacking momentum to break my arm (or dislocate my elbow), as in Pattern 36. I can save my arm (or elbow) by flowing with his momentum (instead of going against it), with another Flowers in the Sleeves, followed by a Horse-Riding Punch as in Pattern 37.

Fig 10.11 Blocking Movement in Flowers in Sleeves

Fig 10.12 Punching Movement in Flowers in Sleeves

Maintaining good balance is extremely important in kungfu. Without good balance it is difficult, if not impossible, to perform some crucial techniques, especially those involving standing on one leg. For example when I execute a left knee strike using the pattern Jade Girl Kicks Shuttle at my opponent as in Pattern 42, Fig 10.13, he swiftly squats on the ground with the pattern Catch a Tiger in the Mountain, counter-attacking my genitals as in Pattern 43, Fig 10.14.

If not for my good balance I might have lost my genitals; but I jump to stand on my left leg, and raise my right knee to ward of his brutal attack, Fig 10.15. Instantly I kick out my right pointed toes at his under-chin, Fig 10.16. This kick is meant to strike the throat, which may maim him, but although he is brutal, I need not have to be a brute like him to cause more than necessary injury.

Fig 10.13 Jade Girl Kicks Shuttle

Fig 10.14 Catch a Tiger in the Mountain

Fig 10.15 Golden Cockerel Stands Magnificently

Fig 10.16 Kicking at his Under-Chin

As in many other aspects of Shaolin Kungfu, the principles behind these fundamental combative skills can also be applied to our daily living. If we carry ourselves well (correctness of form), be present at where the action is (correct spacing), do the right things at the right time (right timing), be harmonious and elegant (fluidity of movement), and be emotionally stable (good balance), we certainly have a better chance to succeed in our work and play than those who are shabby, unavailable, not punctual, clumsy and unstable.

Examples of Crucial Points in Sparring

There are other important points we can learn from practicing sparring sets. The following are just some examples from the Four Gates Sparring Set.

In Pattern 8, for instance, when I move forward to attack the opponent with an elbow strike using the pattern called Phoenix Flaps Wings, Fig 10.17, I must not neglect the following two points.

One, I must be careful of *his* possible elbow strike on my face, as in Fig 10.18. I can guard against this possibility by pulling his arm away from me or placing the palm of my striking elbow against his elbow.

Two, I must place my front leg in such a way that I guard against his possible Horse Back-Kick against my groin. Fig 10.19 shows the right placing of my leg; Fig 18.20 shows the wrong position, which may result with a Horse Back-Kick, Fig 10.21.

Fig 10.17 Phoenix Flaps Wings

Fig 10.18 Elbow Strike to Face

Fig 10.19 Right Placing of Leg

Fig 10.20 Wrong Placing of Leg

Fig 10.21 Horse Back-Kick

What would you do if your opponent strikes your face with his elbow, as in Fig 10.18 above. One good counter is to follow his momentum, bend his arm behind and grip the carotid artery at the side of his neck; but you must be very careful not to grip too hard, or else you may cause serious damage or even kill him. Figures 10.22 and 10.23 show the process of this arm-cum-neck hold.

Fig 10.22 Bending his Arm for an Arm Lock

Fig 10.23 Gripping his Neck from Behind

The following is a useful counter against the Horse Back-Kick. As the opponent moves forward to kick backward and upward with his right heel, use your front left leg to block or deflect his kick, Fig 10.24. At the same time push him to fall forward face-on. Step on his leg, but be careful not to dislocate his ankle, hold his arm away from you to prevent his possible backward elbow strike, and grip a vital point on his body, in a pattern called Entering the Sea to Catch a Dragon, Fig 10.25.

Fig 10.24 Deflecting his Horse Back-Kick

Fig 10.25 Entering the Sea to Catch a Dragon

Let us now reverse roles; your opponent moves forward with an elbow strike using the pattern Phoenix Flaps Wings to strike you, as in Fig 10.17 above.

To counter this attack, move forward slightly with your front right leg, thus moving your body away from his attack, bend your right elbow behind and rotate your body towards your right at the same time, and thrust back a Tiger Tail Kick at your opponent, Fig 10.26. Immediately roll away. It is necessary for you to bend your elbow and rotate your body, or else it is difficult to execute this pattern effectively.

(a)   (b)   (c)

Fig 10.26 Tiger Tail Kick

Hence, combat sequences and sparring sets are very useful in our training to be effective fighters. Combat sequences provide opportunities for us to practice making variations in our fighting techniques to suit the current combative situations. Sparring sets enable us to develop the fundamental combative skills to execute these techniques efficiently. When we have these techniques and skills, we have a good chance of winning in most ordinary combats.

However, if the opponent is a master he too will be familiar with techniques and skills; he knows how to neutralize any techniques applied on him, and he does not expose any weaknesses that can be exploited. How, then, can we have an edge over an expert opponent? If the opportunities for defeating him are not presently available, we will have to create them, and this can be realized through an understanding and application of tactics and strategy to be explained in the next chapter.

11
Creating Opportunities To Secure Victory

(Applying Tactics and Strategies in Fighting)

We can see the particular technique employed to secure victory, often we also know the tactical considerations behind the techniques used, but most of us may not be aware of the underlying strategy from which the tactics and techniques are evolved.

Sun Tzu's Advice

Taking about tactics and strategy, we would get much benefit from reading the work of Sun Tzu, the 6th century BCE Chinese general considered by many as the greatest military strategist of all times. The principles that contribute to the success of an army, Sun Tzu explained in his "Art of War", are also applicable to the success of a single combatant. In the section on Tactics, Sun Tzu says:

The efficient warriors first put themselves beyond the possibility of defeat, then seek the opportunity to defeat the enemy. To secure ourselves against defeat lies in our own hands; the opportunity to defeat the enemy lies with the enemy.

Sun Tzu's teaching is the same as the Shaolin philosophy on combat explained in the previous chapter, i.e. first we make sure that our actions are flawless, then we seek and exploit any weakness in the opponent's actions.

For our purpose here, tactics refers to a planned disposition of techniques to achieve some desirable objectives. Strategy refers to a general design to maneuver the opponent to respond in certain manners.

For example, if I meet an opponent who is very skillful in kicks, a useful tactic I can adopt is to stay close to him to minimize the advantages of kicks, so that if he use kicks it would be disadvantageous to him despite his skill. In this way I put myself beyond the possibility of defeat, which is the first part of Sun Tzu's advice above.

Next I devise a strategy to tempt him to use kicks at the time I am ready to exploit them to secure a victory. This is the second part of Sun Tzu's advice, where the opponent provides the opportunity for his own defeat.

The classification into tactics and strategies, however, is for the sake of convenience; the principles and Shaolin secrets described below can be classified as tactics or as strategies depending on their function.

During combat, even among masters, the combatants have little time to consider at great length the kinds of tactics and strategies to employ. Even if time is available, it is not recommended to be used for deep thought, because it would then distract the combatants from their focus on the combat. Kungfu masters who also excel in meditation, often attain a state of non-thought in combat whereby their mind, free from thoughts, permeates the whole combative environment and process. If they have to be engaged in thoughts, they would do so in a meditative state, quite different from the type of thinking a candidate does in an examination or a politician in working out a policy speech. Such a meditative state of a Shaolin Kungfu master elevates him to a spiritual level, in accordance with fact that the highest aim of kungfu is spiritual development.

Principles to Guide Combat

Then, how does a master assess the current situations and decide on what tactics and strategies to be used? He does all that before the actual physical fighting begins!

As in the case of the techniques and skills that have been discussed in previous chapters, a Shaolin disciple benefits from the accumulated wisdom of past Shaolin masters regarding tactics and strategies through his Shaolin training, as such wisdom has been ingrained in the Shaolin tradition. He is trained to understand and apply various principles and "songs of secrets" (like the examples in Chapter 6 and 9) which summarizes the essential information into poetic expressions. Some examples of these principles, which can be used as tactics or as strategies depending on our purpose, are as follows:

1. Avoid the strong points of the opponent; attack his weak points.
2. If he is powerful, enter from the sides; if he is weak, enter from the front.
3. Move the stance, change the step; shift and dodge, advance and retreat.
4. Use the orthodox in combat; use the unorthodox to secure victory.
5. Trick the opponent to attack unsuccessfully; strike him when he is unprepared.
6. If there is form, strike the form; if there is no form, chase the shadow.

Avoiding the opponent's strength and attacking his weakness is so obvious that it may seem trite; yet many uninformed combatants do the opposite. From my past experiences I notice that in a match against an opponent who specializes in kicks, such as a Taekwondo or a Siamese Boxing exponent, many combatants usually retreat or try to block with their hands when meeting powerful kicks.

It is no surprise that these combatants were forced to be on the defensive most of the time, and they usually loose — often helplessly, as they do not know how to defend against powerful kicks effectively, and they had little chance to counter attack.

Suppose you are in combat with a Taekwondo exponent. If you retreat as he kicks, you may escape being hit, but you will grant him both the advantage of length and the initiative of attack. By retreating and thus maintaining some distance between you and him, it is advantageous to your opponent who specializes in kicks because a kick, as many Taekwondo exponents are fond of saying, has longer reach than a punch.

Unless you can overcome this setback, your opponent will be kicking you most of the time. Assuming all other factors being equal (which is almost never valid in real situations), if he attacks you ten times and you attack him only once, his chances of beating you is 10 to 1.

You have such a high chance of defeat because you fail in both points advised by Sun Tzu above: without some effective tactics you have failed to put yourself beyond the possibility of defeat; and by giving your opponent the convenience of attack, you have provided the opportunity for him to defeat you.

If you blocks his kicks with your hands, you are using your weak points against his strength. I recall watching a few movies where the heroine used two hands to block the powerful round-house kicks of an aggressor.

If this happens in a real situation, most likely the powerful round-house kick will bounce away the dainty hands and strike her head; if her arms are strong enough to provide some resistance, they will ironically be fractured or her wrists dislocated.

Similarly she failed to follow Sun Tzu's advise. She does not have an effective counter against the kick to put herself beyond the possibility of defeat; and she provided the opportunity for the enemy to defeat her by failing to move her head away or placing her hands in the way.

Tactical and Strategic Considerations

There are many effective counters in Shaolin Kungfu for you to reverse your defeat to victory.

First, let us examine some strategic and tactical considerations. His strong points are the power of his kicks and the length of his reach. What then are his weak points? Whenever a person kicks, especially if he has to turn his body to achieve momentum as in a side kick or a round-house kick, his balance is affected, which means that at this moment he is less mobile.

Secondly, the requirements of effective kicks usually posit his body in such a way that the flexibility range of his other three limbs are affected. For example, at the time when a person executes a side kick or a round-house kick, it is very difficult for him to use his other leg, and the application of both his hands are also limited. For comparison, when he executes a punch, he can use any one of the four limbs with ease.

Thirdly, if he does not guard his groin when he kicks, it will be a good target; when he guards it he further limits the use of his hands.

A good strategy, therefore, is to avoid his strong points and attack his weak points; and a good tactics is to enter from the sides. "Avoid" does not mean running away, as is often the case with uninformed combatants.

We may differentiate two types of avoidance: one, avoiding direct contact with his kicks, such as not blocking them with our comparatively weaker hands; and two, maneuvering in such a way that he has little opportunities to use kicks.

Attacking his weak points means that we will attack him when he is less mobile, when the full use of his limbs is limited, and when he exposes an unguarded target. As he is likely to have these weakness when he kicks, but the first part of our strategy suggests avoiding his kicks, we shall therefore have to make some adjustment.

If we find that he is very skillful in kicking techniques, but his hand techniques are poor, we may stick close to him so that he has little opportunity to use his kicks, and force him to use his poor hand techniques most of the time so that we can readily defeat him.

However, if we can counter his kicks despite his skill and power, we may allow him to use his kicks often so that he will reveal those weaknesses we are looking for to defeat him. You will notice that these strategic considerations fulfill Sun Tzu's both points: placing ourselves beyond defeat, and maneuvering the opponent to provide the opportunities for us to defeat him.

To implement our strategy we can use the tactics of entering from the sides, and avoid entering from the front. This means that if we want to counter attack the opponent as he kicks, we shall *not* block the kick and move right in frontally; instead, we avoid contact with the kick by dodging and move in from the side.

If we want to stay close to the opponent to prevent him from using kicks, a useful tactics is "move the stance, change the step; shift and dodge, advance and retreat."

Translated into English, this tactics may appear circumlocutory, but in its Chinese original it is both poetic and concise.

An example of its application is as follows. As he kicks, you dodge; and as soon as he places his kicking leg on the ground, you have move close to him. If he tries to widen the space between you by retreating one step, you move forward one step simultaneously with the corresponding leg.

If he moves back x number of steps, you follow correspondingly with x number of steps; if he moves aside y number of steps, you too move to the same side y number of steps.

If he charges head-on at you, you shift your stance in such a manner that you are right behind him. Meanwhile you engage him in hand combat, and as he is weak in hand techniques whereas you are prepared and have the initiative, you would defeat him. "Having the initiative" means that on the whole you decide and influence the types of patterns to use in the combat.

The following are some examples of how we can implement our strategy and tactics. As the opponent inflicts a powerful round-house kick, I dodge to the exposed side, moving diagonally forward, Fig 11.1.

As soon as he places his kicking leg on the ground, I will move in according to where he has placed his leg and strike him with a leopard punch (formed by bending the fingers at the second joints instead of at the third as is done in a normal fist), in a pattern known as "Golden Leopard Speeds Through the Jungle", Fig 11.2. I may, if I wish to be nasty, immediately follow up with a second leopard punch with the other hand at the same spot, frequently before the opponent realizes what has happened.

Fig 11.1 Dodging a Round-House Kick

Fig 11.2 Golden Leopard Speeds Through the Jungle

But if he can defend against this double attack, I shall instantly continue with combat sequences that I have planned before-hand. I shall stick close to him, and maintain my initiative, but not forgetting to cover myself sufficiently amidst my raining attacks.

For example, as soon as he defends one attack, another planned attack follows instantly, giving him no chance to recover. If he is skillful enough to break this *planned* continuous attacks and attempt a counter attack, I shall revert to my initiative immediately by taking his counter-attack as the start of another of my attack sequences.

Alternatively I may tempt him to exercise his kicks so that I can exploit his weaknesses to defeat him. Fig 11.3 illustrates the opponent executes a powerful side kick; I dodge by moving diagonally forward. As soon as he places his kicking leg on the ground, I have move in accordingly and placed my front leg behind his front leg, Fig 11.4.

Notice that my hands guard against his possible attack. Immediately I fell him onto the ground by pushing his body backward and tripping his leg, using a pattern called "Uprooting a Tree", Fig 11.5. I have my finger-hook on his throat and my knee on a vital point of his body which will cause him pain if he tries to move.

Fig 11.3 Dodging a Side Kick

Fig 11.4 Moving in for a Felling Technique

Fig 11.5 Uprooting a Tree

One must realize that merely knowing strategies and tactics is not enough; the combatant must be skillful in his techniques. Indeed, one who can apply strategies and tactics in combat is usually of a master's level. For ordinary combat situations, being familiar with the principles and practice of combat sequences and sparring sets is generally adequate for securing victory.

Defeat Due to Wrong Choice

While the strategy and tactics described above which advocate close body fighting, may be effective against someone like a Taekwondo exponent who frequently uses side kicks and round-house kicks, they may not be suitable against an opponent like a Siamese Boxing practitioner, who uses other types of kicking techniques, because with his elbow and knee strikes, a Siamese Boxing exponent is also versatile in close range combat. This of course is no implication that Siamese Boxing is superior to Taekwondo: it just illustrates that we must select the right strategy and tactics according to the fighting styles of our opponent.

The kinds of side kicks and round-house kicks typically found in Taekwondo are not commonly found in Siamese Boxing. Their close equivalents in Siamese Boxing are similar to what we call whirlwind kicks and thrust kicks in Shaolin Kungfu. We still can use our same techniques against these equivalents, but then we may not get the same advantages as before, and we must also be careful that the versatile Siamese Boxing opponent has effective counters against our moves. The following show some illuminating examples.

As the opponent executes a whirlwind kick, I dodge by moving diagonally forward as before, Fig 11.6. Immediately I move in with a leopard punch, Fig 11.7. But the versatile opponent sweeps aside the leopard punch and simultaneously jumps up with a typical Siamese Boxing knee strike at my side ribs using a pattern similar to what is known as "Jade Girl Kicking Shuttle" in Shaolin Kungfu, Fig 11.8.

Fig 11.6 Dodging a Whirlwind Kick

Fig 11.7 Leopard Punch to the Opponent's Ribs

Fig 11.8 Knee Strike to My Side Ribs

In Fig 11.9, the opponent inflicts a thrust kick; I dodge by moving diagonally forward. As soon as his kicking leg is back on the ground, I would have moved in and placed my leg behind his leg and I am about to fell him to the ground, Fig 11.10. However, he neutralizes my felling technique with a little jump and simultaneously strikes his elbow into my face using a pattern known in Shaolin Kungfu as "Fierce Tiger Enters Rock", Fig 11.11.

Fig 11.9 Dodging a Thrust Kick

Fig 11.10 Getting Ready for a Felling Technique

Fig 11.11 Fierce Tiger Enters Rock

My defeat in both cases was due to my failure to follow Sun Tzu's advice: I did not ensure myself against the possibility of defeat; and I provided the opportunity for him to secure victory. The failure was the result of strategic, tactical and technical errors.

I used the wrong strategy; I attacked his strong points and was ignorant of his weak ones. Knee strikes and elbow strikes are the forte of Siamese Boxing, and these techniques are best applied in close-body combat.

My tactics of entering from the sides and attacking him when he had not recovered his balance, was also a mistake because knee and elbow strikes can be effectively applied to both the sides and the front, and a nimble Siamese Boxing exponent can recover his balance easily.

Thirdly, in my attack I committed the technical fault of not providing sufficient cover or retreat for myself. The overall cause of all these mistakes was that I had not understood my opponent adequately.

Sun Tzu's famous axiom, "Know thyself and know thy enemy; thou will be victorious a hundred times in a hundred battles" is as important in warfare as in individual combat.

A basic requirement of a master whenever he executes any attack is the ability to neutralize any resultant counter-attack from the opponent. Applying this principle, I can reverse my defeat to victory in the above combat. There are many ways to counter the knee strike and the elbow strike; the following are just two examples.

As shown in Fig 11.12, which is a continuation of Fig 11.8, as the opponent inflicts his knee strike, I move my front leg backward and simultaneously deflect his attacking knee with my right hand. Continuing the movement, I squat down and strike his other knee at its side with my left leopard punch, in a pattern called "Angry Leopard Charges at a Rock", Fig 11.13. It must be noted that Fig 11.12 and Fig 11.13 should be performed in a split second.

Fig 11.12 Angry Leopard Charges at Rock

Fig 11.13 shows my counter against the opponent's elbow strike. I move my *back* leg a small step backward and lower myself into a Horse-Riding stance, thus moving my face away from his attack. Simultaneously I "float" his attacking elbow and strike his side ribs in a pattern called "White Horse Turns Around Its Head".

Fig 11.13 White Horse Turns Around Its Head

Choosing the Right Strategy and Tactics

However, even though I could reverse defeat to victory, I would not take this risk, because in the above sequences I was in disadvantageous situations.

Although Siamese Boxing may appear simple, it is actually an extremely effective art for fighting. Its simplicity is deceptive: Siamese Boxing attacks are brutally powerful, yet bafflingly subtle.

Luckily there are two invaluable factors helping me to equip myself against Siamese Boxing opponents. One, virtually all Siamese Boxing techniques can be found in Shaolin Kungfu, thus enabling me to be familiar with the operation of this art. Two, before his commitment to Shaolin Kungfu my own Shaolin master, Sifu Ho Fatt Nam, was a professional Siamese Boxer, earning his livelihood and a number of championships from the Siamese Boxing ring.

Thus I learnt from him many important secrets Siamese Boxers use in their fight.

When facing a powerful, subtle and agile opponent, I would try not to meet him directly. I would tempt him to attack, but make sure that his attacks are futile, and strike him when he least expects it.

A helpful strategy, therefore, is a combination of the following two principles: "Trick the opponent to attack unsuccessfully; strike him when is unprepared" and "Use the orthodox in combat; use the unorthodox to secure victory". A tactical approach to realize the aims of the strategy is "If there is form, strike the form; if there is no form, chase the shadow".

So, when my Siamese Boxing practitioner initiates his attacks using kicks, which happens to be a common strategy in Siamese Boxing to assess or confuse the opponent, as well as to open the way for subsequent killing strikes, I will *pretend* to block or to retreat.

These blocking and retreating moves are different from those of the uninformed combatant facing a skillful Taekwondo exponent described earlier, because here they are meant to trick the attacker. These moves appear to be orthodox to my Siamese Boxing opponent, as he has probably met countless combatants reacting in these ways to his attacks. This may give him a false impression that I am incompetent, and may cause him to be less vigilant.

Then when the opponent least expects it, but when I have been building up to this opportunity, I will strike him decisively to defeat him. Fig 11.14 to Fig 11.16 provide an example of using the unorthodox to secure victory.

When he executes a right thrust kick, instead of retreating as he may have expected, I withdraw my body without moving back my legs so as to "swallow" or avoid the full impact of his momentum, and simultaneously with my right leopard punch strike his knee (at its side) or ankle, which are soft spots of his leg, Fig 11.14. (Striking his hard, trained shin may fracture my knuckles if they are not tough enough.) This is the tactics of striking the form if there is form — the form here being his extended leg.

Irrespective of whether I hit his knee or ankle or nothing at all, he is likely to withdraw his leg. I move forward to squat down, change my right leopard punch to a right cup fist and following the movement of his withdrawing leg, strike his "dan tian" or the vital point at the abdomen, with internal force channeled from my cup fist, Fig 11.15.

This dan tian is the focus of his chi or intrinsic energy. An appropriate strike at his dan tian can shatter his internal energy field, thus putting him out of combat. This tactic is known as chasing the shadow if there is no form — form being his withdrawing leg.

Notice that my other hand guards his withdrawing leg. It does not matter if he does not withdraw his leg; I would still follow up with the same pattern, which is called "Hitting a Tiger".

He may, despite being hit, spring up his other left leg for a knee strike at my head. I will be ready for this anticipated move: I change my right fist to an open palm and "float" or deflect his left knee, and simultaneously strike the same spot (i.e. his dan tian) with my left cup fist. Fig 11.16.

Fig 11.14 Striking the Knee

Fig 11.15 Hitting the Tiger

Fig 11.16 Striking the Dan Tian Again

Overcoming Throws and Multiple Attacks

My master, Sifu Ho Fatt Nam, once told me that many years ago a Judo expert from Japan specially paid him a visit to test his Shaolin Kungfu. As they walked along, the Judo expert put his arm round my master like an old friend.

"Did he know you before?" I asked innocently.

"No," my master said, "but he was trying to throw me many times as we walked along."

"You could easily have given him an elbow jab or a kick to his shin," I said.

"I did not, because his gesture was friendly, and you do not do such things to a guest who have come from very far away to put his arm around you."

"Did he succeed in throwing you?"

"He did not. It is actually quite easy to neutralize throws. You just apply the principle of `Move the stance, change the step'. The Judo expert was simply amazed."

I was very keen to test the validity of my master's teaching on myself, and found that it works excellently. It is indeed amazing that just one principle, when applied skillfully, can be used to overcome countless combative situations. Basically the principle of "Move the stance, change the step", which sounds poetic in Chinese, means that whenever an opponent attempts to throw you, you can frustrate his effort by regaining your balance as soon as he tries to off balance you. This can be achieved by adjusting your foot position and sitting low on your stance. Figures 11.17 to 11.22 illustrate two examples.

In Fig 11.17 the opponent tries to throw me over his shoulder, similar to a Shaolin pattern called "Farmer Digs the Ground". I push my front leg right into and between his two legs, sit on a Reverse Bow-Arrow stance, and grip his hair from behind, Fig 11.18, in a pattern called "Pulling a Bull's Tail".

Fig 11.17 Farmer Digs the Ground

Fig 11.18 Pulling a Bull's Tail

In Fig 11.19 the opponent attempts a backward throw by tripping my leg, resembling the Shaolin pattern "Uprooting a Tree" which we have met earlier except that in the Shaolin pattern the exponent uses the Horse-Riding stance or the Bow-Arrow stance for better stability.

I lift up my attacked leg, Fig 11.20, swiftly bring it far back behind me, Fig 11.21, simultaneously pull the opponent to fall forward face-on, immobilize his pushing arm by squatting on it and grip his neck with one hand, Fig 11.22, in a pattern called "Catching a Snake on the Ground". All these actions are done continuously in a split second.

Fig 11.19 Opponent Tripping Me to Fall Backward

Fig 11.20 Lifting up the Attacked Leg

Fig 11.21 Pulling the Opponent to Fall Forward

Fig 11.22 Locking Arm and Gripping Neck

This principle of "Move the stance, change the step; shift and dodge, advance and retreat" can be used as an excellent strategy against multiple opponents. There is a kungfu saying that "it is difficult for two fists to match four hands", which means that even if your are a good fighter, you may not match two opponents attacking you *at the same time*, although you can easily defeat them one at a time.

Now imagine you are surrounded by six opponents. If three of them attack you at the same time, what are you going to do? You can fight them *one at a time* if you swiftly move away from you original position into any one of the six opponents. Because you have moved away, the three simultaneous attacks cannot reach you, so you need *not* have to use "two fists against six hands". You will have to be constantly on your move, making full use of "shift and dodge, advance and retreat", to avoid more than two hands attacking you at the same time.

If you have confidence in defeating your opponents, go for their leader (irrespective of whether he is currently attacking you) and strike him before the others close in on you. Once the leader is beaten, the others usually chicken away. However, if you think they are formidable, go ferociously at their most timid member, not so much to strike him but to get him out of your way so that you can escape immediately.

Frustrating Locks and Fast Punches

If you know how to apply effectively just one tact-cal principle, "Follow his momentum, break his flow", you can frustrate most attempts to hold or lock you! Technically speaking, executing a lock is more advanced than executing a punch or kick, because it necessitates making many movements whereas punching and kicking need only one. This explains why punches and kicks are more frequent in most fighting, and also why it is harder to get out of a lock than to defend against a punch or kick.

Let us briefly examine an example each on how to apply the above tactics to prevent getting into a hold, as well as getting out from one. Fig 11.23 shows an opponent pulling me to fall forward, trying to lock my arm with the pattern "Catching a Snake on the Ground", as in Figures 11.21 and 1.22 above.

Instead of resisting, I follow his pulling momentum and move one leg forward to regain balance, Fig 11.24. Then, I swing my held arm upward in an arc to break his hold on my arm, simultaneously strike his face with my other fist and move one leg backward into the Bow-Arrow stance (so as to eliminate the exposure of my groin) in a pattern called "Old Elephant Drops Tusk", Fig 11.25.

Fig 11.23 Opponent Pulling Me to Fall Forward

Fig 11.24 Following His Momentum to Regain Balance

Fig 11.25 Old Elephant Drops Tusk

In Fig 11.26 the opponent holds my head from behind in a pattern called Two Dragons Carry a Pearl. If he forcefully turns my head, he can break my neck and that would be the end of me — physically. This is a deadly technique, and should never be used by Shaolin disciples unless it is absolutely necessary.

If I try to resist his turning, it is using the weakness of my neck against the strength of his two arms. (Although his hands are holding my head, if he locks his wrists it is actually the arms that provide the strength.) So I follow the momentum of his turn, then break his flow by putting my front arm round his two arms to lock them, and, placing my front leg behind his legs to trip him and stabling my stance, I fell him onto the ground with a push and twist, Fig 11.27, in a pattern called Holding the Moon Close to the Body.

When he is caught unprepared on the floor, I could jab two fingers into his eyes, but I stop just an inch away, Fig 11.28, demonstrating that Shaolin disciples do not return a tooth for a tooth.

Fig 11.26 Two Dragons Carry a Pearl

(a)   (b)

Fig 11.27 Holding the Moon

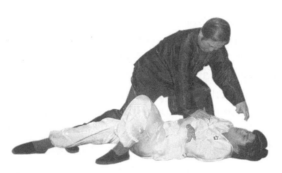

Fig 11.28 Do Not Return a Tooth for a Tooth

Like other kungfu principles, this tactics of following the enemy's momentum, then breaking his flow, can be fruitfully applied to our daily lives. Suppose some envious colleagues are scheming to trap you into a quagmire. Instead of flaring out immediately, which may force them to employ more drastic measures, you follow their scheme a short way on save ground, and when you are with their momentum, you break their flow (such as by removing some essential intermediate steps). Your enemy would have to abandon their scheme.

What would you do if you meet an expert who has fast, powerful punches, such as a skillful boxer (using Western Boxing)? If you try to block his punches, you commit the error of confronting his strong points. One useful strategy is to ignore his punches and concentrate on attacking his lower body, as illustrated in Figures 11.29 and 11.30. You will notice that the strategy here is "Avoid his strong points, attack his weak ones"; and the tactic is "Long against short".

Fig 11.29 Side Kick to the Opponent's Abdomen

Fig 11.30 Clutch Kick to the Opponent's Knee

We started this chapter on tactics and strategies with some invaluable advice from Sun Tzu; it is also fitting to conclude with another quotation from this great strategist, who provides us with the insight that when we observe a master defeating a formidable opponent, we can see the particular technique employed to secure victory, often we also know the tactical considerations behind the techniques used, but most of us may not be aware of the underlying strategy from which the tactics and techniques are evolved.

People know the tactics I employ for securing victory, but no one knows the strategy from which victory is evolved.

12
The Fascinating Force Of Shaolin Masters
(Various Kinds of Force in Shaolin Kungfu)

Shaolin Kungfu is not meant for hurting others but for saving lives and helping people towards enlightenment.

Basic Force and Specialized Force

To be a good fighter it is not enough to know fighting techniques, possess combative skills like spacing, timing and fluid movement, and have a sound understanding of tactics and strategies. The successful fighter must also have sufficient force to back up his techniques and skills, and good speed to execute them efficiently.

Skills, force and speed are closely related, and are collectively known as *gong* (pronounced as "kung"), a Chinese concept that has no suitable equivalent in English, but for want of a better term, is translated here as "force".

The importance of *gong* in kungfu is evident from the fact that the term "kung-fu" (spelt as "gongfu" in Romanized Chinese) actually refers to the attainment of *gong*, rather than an accumulation of fighting techniques.

Gong or force may be classified as basic or specialized; external or internal; and as arts of power, arts of energy or arts of lightness. These different classifications and descriptions of force are meant for the convenience of study, and should not be taken as rigid compartmentalization, as some people used to exclusive division in western science may presume.

Moreover, because of the cultural and linguistic differences between English and Chinese, terms or concepts that are perfectly logical in Chinese may appear odd in English.

As one of the objectives of this chapter is to present to western readers some important concepts of force originally expressed in the Chinese language, readers are requested to exercise some patience if they come across terms or descriptions that may be problematic due to cultural and linguistic differences. But their patience will be amply rewarded as these concepts, little known in the west, are of much philosophical as well as practical value. The methods to develop some examples of this fantastic force are explained in the next three chapters.

Basic force is holistic and transferable: it may be applied to any part of the body, and for different functions. For example, if you have a good storage of intrinsic energy you may, if you know the methods, channel it to your head for clear thinking, to your hands for powerful strikes, or round the ren and du meridians for stamina (see Chapter 20).

Specialized force, on the other hand, is localized and particular; it is usually focussed at one specific part of the body and for a particular purpose. For example if you have developed specialized force at your head in an art called Iron Head, it is specifically used to break an opponent's bones in combat or granite slabs in impressive demonstrations; but not normally used for clear thinking or channeled to other parts of the body for other functions.

Certain types of basic force are essential to kungfu training. In the English language, they are more appropriately referred to as basic skills, indicating that the Chinese concept *gong* incorporates both force and skills.

At the beginning stage of kungfu training, these skills include various stances and foot-work, fundamental techniques and simple methods to develop the minimum power to apply these techniques. At a more advanced stage where kungfu patterns are applied for combat, these basic skills include timing, spacing and fluid movement that we have learnt in Chapter 10.

"Basic" here means "forming the foundation" or "very important". Hence, anyone who wishes to excel in kungfu should pay much attention to these basic skills, which are referred to in Chinese as "basic force" in one of the main ways in classifying force.

Three Levels of Force

Another main way is to classify force into external and internal. External force is sometimes called "gang" or hard force; and internal force called "rou" or soft force.

The division is arbitrary, and the description is provisional, because sometimes it may not be easy to classify certain force as external or internal, and internal force can be very hard too. Besides, the English equivalent "soft" does not adequately convey the meaning of the Chinese concept "rou"; thus expressions like "soft force can be more powerful than hard force", which is perfectly acceptable in Chinese, may seem funny in English.

In the Shaolin teaching, the lowest level of force is hard, external force, such as Iron Legs for whirlwind kicks, developed after having kicked at a tree trunk more than a million times.

Such kicks are extremely powerful and fast, and very effective for fighting; yet, this type of force is not highly valued in Shaolin Kungfu because its training is not only rough and painful, but may cause irreversible damage to the legs; its application is limited (unless you want to be a professional kick-boxer) and is therefore not cost-effective; and the nature of training tends to make the practitioner violent and aggressive.

The intermediate level is soft force, which may be external or internal, such as fast, agile movements (which is considered as external) or well coordinated breathing resulting in good stamina (considered as internal).

This type of force is superior to hard, external force like Iron Legs because not only it is useful for fighting, it also contributes to our work and play. Moreover, all the setbacks of hard external force mentioned in the previous paragraph are absent. Someone with Iron Legs may break the opponent's hands or head if the opponent is ignorant enough to block them or too slow to move away.

But if you are fast and agile, and have good stamina, you have a good chance to defeat Mr. Iron Legs if you are trained in the various Shaolin techniques, skills and strategies described in the previous chapters. If both of you are totally untrained, but you are fast and agile, and he only has iron legs, you are still in a superior situation — in combat as well as in daily living.

The highest level of force is both hard and soft, external and internal, such as Cosmos Palm, where the exponent can cause serious damage without leaving any outward mark, and Golden Bell where the exponent can withstand strikes and even weapon attacks without sustaining injuries! This type of force usually begins as soft and internal, and is often so described, but it can manifest as hard and external at the advance stage.

Someone may ask, not without good reasons, what happens if a master with Cosmos Palm strikes another master with Golden Bell. This depends on the relative force of the two masters. If the Cosmos Palm is *very much* more powerful, it will damage the Golden Bell. If it is the reverse, the Golden Bell will bounce back the force and hurt the Cosmos Palm! But the injury of either one, if any, will be far more serious if he had not been trained in the respective advance force.

Nevertheless, it is not just because of their highly desirable martial functions that these arts are considered to be of the highest level of force. These arts are excellent for promoting health, vitality and longevity, enabling the exponents to put more life into their years, and more years into their lives. It is obvious that the kind of force that is both hard and soft, external and internal is superior to force that is only soft externally or internally, as the former includes and surpasses the latter.

Power, Energy and Lightness

Another useful practice is to classify force as the arts of power (ying gong), the arts of energy (qi gong or chi kung) and the arts of lightness (qing gong). In this classification, the translation of the Chinese term *gong* into English as "force" is most inadequate; thus I prefer to use the word "arts" instead of "force".

The arts of power refer to hard force, which is usually external but may sometimes be internal. Some examples of these powerful arts include Iron Palm, Iron Arm, Iron Head, Iron Leg, Stone Lock and Eagle Claw. It is commonly said that Shaolin Kungfu is well known for its arts of power, which is true but which may be misleading if understood superficially, for it may wrongly imply that soft and internal force, and the other arts of energy and of lightness, are not significant.

The arts of energy, sometimes called internal arts or *nei gong*, refer to the application of intrinsic energy to enhance combat efficiency. Some examples of famous Shaolin energy arts are Iron Shirt, Golden Bell, Cosmos Palm, Diamond Palm, One Finger Zen, Golden Finger, Marvelous Fist, Cosmos Breathing, Small Universe and Big Universe.

As mentioned earlier, Chinese terms and descriptions are often used provisionally; they should not be taken as rigid scientific names meant for exclusive sets. The Chinese term for this class of energy arts is referred to as chi kung, sometimes as hard chi kung; the term "chi kung" is also used collectively for all kinds of arts dealing with energy which may not be related to kungfu.

In fact in later chapters we shall read about some aspects of Shaolin Chi Kung that are specially meant to cure illnesses, promote longevity and develop spirituality, and have no combative functions normally.

A similar example of such linguistic complication can also be found in the use of the term "Chinese" in the English language. When we refer to a citizen of China as a Chinese, he may not actually be Chinese, i.e. of the Chinese race (e.g. he may be a Manchurian or a Mongolian); whereas a Chinese (like one staying in America or Australia) may not be a Chinese, i.e. a citizen of China.

The third class in this classification is the arts of lightness, which is a figurative term to describe a class of specially trained abilities that may be generally summarized as being exceptionally fast and agile.

Some examples of these lightness-arts include Thousand Steps, Running on Grass, Running on Water, Plum Flower Formation, Through the Woods, Walking on Baskets, and Light Body Skill. In Chinese, these terms are poetic and meaningful. In the history of kungfu, some Shaolin masters were known for their ability to run extremely fast, run for very long distance, and jump very high.

My master lived near a river when he was a small boy. One day he saw an old man literally run across the river which he knew was deep. He told me he actually pinched himself to ascertain he was not dreaming. Even at that early age, my master knew he witnessed a very advance kind of *qing gong* or the art of lightness called "Running on Water as if on Land". For many months he waited for the old man to appear again, but to no avail. Understandably, most people would not believe it is possible to run on water unless they have seen it with their own eyes.

An Invaluable Lesson

My master also told me a lesson that he would never forget. He started to learn Northern Shaolin Kungfu very early. His was a traditional way whereby the student followed the master like an apprentice, serving the master in all his personal needs, and getting two square meals in return, besides learning the master's art. Every morning he had to wake up early to run with the master. First they ran along the sleepers of a railway track, skipping over one and then more sleepers as they progressed, so as to widen their steps.

Later his master marked out ten trees in a circle in a forest. They started running together, but soon his master, despite his age, was far ahead. Then the old master would be out of sight. Next the old master would come up from behind, and as his old master over-took him, he would be given a whack and be scolded for being slow. This went on for many months.

One day my master, who was then a young student, decided that he had enough. When the old master asked him to train, he said, "No, I have enough of your beating!"

"You have been making good progress," the old master said.

"What progress? You said you would teach me kungfu, but all that I have learnt was running and being hit."

"But I have been teaching you kungfu. If you stop half way, you will waste all your previous efforts. Are you going to train?"

My master could catch a wink from his master's wife, signaling to him to carry on training. But he had made up his mind. He told me that at that time, kungfu to him meant punches and kicks and elaborate patterns, just like what many students erroneously believe today. "No, I am not going to continue," he insisted.

The old master was getting angry. "I am asking you seriously the third and last time. Are you going to train with me? I want to remind you again that if you stop now, you are going to waste all your previous efforts in your kungfu training, which is a great pity."

"What kungfu? It is just running and being hit. No, I am not going to train, even if you skin me!"

"Since you have made up your mind, follow me and I will show you what kind of kungfu I am teaching you."

They went to an open space at the back of the house. There was a high wall with pieces of broken glasses on top of the wall purposely placed by the builder to prevent burglary.

"Now watch carefully. Do not blink your eyes," the old master said. He went to the bottom of the wall, folded his long robe and tucked it into his waist slash, bent his knees slightly and sprung up from the spot high into the air, with a sweep of the long smoking pipe he habitually carried with him, he brushed aside some pieces of glasses and stood motionlessly on the high wall with one leg and arms spread out like an elegant crane! The old master stood majestically on the wall for a few seconds, then jumped down and landed gracefully without making any sound!

Immediately my master knew this was *qing gong*, the arts of lightness. He prostrated before the old master, apologized profusely for his rashness, and begged the master to accept him again. No, the master said. It was a tradition among old masters that if they asked you three times, thus giving your an opportunity thrice, and yet you refused, they regarded that you were not destined to learn their art.

My master said that was his greatest regret for failing to learn a priceless art, but it provided him with an invaluable lesson: he resolved that if found a good master next time, he would do whatever the master commanded.

Hence, years later when he met a good master of Southern Shaolin Kungfu, at a time when he himself was already an accomplished fighter, he did just a seemingly simple movement with a finger on the horse-riding stance (the "Art of One-Finger Shooting Zen" explained in Chapter 5), and hardly anything else, for three years, because his master asked him to do so.

His effort was richly rewarded as he succeeded in the rare, advanced art of One Finger Zen, which is applied to the technique of *dian xue* (or *dim mark* in Cantonese) where the exponent can cause serious injury with only a finger and often without the opponent knowing.

He also had an immediate consolation. Pitying him, his *simu*, the old master's wife who tried to help him by signaling with a wink, taught him a kungfu set called Seven Stars.

Indeed it was while teaching me Seven Stars that my master told me this case history. He also asked me, "Suppose a fragile-looking lady meets an agile, powerful kick boxer in combat. How could she defeat the opponent?" The Shaolin Seven Stars Set is a good answer because it is built upon techniques and tactics meant for a woman or a comparatively weaker person against an exponent with hard, external force.

Iron Palm and Cosmos Palm

Probably the best known example of hard, external force in Shaolin Kungfu is the Iron Palm. It is classified as external because the main part of its training is by external means, such as hitting sandbags and thrusting the palm into iron filings.

It is classified as hard because its function is visibly destructive, such as breaking bricks and smashing bones. Yet, in the hands of a master, Iron Palm can be manifested as soft and internal force. For example, meeting the challenge of a Russian who had brought in a trained horse to insult the feebleness of the Chinese people in this early twentieth century, the famous Shaolin master, Gu Ru Zhang, used his Iron Palm to hit the horse only once.

The poor horse dropped and died. There was not a trace of injury on the surface of the horse, but when it was operated on, it was found that its internal organs were badly damaged.

Ordinarily, if a master strikes his Iron Palm on a horse, its flesh will be smashed up. Although Gu Ru Zhang used Iron Palm, what he demonstrated was actually the effect of Cosmos Palm. Someone has given a vivid, albeit exaggerated, description to contrast the Iron Palm with the Cosmos Palm as follows.

If a master strikes an Iron Palm on a wall, the wall will collapses. If another master strikes the same wall with a Cosmos Palm, nothing will happen to the wall, but the furniture behind the wall will be damaged.

The Cosmos Palm is internal and soft. It is generally classified as internal because its main training is by internal means, such as breath control and meditation. It is classified as soft because the actual palms of a master of this art are soft and gentle, without tell-tale signs like disproportionate large size, callus and toughness which are common characteristics of the Iron Palm, and the effects of its applications are without the potent destructive features of a hard force.

In Sifu Ho Fatt Nam's school, Iron Palm training was one of the basic requirements for his advanced students. I had practiced the Iron Palm for some time, striking my palms on a bag of iron fillings when one night he said to me, "You have fine palms like a lady's. Do not spoil your palms with this hard training." For a moment I thought that would be the end of my force training. But my master continued, "I will teach you Cosmos Palm instead."

I bet many people would be very surprised if shown some training steps of the Cosmos Palm; they seem so unrelated to developing force. I was taught to move my arms in an apparently simple manner, coordinating my breathing and making appropriate sound.

There was no hitting of sandbags, thrusting palms into granules, or any hard conditioning at all. I was more surprised when a few months later I could break a brick with my lady's hands.

Then my master taught me Cosmos Breathing, which led me to the wonders of Shaolin Chi Kung, and later he taught me meditation, which gave me glimpses of the greatest achievement any being could attained here or anywhere! This change of training from Iron Palm to Cosmos Palm was certainly one of the best blessings in all my Shaolin practice.

I am glad that I had no need to use the Cosmos Palm in combat although I was involved in real fighting a few times. Nevertheless there were two interesting occasions that confirm for me the potential damage the Cosmos Palm can inflict.

There was an old, unwanted papaya tree in my garden to be cleared away. For fun, I struck the tree trunk a few times using my Cosmos Palm. When a workman sawed the trunk to discard the tree in parts, he was surprised to find that the interior of a certain section was blackened although its exterior was intact, and all other parts were normal. This section was exactly where I applied the Cosmos Palm on the trunk.

After kungfu training a few of my advanced disciples and I discussed the application of the Cosmos Palm in an incredible art known as "Hitting a Buffalo Behind a Hill", where force could be passed through a person unhurt to injure another person behind!

As some were keen to know how the first person could be unhurt, I demonstrated this to them. I hit them on one arm near the shoulder and asked them to feel the effect on the other arm. But it was very important that they must be relaxed, for if they tensed their body, their tension could block the flow of internal force thereby hurting them. All of them felt the effect on the other arm; some even felt a flash of energy across their body. Wong Yin Tat, my senior disciple who specializes in the art of Iron Shirt whereby he can take punches and kicks without sustaining injuries, tensed for a moment.

Two days later Yin Tat, who had never been sick since practicing Shaolin Kungfu, felt feverish with cough and pains in his chest. At once he knew it was due to our experiment with Cosmos Palm. I opened some relevant vital points and transmitted chi (or energy) into him to clear away his energy blockage.

It is interesting to add that my son, Wong Chun Nga, who could see into organs, saw a cloud of dark energy inside his chest, and when I transmitted chi into Yin Tat, he saw a beam of greenish golden energy issuing from my fingers to disperse the dark energy. Yin Tat also performed some remedial chi kung exercises, and a few days later he was completely cured. Some people may find this hard to believe, but it was all true.

As I have spent many years practicing the Cosmos Palm, but have never used it for actual fighting, is it a waste of my time? Certainly not. The internal force that I have developed in my Cosmos Palm has enabled me to help countless people: for example, children with various types of pains often had their pains relieved after I had placed my palm over their troubled spots; many adults at my chi kung seminars had an immediate experience of chi after I had transmitted chi to them; old people with degenerative illnesses usually sped up their recovery remarkably after I had improved their energy flow using the energy of my Cosmos Palm.

These performances reduces my intrinsic energy, thus making my Cosmos Palm less potent for combat, but as many Shaolin masters have said in different words, Shaolin Kungfu is not meant for hurting others but for saving lives and helping people towards enlightenment.

13
Principles And Methods Of Power Training
(Shaolin Iron Palm and Iron Arm)

Have mercy on your opponent if ever you have to use your kungfu on them.

Important Factors for Force Training

After reading about the fantastic effects of kungfu force in the previous chapter, many readers would have the impressions that the methods to develop kungfu force must be elaborated and kept as top secrets.

They would probably be very surprised if shown the once-secretive methods, for except some internal arts, the training procedures of most types of kungfu force are so bafflingly simple that many people may question whether these methods really produces the incredible results claimed for the various types of force.

I can assure them that if they practice the recommended methods *correctly* and *persistently* over a reasonable period of *time*, they will certainly derive the effect attributed to the force. Indeed, the "top secret", without which no one who attempt force training will ever succeed even if he knows the method, is "training correctly and persistently over a reasonable period of time."

The "correct" methods of many interesting types of kungfu force are explained in some detail in this and two subsequent chapters.

The "persistent" training will of course have to be done by you yourself. A good book may supply invaluable information, a master may provide the personal guidance that will enhance your development, but no one (and no drugs) can do the training for you.

Persistent training means practicing for about half an hour (some force may need a longer time) every morning and evening or night without fail. You may practice just once every day; but the attainment of your force, understandably, will take a longer period. It is permissible if you miss your practice once a while, but your overall training must be regular. On the other hand, it is not necessary, sometimes even injurious, to train more than required.

Regarding a reasonable period of time needed for attaining the force, masters in the past advised that "three years is required for small success; ten years for great success."

If you train for the Iron Palm, "small success" is something like making a big hole in a brick wall with one strike; "great success" will cause the whole wall to collapse. Translated into fighting situations, an Iron Palm of small success can kill an ordinary person with just one strike.

This explains that in kungfu philosophy, the exponent would take great care not to be hit even once; exchanging blows generously as is quite common amongst combatants nowadays was unthinkable in kungfu fighting of the past.

Because of changed conditions, the standards of kungfu then and now are vastly different. Even an average student in the Shaolin Monastery could easily strike a hole in a wall; a master's power would be unbelievable to a modern, uninitiated person. But nowadays breaking a brick with a palm strike is already a remarkable achievement. Hence, for our modern purpose, if you train daily for one year, you should attain small success; and three years for great success.

A common question many students have in mind, but feel uncomfortable to ask, is whether they can have sex during the period of training.

In the past masters asked their students to abstain from sex during the training period; if this proved too demanding, they should at least abstain for the first hundred days, which constitute the foundation-laying stage.

As mentioned above, conditions as well as standards aimed at are now different; nowadays masters generally advise their students to carry on their normal sex lives in moderation. With sex added to the training, the period required to attain the desired force will be longer, but most agree that it is wiser to maintain sanity (and sometimes family harmony) than sacrifice it for rapid force development.

Of the three kinds of classification of force described in the previous chapter, the triple division of force into the arts of power, the arts of energy, and the arts of lightness is most comprehensive, as it also incorporates the principal features of the other two classifications, such as basic and specialized, external and internal.

Hence, we shall adopt this classification for the purpose of describing force training. Two examples of the arts of power are explained in this chapter, and other examples of the arts of energy and the arts of lightness are explained in the following two chapters.

Training for Iron Palm

The methods for the training of the various arts of power, or hard force, such as Iron Palm, Iron Arms, and Iron Leg, are astonishingly simple.

Although there are some finer points that most students would not know unless revealed by a master, and which we shall study presently, generally if anyone, who does not know anything about martial arts, persistently strikes his palms, arms or legs on a sandbag, pole or some suitable objects a hundred times everyday for three years, he will inevitably develop the Iron Palm, Arm or Leg.

If he is aware of the finer points, he will not only attain his force in a much shorter time, but also avoid the unfavorable side-effects that uninformed practice may bring. Why, then, very few people achieve such powerful arts as the Iron Palm or Iron Leg? It is because very few people have the patience and self-discipline to sustain training for the required length of time.

Prepare a rectangular striking bag made of canvas about one foot by two feet. It is preferable for the bag to be of two layers, so as to prevent its content which will have been rendered to dust after repeated hitting, from filtering through the bag into your nose.

Fill the bag with a mixture of black beans and green beans of about equal portions. Place the bag at a suitable height (about two and a half feet) on a firm support. Place a piece of clean canvas over the bag, so as further prevent its dust from getting into your lungs.

Shaolin philosophy insists that no matter what or how we train, it should contribute to our well-being, and must never affect our health or physiological function unfavorably. We do not want students to have, for example, powerful palms but suffocated lungs.

Go into the horse-riding stance in front of the bag, which should be at about your waist level. Take a few deep breaths and focus your mind at your *dan tian*, which is an energy field about three inches below your navel. Be alert and relaxed.

Then, raise your whole arm high above your head, gently breathing in as you do so, Fig 13.1. Focus your *chi* or intrinsic energy at the center of your palm, where there is a vital point known as *lao gong*. Drop your arm smoothly and strike the bean bag firmly, gently breathing out as you do so, Fig 13.2.

It is very important that you must *not* use strength, and must *not* tense your arm or any part of your body! This is a crucial secret of the training method. Most people erroneously think that the more strength you use, the more force you will develop. It is not so. If you use strength or tense your arm, you impede the flow of internal force from your dan tian to your palm.

Fig 13.1 Raising the Palm High Before Striking

Fig 13.2 Striking the Bag Firmly and Squarely

Let your palm strike the bean bag firmly and squarely; look at the palm with your eyes and focus your chi at the center of the palm. Leave the palm in contact with the bag for a few seconds and relax. Then raise the same arm above your head and repeat the procedure for about ten times.

After about ten strikes with one palm, repeat the routine with the other palm. This constitutes one form of striking with the palm known as *pai*, or "slap" in English.

Repeat the same procedure, first with one palm and then with the other, using another form of striking known as *pi*, or "chop". Here, the striking point is the edge of the palm, Fig 13.3. The focus of chi when the arm is raised above the head, and when the palm is chopped onto the bean bag, is at the striking point.

Fig 13.3 The Striking Point of "Pi" or "Chop"

Then, the third form of striking known as *yin* or "stamp", where the striking point is the base of the palm, is similarly performed, Fig 13.4. Thus, the whole sequence consists of three parts — *pai* or slap with the whole palm, *pi* or chop with its edge, and *yin* or stamp with its base — and each part consists of ten strikes with each hand, making a total of sixty strikes.

Fig 13.4 The Striking Point of "Yin" or "Stamp"

After the whole sequence of sixty strikes, drop both palms at your sides, bend forward slightly from your Horse-Riding stance, Fig 13.5 (a), and jump to bring your feet together, simultaneously breathing in gently with your nose and bringing your hands up in front to your chest level with both palms facing upward, Fig 13.5 (b).

Then, as you gently breathe out through your mouth, turn your palms to face downward and slowly lower them to a position in front of your abdomen, Fig 13.5 (c). Drop your hands and let your arms hang naturally at your sides. Focus your chi at your dan tian in the abdomen, Fig 13.5 (d).

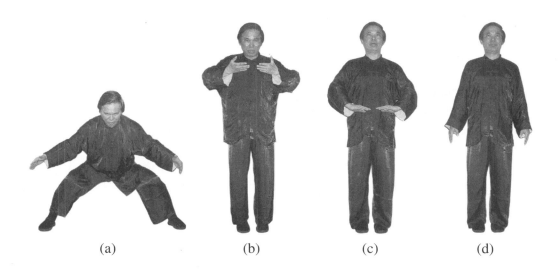

(a) (b) (c) (d)

Fig 13.5 Bringing Chi to the Dan Tian

Next, wash your arms and palms in a basin of warm medicinal concoction, the ingredients and preparation of which will be given later. While your hands are still wet, perform another sequence of sixty strikes. Jump to bring your feet together, drop your hands, and focus your chi at your dan tian as before. Then, gently close your eyes, relax and remain at this Standing Meditation with eyes close for a few minutes. Do not think of anything in your standing meditation; you will probably feel power swelling at your palms.

At the conclusion of the training session, wash your arms and palms in the warm medicinal concoction again. Let the concoction on your hands dry by itself.

If your palm is injured during the training, rub some medicinal wine on to the injured parts *after* the arms and palms are perfectly *dry*. Avoid contact with water on the injured part for about an hour after you have applied the medicinal wine. It is not necessary to apply the wine if there is no injury.

However, if the medicinal concoction is not available, then apply the medicinal wine at the end of the training irrespective of whether there is any injury or not, and keep away from contact with water for an hour.

You must stand properly at the hose-riding stance throughout the process of striking the bean bag sixty times; otherwise your training is merely mechanical, missing the internal part where force is developed at the dan tian and channeled to the palms during striking. Hence, being able to stand at the horse-riding stance for some time is a prerequisite. However, if your stance is unable to last the whole sequence, you may pause after each part.

In other words, after striking with one form of the palm, you may jump up to stand with feet together for a while, before proceeding to the next form. On the other hand, as you progress, you should *gradually* increase the number of strikes with each palm form, so that you may be making hundreds of strikes in one session.

After practicing for about three months, you can change the content of the striking bag from beans to sand. After another three months, change the sand to marbles, pebbles or ball bearings. If these are not available, you can continue with sand.

You should practice twice daily for about a year. In the past, Iron Palm training included thrusting the palm into iron fillings. Such a drastic step is not recommended nowadays.

Preserving Sensitivity and Relieving Injury

At least once a week throughout the training, at any convenient time, place eight grains of beans or sand on a table on your side. Using your thumb and a different finger at one time, pick out one grain and transfer it to the other side.

Repeat with the other hand. Later, use threads or hairs instead of beans or sand. The purpose of this "yin" aspect of the training is to balance the "yang" aspect, so that the sensitivity and utility of the hands are not impaired.

Application of medicine is necessary in hard, external training to serve two important functions: to cure injuries sustained during the training, and to enhance the progress by generating better blood and chi circulation. The Chinese names and appropriate amount of the ingredients of the medicinal concoction, which is called "Soothing Muscles and Livening Blood Concoction for Washing", are as follows:

shen jing cao	12 grams
hai tong bi	12 grams
zuo qin yuan	12 grams
da du huo	12 grams
shan gou teng	12 grams
chuan hong hua	12 grams
da dang gui	8 grams
ru xiang	8 grams
mo yao	8 grams

This prescription is a herbal mixture, not a chemical compound; hence if one or two ingredients are unavailable the mixture can still be used. The ingredients are placed together in a basin with water and brew over a small fire until the concoction boil for a few minutes. It is allowed to cool until lukewarm for use in bathing the arms and palms or other relevant parts of the body for force training.

Immediately after use, add some water to the concoction and boil it again. Cover the concoction to prevent dust and microorganisms from getting in, and keep in a suitable place for use in the next training session, when it is boiled again and then allowed to cool till lukewarm for bathing. Each mixture may be used for about ten times. Add water when necessary.

The following are the Chinese names of the ingredients of the medicinal wine, generally known as medicinal wind for injuries sustained from falling and being hit. Like above, this prescription is a herbal mixture, so it still can be used even if one or two ingredients are not available.

gui wei, ru xiang, mo yao, chuan hong hua, zhi ke, mu xiang, tao ren, chuan gong, jin jie, chi yao, hu gu, ji geng, chen xiang, zhi zi, dan pi.

Obtain 12 grams of each ingredients and soak them in about three pints of white rice wine for about two months. Then pour out the medicinal wine, which is now ready to be used, to be kept in suitable bottles. Discard the residue.

The above kungfu medicine can be used not only for Iron Palm training, but also for other types of hard conditioning like Iron Fist, Iron Arm and Iron Leg. If such medicine is not available, an effective and convenient alternative is chi kung therapy, such as the chi kung exercise known as "Lifting the Sky", explained in Chapter 4.

As a substitute for the kungfu medicine, the chi kung exercise should be performed before and after the hard force training, gently visualizing during standing meditation that chi flows harmoniously down the body and its relevant parts (such as the palms) to cleanse away any injuries.

It is not advisable to practice hard conditioning without kungfu medication or chi kung therapy, because if injuries sustained unwittingly during training are not relieved, they may cause serious side-effects later on.

Rolling Bamboo for Three Years

Having powerful arms is obviously a big advantage for effective fighting. One Shaolin method, which is as effective as its name is esoteric-sounding, is called "Rolling Bamboo". This method is incorporated in the following story, which also reveals some vital lessons of kungfu in general and force training in particular.

A young man from a rich family was very interested in kungfu. His father employed many kungfu instructors to teach him, hoping that one day he would become a kungfu expert. But as expected of rich pampered sons, the young man was not ready to endure the hardship associated with force training, so his instructors, in order to justify the attractive salaries received from his wealthy father, taught him a lot of beautiful kungfu sets and patterns.

"Son, how is your kungfu progress?" the father was fond of asking him. "Very good, father, sifu has just taught me another new set." (Sifu means "master".)

The father was very proud of his son, and whenever there was any social function he would ask his son to demonstrate, and all those present would say what beautiful kungfu he could perform. Soon the father and son became arrogant.

One day the father and son were involved in a brawl with some people. The father asked the son to teach them a lesson, but instead they were badly beaten. The father was very angry with his son for being so useless in actual fighting, and the young man was so shameful of himself that he ran away from home, vowing never to return unless he had become an efficient fighter.

The young man went up a mountain to beg a Shaolin monk, the Venerable Tie Pi, to teach him Shaolin Kungfu. "I have practiced useless kungfu for many years," he said to the monk.

"Show me your useless kungfu."

After viewing the young man's performance, the monk said, "it is you and not the kungfu that is useless!"

"Then, master, please teach me some kungfu that can be used for fighting."

"You are not ready for fighting; you are only fit to roll bamboo!"

"Roll bamboo?"

"Yes. Go to the woods, and bring me some round bamboo stems."

The young man was very happy, thinking that now at last he could learn some real kungfu. Soon he came back with round bamboo stems.
"Now place a bamboo stem on a table. Stand at the horse-riding stance and roll the whole length of your arm over the bamboo. Do it every day," the monk told the young man.

Fig 13.6 Rolling Bamboo on a Table

The young man had heard that great masters taught students only after testing their patience, so he resolved to do whatever the master asked him to. He rolled one arm, then the other, then both arms over the bamboo stem, causing it to roll under his arm along the table. He persisted, and rolled his arms thousands of times over the bamboo stem the first day, but the master paid no notice of him. The next day he did the same thing, yet the master paid no attention.

After the third day, he gathered enough courage to ask the master, "Sifu, I have been rolling my arms over the bamboo for three days. When can I start to learn kungfu?"

"Continue rolling!" the master commanded, "practice your own kungfu whenever you are tired of rolling the bamboo."

So he kept rolling the bamboo every day. After three months, he asked the master again, "Sifu, when can I start to learn kungfu?"

The master told him angrily, "Continue rolling! If you do not want to roll bamboo, you can go home."

Going home without becoming a good fighter was the last thing he would do. He had no choice but keep rolling bamboo. Soon he found that the bamboo break easily when he rolled his arm over it. But what impressed him most was the kungfu performance of his shih-xiong (senior classmate), who attended to his master in the temple.

He'll Break Your Arms

After one year he approached his master again, "Sifu, I have been rolling bamboo everyday for one year; and I have broken many bamboo stems and also a few tables. Can I start Shaolin Kungfu, or at least can I practice sparring with Shih-xiong?"

"He will break your arms! Now place the bamboo below the table surface, instead of on it, supported by one or both of your arms, and keep on rolling. You can leave any time if you are dissatisfied."

Fig 13.7 Rolling Bamboo Below a Surface

Another year passed, with more bamboo stems and tables broken. After rolling bamboo for two years, the young man thought he would at last begin Shaolin Kungfu. But when he approached his master, the monk asked him to roll stone rollers on a stone table instead of rolling bamboo; nevertheless, the master allowed him to spar with his shih-xiong. The young man was surprised his shih-xiong had so much internal power.

The third year passed, and he had also broken a few stone rollers. He gathered all his courage he had and asked his master, "Sifu, I have been rolling bamboo and then stone rollers for three years. When can you teach me kungfu?"

"You can pack your things and go home," the master said. The young man was astonished. He knelt and apologized for his rashness. "Sifu, I am sorry if I have annoyed you, but I really want to learn Shaolin Kungfu. Please have mercy on me."

"I have taught you Shaolin Kungfu, and you have done remarkably well. Go home, your parents are waiting for you. Have mercy on your opponent if ever you have to use your kungfu on them."

On his way home, the young man encountered four robbers. Finding no money on him, the robber were angry. One of them started to punch him. Spontaneously the young man blocked the punch.

The robber bent down groaning with pain; his arm was fractured. Another robber executed a kick. The young man blocked, and fractured the robber's leg. The third robber smashed his staff onto his head; he blocked and broke the staff. The fourth robber slashed his broadsword at the young man, who deflected it and broke it into two pieces! The robbers begged for mercy.

Only then did the young man realize what wonderful Shaolin Kungfu he had developed. The Iron Arm, like the Iron Palm, is classified as specialized, hard, external force. He prostrated in the direction of his master, and knocked his forehead three times on the ground as a sign of gratitude.

His wealthy father threw a grand party to welcome him home. People were eager to know what he had learnt from the famous Shaolin master, the Venerable Tie Pi. "I only learnt rolling bamboo and stone rollers," he said solemnly. Someone commented, "I thought Tie Pi was a great kungfu master; so he only knew rolling bamboo!"

"How dare you insult my master!" the young man retorted, automatically banging his arm on the table. The solid table broke into a few pieces.

14
Secrets Of The Energy Masters

(Developing Cosmos Palm and Iron Shirt)

Considering all these factors, it is not unreasonable to say that Shaolin Kungfu is the greatest martial art in the world.

The Greatest Martial Art in the World

Many people, understandably, will vehemently oppose the claim that Shaolin Kungfu is the greatest martial art in the world; but if they are willing to listen rationally to the arguments substantiating this claim, they may concede its validity.

First of all, it needs to be clarified that claiming Shaolin Kungfu to be the greatest martial art does not imply that one who practices Shaolin Kungfu is necessarily a better fighter than one who practices another style of martial art. If someone practices even a simple art well, he will probably be more efficient than another who practices a profound art badly.

Moreover, practicing a profound art well usually needs more time; hence, at the early stage, a person practicing an art that is solely meant for fighting usually can fight better than another practicing a martial art that also promises other non-fighting benefits.

For example, a Siamese Boxing student can fight fairly well only after six months of training, and he may easily defeat a kungfu student who has spent six months learning only stances and basic patterns. But if you are looking for greater achievements than mere fighting, then Shaolin Kungfu can offer much more than Siamese Boxing or any other martial art.

Below are the areas where Shaolin Kungfu compares more favorably than any other martial arts:

1. Shaolin Kungfu patterns are aesthetic to watch and of a great variety. A performance of Shaolin Kungfu is power, elegance and beautiful forms in poetic movements.
2. The fighting techniques in Shaolin Kungfu are more extensive than in any other martial arts. While many martial arts specialize on only one category of fighting, such as Western Boxing on punching, Taekwondo on kicking, Judo on throwing, and Aikido on holding, Shaolin Kungfu not only possesses all these techniques, there are some Shaolin techniques (like the Horse Back-Kick, the Crab Hook, and the Phoenix Fist) that are not found in any of the other arts.

3. The range and depth of "force" in Shaolin Kungfu far surpasses those of any other martial arts. The various types of force training in many other arts, like punching sandbags, kicking at poles, and carrying weights, are comparatively simple; many types of Shaolin force, like Cosmos Palm, Golden Bell and One Finger Zen, are incredible to other martial artists.

4. The rich theories for effective combat accumulated in Shaolin Kungfu, like the principles and songs summarizing in poetic expressions effective techniques, tactics and strategies explained in previous chapters, reveal a depth and scope that is not found in other martial arts. (Even Taijiquan, with its exceedingly rich philosophy, cannot be compared with Shaolin.)

5. While the belief that top performance in fighting ability or sport deteriorates after thirty, may be true in many martial arts, it is not true in Shaolin Kungfu. Shaolin masters are youthful and energetic even after fifty, and their fighting competency increases with age! This is because Shaolin training involves the internal besides the external, and internal development is not limited by chronological age.

6. While practicing some martial arts are actually detrimental to health (such as sustaining injuries that are not treated, and becoming aggressive and violent), Shaolin Kungfu training contributes to health physically, emotionally, mentally and spiritually. Taijiquan is also excellent in this respect, but Shaolin is even better because its development is both external and internal, whereas Taijiquan focuses more on internal development.

7. Besides health, Shaolin Kungfu contributes greatly to vitality and longevity. The vitality of a Shaolin disciple is often revealed in the sparkle of his eyes. In comparison, if you observe carefully you may notice that the eyes of martial artists of many other styles are often dull and yellowish, indicating that they suffer from untreated insidious injury endured through sparring.

   Shaolin Kungfu has an advantage in this respect over other martial arts because it incorporates chi kung and medicine, both of which contribute to vitality and longevity, whereas other martial arts do not. Chi kung is also an important aspect of Taijiquan, thus enabling Taijiquan to have this advantage like Shaolin, but there is comparatively less emphasis on Chinese medicine in Taijiquan.

8. Mental freshness as well as mind expansion are significant benefits of Shaolin Kungfu, derived especially from practicing meditation, which forms an integral part of the Shaolin arts. Taijiquan, which also places much importance on meditation, has these benefits too. Meditation is not an integral part of other martial arts; if it is ever practiced, it is usually treated as supplementary.

9. The philosophy of the Shaolin arts is extensive and profound, sometimes touching on aspects that modern science is now rediscovering, such as the concepts of the inter-changeability of energy and matter mentioned in Shaolin Chi Kung, and the various levels of consciousness in Shaolin meditation. Studying Shaolin Kungfu at advanced levels is opening vistas of Eastern wisdom.

10. The highest achievement of Shaolin Kungfu is spiritual fulfillment, irrespective of one's religion. No other martial arts, except Taijiquan, have such a noble aim. Even in Taijiquan this supreme aim towards spiritual fulfillment is not as explicitly stated as in Shaolin Kungfu.

Considering all these factors, it is not unreasonable to say that Shaolin Kungfu is the greatest martial art in the world. We shall have a better perspective if we recall that Shaolin Kungfu was first initiated by the great Bodhidharma as an aid to enlightenment in the Shaolin Monastery, the foremost temple of the Chinese Empire which probably enjoyed the highest level of civilization in the world at that time.

The above ten factors show the potential benefits one can get from practicing Shaolin Kungfu, but of course he must be ready to work hard and be blessed with a generous master. It is a Shaolin tradition that the advanced arts are taught only to selected disciples, so he must also prove that he is worthy of the arts. On the other hand, if someone learns only kungfu form and mistakes it to be Shaolin Kungfu, as many people do, he may not even achieve the minimum requirement of self defense.

Force training is a very important aspect of any style of kungfu. Many people have heard of the saying: "If you only learn kungfu form but never develop kungfu force, your kungfu will be futile even if you learn a life-time"; but not many people really understand its meaning, and less still put it into practice. Two examples of hard force, or the art of power, are explained in the previous chapter; in this chapter two examples of internal force, or the art of energy, are discussed.

The Palm That Can Kill or Heal

An interesting feature of Shaolin Kungfu is that while it is a very effective martial art, fighting is not its only objective. The Cosmos Palm is a remarkable expression of this feature. While the Cosmos Palm can cause serious damage to an opponent in combat, it can also bring much benefits in healing. The Cosmos Palm is an advanced internal art, and should be trained only with the supervision of a master. The methods described below are meant for knowledge rather than self practice.

The foundation of the Cosmos Palm is the continuous flow of cosmic energy in the body attained through the art of the Small Universe or microcosmic flow. If the exponent has not attained the Small Universe, he should at least be able to perform Abdominal Breathing or Cosmic Breathing (please see Chapter 20).

After having acquired the Small Universe (or Abdominal Breathing, or Cosmic Breathing) practice Forceful Windmill as follows. Standing upright with feet together, thrust one palm in front as in Fig 14.1 (a), with a "her-it" sound coming from the abdomen.

Next raise the palm upward, simultaneously breathing in through the nose, Fig 14.1 (b). Then lower the palm in an arc, simultaneously breathing out with a continuous "shss" sound coming from the lungs, Fig 14.1 (c), and ending at the original position, Fig 14.1 (a), with an abrupt "sher" sound.

The performing palm and arm should be terse with force throughout the circulating movement, while the rest of the body is relaxed. Drop the palm and arm after the "sher" sound, and relax. Focus chi or intrinsic energy at the dan tian in the abdomen. Repeat the process about 10 times with the same hand. Then repeat the procedure with the other hand.

Increase the number of repetition as you progress. Close the eyes and remain at Standing Meditation for a few minutes, feeling internal force developing at the arms and palms.

(a)   (b)   (c)

Fig 14.1 Forceful Windmill

Next practice Pushing Mountains. Stand upright with eyes close and channel intrinsic energy to flow round the body in the Small Universe or micro-cosmos a few times.

Then, while the Small Universal flow is going on, place both palms, facing forward, at chest level, Fig 14.2 (a). Breath in and visualize cosmic energy flowing into your abdomen. Push both palms out, Fig 14.2 (b), breathing out at the same time.

Do not use strength, but visualize intrinsic energy flowing from your back through your arms to your palms. Bring back both palms, Fig 14.2 (b), breathing in gently into the abdomen and visualizing cosmic energy flowing into you. Repeat a few times.

After that visualize a mountain in front. As you push out your palms, visualize pushing away the mountains not with any strength but with your chi or intrinsic energy; and as you bring back your palms, draw the mountain towards you. Repeat between twenty to a hundred times.

The Small Universe is simultaeously flowing while you are pushing and with-drawing your palms. Increase the number of repetition as you progress. At the end of this procedure, drop the arms and stand at meditation for a few minutes, feeling the flow of cosmic energy to the palms, Fig 14.2 (c).

(a)   (b)   (c)

Fig 14.2 Pushing Mountain

After a few months of pushing mountains, do not drop the palms immediately at the end of pushing at least a hundred times, but hold the extended palms and arms stationary, as in Fig 14.2 (b) above, for about five to twenty minutes. The palms and arms are at right angles, the elbows straight, and the shoulders relaxed. Imagine that your arms are very powerful.

Then turn your palms so that they face upward, and imagine that you are carrying the sun and the moon in your palms, Fig 14.3 (a). Your elbows are straight and shoulders relaxed. Stand at this Carrying the Sun and Moon position for another five to twenty minutes.

Next bring the sun and moon to the sides of your body, Fig 14.3 (b), and remain stationary at this poise for a further five to twenty minutes. Your elbows should be bent sharply and pointing backward, and your shoulders relaxed. Then turn your palms to face downward, slowly lower them, and remain at Standing Meditation for about ten to thirty minutes. Gently visualize two balls of energy at the center of both your palms, Fig 14.3 (c).

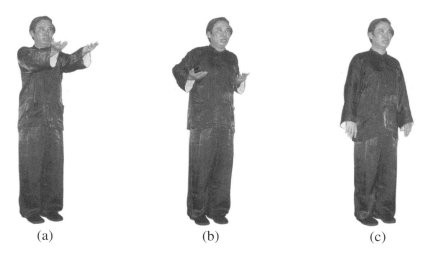

(a)   (b)   (c)

Fig 14.3 Carrying the Sun and Moon

At various parts during your training, you may feel that you are highly energized. But you must not feel any pain, especially at your chest. If you feel pain, which is a warning sign of faulty practice, you *must* stop immediately. Serious injury may result if you do not heal the warning sign of pain. Remedial chi kung exercises, like Lifting the Sky (Chapter 4) and Self Manifested Chi Flow (Chapter 18), can relieve the injury.

After at least a year of daily practice of the above exercises, you may test your Cosmos Palm on a brick. Support the two edges of a brick lengthwise, and place another brick over it, as shown in Fig 14.4. Stand at any suitable stance near the two bricks. Focus your chi or intrinsic energy at your abdomen, and then at your striking palm. Look at the middle of the lower brick and focus your mind there for a few second. Then strike the top brick any way you like with your Cosmos Palm, but visualize your internal force going through the top brick to reach the middle of the bottom brick to break it. You will find the bottom brick broken but the top brick is intact!

Fig 14.4 Breaking the Bottom Brick with Cosmos Palm

When you have succeeded in attaining the Cosmos Palm, you are blessed with a pair of wonderful healing hands. Hence, although the Cosmos Palm is usually classified as a specialized art for striking, its force can be used for many general purposes. For your own sake, do not be so unwise as to create bad karmic effects for yourself by hurting others with your Cosmos Palm; rather, accumulate blessings with your Cosmos Palm by helping others and saving lives.

If you are worried that you may accidentally hurt your sparring partner with your Cosmos Palm, take comfort that the most important factor here is the mind and not the palm. Even if you strike your partner with your palm, but if you do not use your mind to channel intrinsic energy to hurt him, he will not be hurt. A Shaolin poetic expression advises that when your palm is in contact with an opponent,

> Focus energy at dan tian, relaxed and calm,
> When striking, power issues from your palm.

Similarly, if you wish to transmit chi or energy to another person to help him relieve pain or cure illness, first focus your chi at your dan tian (the energy field at your abdomen), be relaxed and calm, then think of chi flowing into him from your pointed finger(s) or palm.

It is a great blessing to do so, as you donate your chi, which is more valuable than blood, but you must be very careful not to drain yourself. You must also avoid the back-flow of negative energy from him, especially if he is gravely sick: this can be done by withdrawing your hand immediately after transmitting chi.

It is advisable to cleanse yourself, especially after treating gravely sick patients, then replenish your chi. One effective way is to perform Lifting the Sky: for the first few times, think of negative chi flowing out of your hands as you lower them; then think of good cosmic energy flowing into your abdomen. You will notice that in all these activities, it is your mind rather than your physical actions that bring about the desired effects.

Withstanding Attacks with Iron Shirt

While it is not difficult to classify Cosmos Palm as soft and internal, and Iron Palm as hard and external, it is not so easy to classify Iron Shirt, the art of energy that enables the exponent to withstand attacks without sustaining injuries.

Many people consider it internal as it involves chi or intrinsic energy; other consider it external as it involves hitting with external tools. But all agree that it is hard force.

Nevertheless, while Iron Shirt is normally categorized as a specialized art for protective cover, its force can be used for purposes of general health, thus reminding us that the various classifications of force is not rigid compartmentalization but for the sake of convenience.

The basis of Iron Shirt is the Small Universe, which is also the foundation for many types of advanced arts. Some students practice Iron Shirt without the Small Universe, or without any chi kung foundation at all. They only use the external methods of conditioning through hitting, as explained below.

This is not accepted in Shaolin Kungfu, because without the internal foundation, not only the exponent cannot advance far and therefore may be hurt by an opponent using hard force, but also the training itself may cause unwitting injuries and if the injuries are not relieved through the accompanying chi kung practice, it will accumulate and result in serious consequences, which contradicts the Shaolin philosophy that any training must contribute to the exponent's health. Iron Shirt, like Cosmos Palm, should be practiced with a master's supervision. The following description, therefore, is meant for knowledge rather than self practice.

The intending practitioner therefore must practice Small Universe for at least a few months. If he does not have the Small Universe, he must at least practice Abdominal Breathing or Cosmic Breathing to enhance his energy level, and Self Manifested Chi Flow to relieve any unwitting injury during practice.

Prepare about eight canes, each about an inch in diameter and fifteen inches in length. Soak the canes in medicinal wine (like the one given in the previous chapter) for about ten minutes. As medicinal wine may be costly, an economical alternative is to hold each cane vertically above a bowl, pour a cup of medicinal wine down the whole length of the cane letting the wine to soak into it, and reuse the wine collected at the bowl. Repeat a few times. When the canes are dried, tie them into a bundle.

Start the training with Small Universe for about five to ten minutes. Then hit the inner side of the whole length of your arm about thirty times from the shoulder to the fingers with the bundle of canes. Repeat with the outer side, upper side and lower side of the same arm, so that every part of the arm has been hit. Repeat the procedure with the other arm.

Fig 14.5 Hitting the Arms

You should be relaxed and your breathing natural during the hitting. Initially the hitting should be gentle, but later as you progress, you should increase the force of the hitting. The increase should be gradual so that you would not sustain any injuries.

After hitting both arms about 240 times, perform Self Manifested Chi Flow, then Small Universe. Complete with Standing Meditation, gently thinking of your dan tian.

After about two weeks of daily practice, add hitting your legs in the same way. Then add hitting various parts of your body, including your head, with an interval of about two weeks for each addition. The procedure is as follow: Small Universe, hitting various parts of the body, Self-Manifested Chi Flow, Small Universe and Standing Meditation. After a few months, you will be hitting yourself hundreds of times per training session.

Fig 14.6 Hitting the Front of the Body

Fig 14.7 Hitting a Side of the Body

Fig 14.8 Hitting the Back of the Body

Fig 14.9 Hitting the Head

If you have someone to help you in your training, ask him to hit you with the bundle of canes. You may find it quite pleasant, especially if he hits you hard! This is not because you have become masochistic, but because the hitting helps to spread chi over your body.

After practicing daily for six months, instead of hitting yourself with the length of the cane-bundle, you can ram yourself using one end of the bundle, Fig 14.10. Later, change the bundle of canes to a bag of pebbles or iron bearings. Use a double-layer bag if possible, to prevent dust of the pebbles or even iron bearing filtering through the bag and getting into your body.

Once every fortnight, soak the pebbles or iron bearing in cold water, so as to remove any dust that may result from constant knocking inside the bag. Dry in a cool place before filling back into the bag for use. Do not dry in the sun, because the heat of the sun absorbed in the pebbles or iron bearing is not conducive to your health when you use the pebbles or iron bearing for hitting.

Fig 14.10 Ramming with One End of the Bundle

If you have no chi kung base in your Iron Shirt training, you must take a herbal concoction once a fortnight to relieve any injury sustained unwittingly during the training. If you include Small Universe or Self Manifested Chi Flow in your training, the concoction is not necessary. The following herbal mixture, known as "Harmonizing Chi and Enlivening Blood Concoction", is helpful:

chuan hong hua	12 grams
su geng	12 grams
ji ke	12 grams
sa ren	12 grams
tou ren	12 grams
xiang fu	12 grams
chi yao	12 grams
gui wei	10 grams
hou bu	10 grams
su mu	10 grams
mu xiang	10 grams

Brew the mixture in three bowls of water over a small fire until about eight-tenth of a bowl of the concoction is left. Drink the concoction when luke-warm. Keep the residue for the next day and brew it again in three bowls of water until about eight-tenth remains. Drink the concoction when lukewarm, and discard the residue.

To test your force, ask a friend to punch you gently at first, then gradually harder and harder until he punches you with all his might. Next ask him to kick you, again from gently to all his might. If you are adventurous, strike yourself with a sharp weapon, such as a meat chopper; you will be surprised that you are not hurt.

There are a few important points to bear in mind. Having Iron Shirt does not make an exponent invincible; although he can withstand attacks from an ordinary opponent, he can still be injured if the opponent has tremendous force.

There are some vital points, like the eyes, throat, and reproductive organ, where even an ordinary opponent can cause injury to an Iron Shirt exponent. Hence, it is folly to let your opponent know that you have Iron Shirt. Similarly, although it may be impressive to demonstrate Iron Shirt publicly, where strangers are invited to strike the exponent, it is not a wise thing to do.

If the benefit of the Iron Shirt is just for you to take punches and kicks, it is not worth the time spent on training it. Unless you harbor such wishes like becoming a stuntman or a professional boxer, and apart from bolstering your ego in risky public demonstrations, there are not many occasions to use this art in our modern law-abiding society. But the Iron Shirt has other invaluable functions. The spread of chi over your whole body gives you radiant health, and your protective iron shield makes you tough — psychologically as well as physically.

15
The Fast, The Agile And The Marvelous

(Marvelous Responses and the Arts of Lightness)

The response is so superb, usually with an element of surprise, that the opponent himself cannot help marveling with awe and admiration at it

Techniques, Force and Speed

Suppose you have four combatants: one is physically strong, another is skillful in using techniques, the third has tremendous kungfu force, and the fourth is fast. Who do you think is the best combatant, and who is the worst?

A Shaolin axiom says, "strength cannot match techniques, techniques cannot match force, force cannot match speed, and speed cannot match the marvelous".

It means that if you can apply techniques skillfully, you can defeat an opponent who depends only on his mechanical strength. If he pushes you, for example, do not resist, but retreat a step, pull him following his forward momentum, and trip him to fall face-on.

If he punches you, do not block his massive fist, but step aside and kick at his side ribs. You must never let him catch you. However, if he ever catches hold of you, grip one of his fingers, strike his weak spot like kicking his shin, then immediately bend his finger outward against its natural leverage to release the hold. All these examples illustrating the first part of the above Shaolin axiom involve the skillful application of techniques. However, if you only know kungfu form but ignorant of its application, you will have little chance against a strong opponent.

The second part of the axiom states that you may know a lot of techniques, and may be skillful in applying them, but in a real fight if your opponent has tremendous kungfu force such as Iron Fist or Iron Leg, he is likely to beat you.

You may be very elegant and stylistic in your movements, and have actually hit him many times; he can be clumsy and unskillful but if he succeeds in ramming his Iron Fist or striking his Iron Leg only once into you, you will be out of action with a few broken bones. You will notice that kungfu force here is different from the physical strength of the earlier combatant.

Imagine a seven year old black-belt fighting a massive brute who has no knowledge of martial art. If it is a non-contact friendly match, the child will easily win on points; in real combat, the brute merely walks in, ignoring the opponent's ineffectual strikes, and fell the child with one merciless blow.

This resembles the situation many years ago of so-called kungfu practitioners, who have never sparred before, fighting professional Siamese boxers in boxing rings. On paper, these so-called kungfu practitioners described how effective kungfu patterns were against the seemingly simplistic Siamese Boxing techniques, but in the ring they could not even survive one kick of the Siamese boxers' Iron Leg.

But if you are fast and agile, the Iron Leg or Iron Fist cannot hit you, and therefore is ineffectual. Obviously, Siamese Boxing exponents are good fighters not merely because of their forceful kicks, but also because they are extremely fast.

Hence the third part of the Shaolin axiom says that even if the opponent has tremendous force, if you are fast enough to avoid his attacks and strike him in return, you are a better combatant. Even if you do not have tremendous kungfu force like the Iron Leg, but if you are fast enough to strike his vital spots like his temples, neck or groin with some ordinary strength, you can put him out of action.

My master, Sifu Ho Fatt Nam, used to remind me that hard force like Iron Leg and Iron Palm is "dead" kungfu whereas speed and agility are "live" kungfu. Of course he did not imply that hard force is not useful (otherwise Iron Palm training would not be an essential practice for his advanced students); he meant that possessing hard force by itself does not necessarily make a good fighter, because an opponent, unlike a granite slab in demonstrations, does not remain motionless to allow you to strike him.

There is another Shaolin axiom which says, when literally translated, that "hundred techniques might as well be one speed". It has two related interpretations, according to the situation.

One, it means that if you intend to practice one hundred techniques, you might as well practice one technique so well that you can execute it in great speed. Two, an opponent may be familiar with countless techniques, but if you are fast you can defeat him irrespective of the technique you use to strike.

There is an interesting story of a classical kungfu expert nicknamed Fast Fist. He specialized in only one pattern — the simple straight punch, but he could inflict it so fast that it became an "ultimate pattern".

It was "ultimate" because if he ever used it, he would surely be victorious. His opponents might attack him in various ways, including some complex moves that would need much skill to escape from, such as a nine-step continuous attack using different parts of the attacker's body to strike different parts of the opponent's body.

If Fast Fist were to counter each of these nine attacks, he would be defeated. But he understood the tactics of avoiding the opponent's strong points, and of employing his own strongest point to strike at the opponent's weakness.

So he did not bother to defend against the nine-step attack, but simultaneously executed his "ultimate" fast punch at a time when his opponent was concentrating on attack and thus might slacken in defense.

Fast Fist won on speed, his punch striking the opponent and therefore hurting and throwing the latter off balance before the first of the nine continuous attacks could reach its target. This split second implementation of his "ultimate pattern" was the result of years of dedicated training. It was "ultimate" not because there was no defense against it, but it was so fast that the opponent could not defend against it though he knew how.

Marvel with Awe and Admiration

Is it logical, then, to forget about force and techniques, and concentrate only on speed? No, mere speed, like mere force or techniques, is not enough to clinch victory. Unless you always aim for his vital spots like his eyes and groin, a strategy which the compassionate Shaolin philosophy prohibits, your strikes will not be effectual even if you are fast, unless your strikes are backed up with some force.

Even if one were to be so inhuman as to maim an opponent by always striking at vital spots, he still needs techniques for the attack. The Shaolin axiom illuminates the relative importance of techniques, force and speed, which are often collectively known as *gong* (or kung), but never suggests that any one of the three factors can replace another.

Moreover, speed is not the highest factor in combat. The fourth part of the axiom says that speed cannot match the marvelous. By "marvelous" is meant that the response is so superb, usually with an element of surprise, that the opponent himself cannot help marveling with awe and admiration at it, although this marvelous response may be natural or spontaneous to a master. The marvelous response gives a sense of being "just right" in all aspects, though it may be directly related to one particular aspect, like that of techniques, force, speed or other factors.

Let us examine some examples. Figure 15.1 illustrates a "hook punch" to an opponent's temple. This is the first of a nine-step attack, and is often a feint move to distract the opponent. My second attack, a two-finger jab at his side ribs, is ready to strike the opponent the instant he responds to my hook punch.

Fig 15.1 Feint Opening with a Hook Punch

But my opponent, Mr Fast Fist, ignores my hook punch, irrespective of whether it is a feint or real attack, and strikes out his lightning straight punch at an important energy field known as *tan zhong* at the middle of my chest. Fig 15.2 shows the effect of his superior speed: his punch reaches me before either my hook punch or my finger jab could complete its course.

Fig 15.2 Victory Due to Speed

However, to his great surprise, this effect of speed does not happen, because I overcome speed with "the marvelous". Instead of landing his punch at my chest, he finds my palm jabbed at his carotid artery, Figure 15.3, and he certainly is pleased that (thanks to the Shaolin teaching on compassion) my palm merely touches his neck instead of jabbing right into the artery.

I achieve "the marvelous" by slightly rotating my waist to move my chest away from his punch and simultaneously changing the hook punch at his temple to a palm jab at his neck, and changing the intended two-finger jab to a hand guard against his arm, all in one smooth action without interrupting the original momentum.

The onus of this marvelous response is on skillful use of techniques, though all other factors are also "just right". Despite its speed, the opponent's fast punch could not hit me because I have moved the target away, and this changed movement is not a new, fresh movement, but a continuation of a movement that is already on its way. Its application, of course, requires much skill.

Fig 15.3 Executing the Marvelous to Clinch Victory

Figures 15.4 and 15.5 illustrate another marvelous response basing mainly on force. In the midst of executing my hook punch, I find his straight punch coming at my *tan zhong*.

Following the forward momentum of my attack, I raise my back heel so that my *tan zhong* is moved slightly upward and forward, Fig 15.4. In this way his punch crashes not into my *tan zhong*, which is a vital spot with an important energy field, but into my upper stomach which, if I have protective force like Iron Shirt or Golden Bell, can take his punch without sustaining serious injuries.

Fig 15.4 Moving the Tan Zhong away from Attack

As his punch comes into contact with my body, I move my front leg a slight step forward, bend my body diagonally downward, change my hook punch at his temple into a tiger claw at his neck, and change my two-finger jab into another tiger claw at his elbow — all these actions are performed simultaneously, Fig 15.5.

Hence, at the very moment my opponent expects his lightening punch to hit me, he finds his attacking wrist dislocated, while one tiger claws grips crucial vital points at his neck preventing him from moving away freely, and another tiger claw grips his elbow preventing him from bending his arm to nullify my body attack on his wrist. Of course, I must earlier make sure that my protective force can take his striking force.

Fig 15.5 Dislocating the Wrist with the Body

Figure 15.6 illustrates why the combined forward movement of the opponent's arm and the diagonally downward movement of my body dislocate the opponent's wrist.

Fig 15.6 Mechanics of the Dislocation

Another example showing that speed cannot match the marvelous is illustrated in Fig 15.7. As I find a fast punch rushing at me while I am executing a hook punch, I immediately discontinue the hook punch, move my body backward by shifting my body weight to my back leg (thus moving my chest away from the opponent's punch), and kick up with my toes at the elbow of the opponent's attacking arm, Fig 15.7, hence dislocating the elbow.

Fig 15.7 A Marvelous Response Basing on Speed

It may appear that this kicking at the opponent's elbow to dislocate it, is the easiest of the three examples of marvelous responses. But if you try out the three sequences, you will probably find it is the most difficult.

The difficulty lies not in the technique which is comparatively simple though unexpected, nor does it need specialized force to dislocate an elbow with a kick. The difficulty is in its speedy performance. Unless you are well trained, you are likely to be hit before you can shift your body backward, because this shifting involves stopping your forward movement, then starting a reverse movement backward.

As it involves two opposite momentum, it needs much skill and more time to perform than the other two examples of spontaneous responses where the action is continuing the original momentum. Hence, the onus of the marvelous in this case is speed, whereas that of the other two is technique and force respectively.

Some Considerations in Speed Training

Speed, of course, is a very important factor in any martial art. Even in Taijiquan, where practitioners normally perform Taiji patterns slowly during practice, speed is essential in combat — a fact unfortunately and surprisingly many Taiji students themselves are not aware! In Shaolin Kungfu, the arts of lightness incorporate specialized methods to train speed and agility.

Attaining speed is not simply trying to be fast. If you try to perform your kungfu movements fast without proper methods, you are likely to be panting for breath, practicing incorrect form, and lacking in force.

It is not uncommon to find that when martial artists try to execute their techniques with power, they generally slow down their movements; when they try to be fast, they generally become short of breath.

Properly trained Shaolin disciples, on the other hand, come out of their fast, forceful kungfu performance in solo practice or sparring as if they have come back from a leisurely walk! A Shaolin tenet advises: "Powerful but not tardy; fast but not breathless."

Before attempting a program of speed training, it is helpful to consider some important principles.

1. The lung capacity must be enlarged to hold more air to meet the extra requirement of speed; otherwise the exponent will be short of air.
2. The breathing rate must not quicken when movements quicken; otherwise the exponent will be panting.
3. The meridian system, which may be translated as the circulatory and respiratory systems in this case, must be improved so that not only more chi, or extra oxygen, can be effectively channeled to the relevant tissues, but also toxic waste can be readily disposed off; otherwise the exponent becomes tired easily.

4. There must be adequate preparatory exercises to stretch the necessary muscles; otherwise the exponent becomes muscle-bound and clumsy.
5. There should be meditative exercises to develop mental freshness; otherwise bodily speed will be hampered by mental indecision.
6. There must be sufficient practice so that reaction is not only fast but spontaneous; otherwise the exponent becomes hesitant.
7. The training should be gradual so that the various body systems have sufficient time to adjust to new levels of speed and power; otherwise there may be insidious ill effects on the exponent's health due to sudden stress and tension.
8. The attainment of speed must not be at the expense of other combat factors, like form, force, balance and flexibility; otherwise the advantages gained in speed will be off-set by the resulting weakness of these other factors.
9. Breathing must be regulated and well coordinated with movements; otherwise both speed and force will be effected.

The first four above points are well provided for by Shaolin Chi Kung, Point 4 also suggests that weight training which develops big muscles are not suitable for speed. But if employed appropriately, weights can be of much help to speed and force training. The fifth point is provided for by meditation. The last four points concern training methods and will be discussed below, whereas the other points are explained in various parts of the book.

How to Attain Speed

Can you remember how you put on an attire yourself when you were a child? You might have taken half an hour just to put on a shirt or a dress, but now you can do so in a minute. The amazing thing is that you have never consciously attempted to increase the speed, yet you can now put on your attire so much faster.

The reason is that all this time you have been practicing unconsciously, with the result that putting on your attire has become a habit and is therefore rapid. This gives an idea that if we practice our kungfu patterns until we have become very familiar with them, then we can perform them rapidly.

The following is a useful method for training speed, without sacrificing form and force, in solo set practice; the same principles can be applied to combat sequences and sparring. Understandably, unless you are already familiar with kungfu training, it is difficult (but not impossible) to learn such arts as correctness of form, force and speed from a book; it is therefore advisable to seek the help of an instructor.

The basic Shaolin set, Cross-Roads at Four Gates (Chapter 6), is used as an example. At the first stage, perform the set with special attention to correctness of form. The whole performance takes about 3 minutes.

You need to practice this stage daily for about three months, towards the end of which you should perform the whole set in a rhythmic flow of beautiful form.

At the second stage, which will also take about three months, you should practice the set correctly with special emphasis on force. For example in Pattern 3, Thrice Threading of Bridge, channel inner force to the two fingers; in Pattern 7, Single Dragon Emerges from Sea, punch out with all your might.

You must of course maintain correctness of form in your set. Initially you take one breath for each pattern, breathing in at the start and breathing out at the completion of the pattern. You should also remember that force is different from brutal strength.

As you progress, you will find that your one breath may be sufficient to last you for two or three patterns; but you must not at any time be out of breath. Hence, whenever you feel that you have used up about seventy percent of your current breath, gently take another breath.

Generally, when you strike, as in Single Dragon and Black Tiger, breathe out explosively with a "her-it" sound from your abdomen, and immediately let about 30 percent of your chi sink into your abdominal dan tian (energy field). It is *very* important that this sinking of chi into your abdomen must *not* be forced; feeling pain in your groin is a warning that you have forced down the chi.

You also need about 3 minutes to perform the whole set with accurate form and force. Towards the end of the third month (or the sixth month from the beginning stage), you will be able to perform the set correctly and forcefully, yet you will not be tired at the conclusion of the performance.

At the third stage, which also takes about three months, you concentrate on speed, of course without neglecting correctness of form and force. The general procedure is as follows.

Perform a series of related pattern while comfortably holding one breath; explode with a "her-it" sound as you strike; immediately let the remaining chi sink into your abdomen (it is *very* important *not* to force the sinking); breathe in deeply but gently as you begin the next series of related patterns.

In the Four Gates Set, the general procedure described above does not apply to the first three patterns, because they are meant to generate overall chi flow for the whole set and have special breathing techniques of their own. Briefly, breathe into the dan tian in Pattern 1, breathe out and sink the breath in Pattern 2, have three breaths in Pattern 3 to coordinate with channeling chi to the two fingers and complete the pattern with focusing chi at the dan tian.

The general procedure starts with Pattern 4. Take the first deep breath at the start of Pattern 4, and perform right through to Pattern 10 with 70 percent of this breath, sinking the remaining 30 percent after the Horse-Riding Punch so as to store the chi at the abdominal dan tian (energy field). Take the second deep breath and perform till Pattern 15, storing 30 percent of chi at the dan tian as before.

Take the third deep breath and perform till Pattern 20. Patterns 21 to 26 are to be performed with the fourth deep breath. Perform Patterns 27 and 28 without worrying about your breathing, then breathe in fully, i.e. the fifth deep breath, as you jump back, and continue till Pattern 33 with the same breath. Perform Pattern 34 without worrying about breathing, breathe in at Pattern 35, and breathe out with chi focussed at the abdominal dan tian at the completion of the set at Pattern 36.

Hence, besides the special breathing techniques at the beginning three patterns to generate chi flow, and the concluding two patterns to store chi at the abdomen, the whole set is to be performed in five breaths. The sequence of patterns between the breaths are executed as if they are each one long continuous pattern.

In other words, the whole set is performed in five breaths as if it consists of five patterns. If you practice well, you can perform the set correctly and forcefully in less than a minute, which is more than three times faster than when you first started nine months ago.

Although this method, which I learnt from Sifu Ho Fatt Nam, is very effective for training speed, it is not usually regarded as an art of lightness, and not even labeled with a special name, because it is a basic procedure in our kungfu set practice.

Nevertheless, the expression "completion in one breath" is frequently used in connection with this method. We may, therefore, for the sake of reference, call this method the "one-breath technique".

Plum Flower and Through the Woods

Plum Flower Formation is one of the well known Shaolin specialized arts of lightness. Its special purpose is to train agility.

Draw five circles, about a foot in diameter, on the ground in the pattern of a plum flower, Fig 15.8. Move about in various stances and directions on this plum flower pattern, but your feet must at no time step outside the circles. After about a month of daily practice, draw more circles and practice similarly.

Fig 15.8 Moving About on Drawn Circles

After another two months, use five inverted bowls instead of circles, and move about freely on the inverted bowls. Your feet must at no time be off the bowls. Remember to wear suitable shoes so that if you accidentally break a bowl, its broken pieces would not cut your foot. After one month, add more inverted bowls to your practice, Fig 15.9.

Fig 15.9 Moving About on Inverted Bowls

After three months of daily practice on the inverted bowls, insert five short poles in a plum flower pattern into the ground about a foot high, Fig 15.10. Practice various foot work on the poles. Add more poles after a month, and practice for another two months.

Fig 15.10 Moving About on One-foot Poles

Next, practice on five poles about four feet high, Fig 15.11. Add more poles after a month, and practice various kungfu movements, including kicking and jumping, on the poles for another two months.

Then, practice on five poles about seven feet high, Fig 15.12. After a month, add more poles to practice kungfu sets or combat sequences for at least two months. If you have a partner who also practices Plum Flower Formation, spar with him on the poles. Needless to say, any slip may cause injuries.

Fig 15.11
Kungfu Movements on Four-Foot Poles

Fig 15.12
Plum Flower Formation

You can also use these seven-foot poles for another art of lightness known as "Through the Woods", which is also useful for training speed and agility. Although it is better to practice "Through the Woods" only after you have succeeded in "Plum Flower Formation", or vice versa, so that you can concentrate in one art at a time, you may, for various reasons, practice them together. For this specialized art of "Through the Wood", instead of practicing on the poles, you practice on the ground in the midst of the poles.

There are three parts in this training, and you should practice daily for at least four months for each part. You may, if you are ready, practice two or all the parts at the same time.

First, plan out a sequence of useful and varied foot movements. Go into the "woods" of these poles and perform these foot movements, without touching any poles at all, Fig 15.13.

If you touch a pole, you have to start all over again. Initially move slowly, but increase your speed as you progress so that eventually you move very rapidly. Also, lengthen the sequence and make the movements more elaborated. Practise for at least three months.

Later, incorporate appropriate hand movements as you go over your footwork sequence. You may strike the poles as if they were opponents, but any strikes, by your hand, leg or any part of your body, must be performed while you are on your move; you must not let any striking affect your continuous, fast movements through the woods.

Fig 15.13 Moving Through the Woods

Then, move about freely in the woods of poles performing various kungfu patterns for a period of five minutes without touching any poles, except your purposeful strikes on them which must not affect your smooth movement. If you touch any pole (except your striking), start afresh.

In other words, you can move about in any direction in the woods for a set period of time without touching any pole. Gradually increase the speed of your movements and the period of time.

Next, move from one end of the woods to the other end without touching any poles (excepting striking them), imagining that these poles were armed enemies and you were going through them untouched. The arrangement of the poles should be fairly long for this practice.

Move slowly at first, paying attention more to agile shifting and dodging than to speed. Gradually increase your speed so that you can pass through the columns of armed enemies swiftly. If you have wondered how kungfu experts could escape unhurt from swarms of armed attackers, as is sometimes depicted in movies, you now have a method to develop such an ability.

16
Dragons, Phoenixes, Tigers And Crescent Moon

(A Brief Survey of Kungfu Weapons)

Besides the hedonic principle to preserve tradition, there are also practical reasons why weapons are practiced in kungfu today.

Why Classical Weapons Are Still Practiced Today

When we mention martial arts in our present twenty first century, we usually think of unarmed combat for sport, and sometimes for self defense. Hence in most martial arts today like karate, judo, aikido, taekwondo, kick-boxing and taijiquan, weapons play a minor role in their practice. This is not the case in Shaolin Kungfu, especially if it is taught in the traditional manner, because weapons form a significant part of the training.

In classical China, martial arts in general, known at different times as wuyi, wushu or jiji, referred not just to unarmed and armed combat among individuals, but also included horse-back fighting, archery, mass attack and defense, maneuvers and traps, and military strategies. Specialized martial *sports* like wrestling and boxing, which were performed for entertainment rather than for actual fighting and were already popular as early as the time of Shih Huang Di in the 3rd century BCE, were known as "juedi" and "shoupo" respectively.

But after the invention of firearms in the modern period, classical weapons like spears and swords have lost their former importance in mass warfare or individual fighting. Why then are classical weapons still practiced in Shaolin Kungfu?

Classical weapons have become an integral part of the kungfu tradition, so that even if there were no practical functions, many masters consider it a moral obligation to preserve the tradition and teach kungfu weapons as an art form by itself.

Indeed some masters consider one's kungfu training is incomplete if he has not learnt any kungfu weapons. A performance of kungfu weapons is also very spectacular to watch. Kungfu literature has often described an artistic performance of a spear as a wandering dragon, of a sword as a nimble phoenix, and of a scimitar (often called a broadsword) as a ferocious tiger.

Besides the hedonic principle to preserve tradition, there are also practical reasons why weapons are practiced in kungfu today. Training with weapons is a continued development of unarmed training.

For example, after a student is proficient in his unarmed kungfu set practice, he can further improve his force, speed and stamina if he performs the same set by holding some weights such as dumb-bells.

A more interesting and profitable way is to practice a set holding some short but heavy weapons, like "round hammers" and "double rods", Fig 16.1.

When he can perform such weapon sets well, he will even be better when he perform unarmed sets without having to hold these weighty weapons. If he uses a heavy long weapon instead of a short one, such as a "crescent-moon spear", a "guan-dao" (a form of halberd) or a trident, Fig 16.2, he will further improve his stances and footwork, which of course can be profitably transferred to unarmed combat.

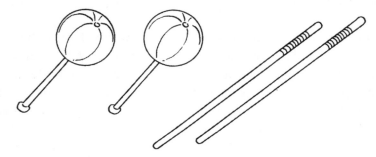

Fig 16.1 Round Hammers and Double Rods

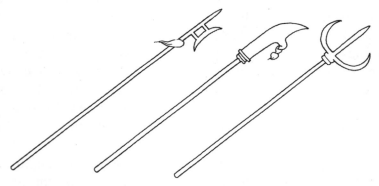

Fig 16.2 Crescent-Moon Spear, Guan-Dao and Trident

Thirdly, each type of the wide range of kungfu weapons is constructed for at least one but usually more combative functions. Daggers, for example, are used mainly for stabbing, round hammers for hitting, spears for piercing, and battle axes for chopping.

You may use a dagger to chop your opponent, or a battle axe to stab him, but you are unlikely to achieve desirable result. As different weapons exhibit special features, training with weapons develops those skills as well as emphasizes those techniques that are particularly related to the weapons.

For example, if you wish to use a dagger effectively, you need to maintain close range with your opponent so that you can stab him easily; but if you use a spear, you would keep a distance from him so that you can take advantage of the length of the spear. Thus, training with a dagger or a spear will provide you with the skills and techniques which you can transfer to unarmed fighting for close or long range fighting respectively.

Some weapons require special skills, or *gong*, to use them efficaciously. Sharp eyesight is required for spears, agility for swords, and good horse stance for halberds.

These skills are of course needed for other weapons and unarmed combat too, but they are particularly necessary for these weapons. In a good training program, besides practicing a spear set, the exponent should also practice the relevant skills, just as in an unarmed set, he should also practice such skills like speed, spacing and fluidity besides merely performing the patterns of the set.

One helpful method to develop sharp eyesight in using a spear is to suspend a ring about six inches in diameter and pierce the spearhead into this ring using various patterns from different directions.

When the exponent can be successful every time he pierces his spear into the ring, he proceeds to piercing into a moving ring. Then he uses three rings instead of just one, and later he may use more rings arranged in different patterns.

As he becomes proficient, he reduces the size of the rings. He may suspend the swinging rings from a fixed point, hang them from a slowly moving ceiling fan, or arrange them in four directions.

Fig 16.3 illustrates a continuous piercing of the spear into predetermined rings using different patterns. When such a skill is transferred to unarmed combat, the exponent would be able to strike at predetermined spots on the opponent's body accurately. This transfer of skills from weapon training to unarmed combat is another reason whey weapons are still practiced today.

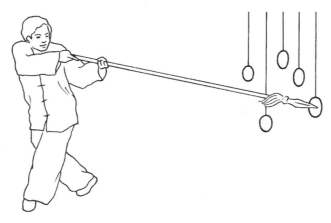

Fig 16.3 Training in Sharp Eyesight with a Spear

The fifth reason is that many common things can be improvised as weapons. A broken bottle, for example, can be used like a dagger, a spike like a spear, a bicycle chain like a "soft-whip", a hard stick like a "copper rod", and a meat-cutter like a scimitar.

Training with classical weapons therefore enables us to defend ourselves efficiently against opponents using such improvised weapons, as well as enables us to use improvised weapons if necessary. Hence although classical weapons are not normally found in public, some knowledge of and practice in their use are still useful for self defense.

Classification of Weapons

The range of kungfu weapons is both extensive and bewildering. In a documentary text of the Shaolin Monastery, *The Secret Book of Complete Shaolin Weapons*, hand written and illustrated by Venerable Su Fa and Venerable Te Qian, who described the weapons used by well known Shaolin masters, 220 different types of weapons were recorded.

Many of these weapons are exotic. Fig 16.4 illustrates some of such exotic weapons: Mountain-Chasing Whip used by Venerable Fu Ju of the Song Dynasty, Eight-Branched Tree used by Venerable Hui Ju of the Yuan Dynasty, Tortoise Ring used by Venerable Xuan Jin of the Ming Dynasty, and Snake-Shaped Key used by Venerable Jing Xiu of the Qing Dynasty.

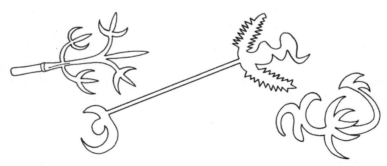

Fig 16.4 Exotic Shaolin Weapons

There have been many attempts in kungfu history to classify the diverse range of weapons. The popular phrases "five weapons" and "eighteen weapons" represent some of these attempts at classification.

During the Zhou Dynasty (11th to 5th century BCE), the "five weapons" as mentioned in the Book of Rites referred to ge (long weapon with a sickle-like blade at the end), shu (long weapon with a horn-like structure), ji (crescent-moon spear), mao (lance), and gong-shi (bow and arrows). As there are often no English equivalents for the Chinese weapons, Chinese terms are used in this chapter to name the weapons.

Fig 16.5 Five Weapons in Ancient Times

Much later during the Han Dynasty (3rd century BCE to 3rd century CE), the Book of Han referred to the "five weapons" as mao (lance), ji (crescent-moon spear), gong-shi (bow and arrows), jian (sword) and ge (long sickle-like weapon).

The term "five weapons" was used idiomatically to suggest a variety of weapons, and should not be taken to mean that there were only five types or groups of weapons. For example, jian (sword) was widely used in prehistoric times; archaeological finds reveal a lot of copper swords, but jian was mentioned as one of the "five weapons" only in the Han but not in the Zhou period. Weapons like yue (battle-axe), chui (mace) and dang (spear with a crescent blade), Fig 16.6, were already popular in ancient China, but they were not mentioned in the "five weapons".

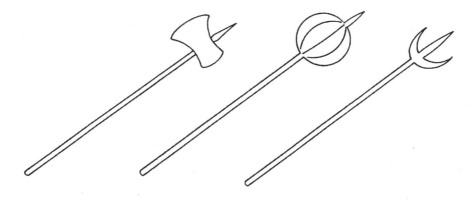

Fig 16.6 Yue, Chui and Dang

The term "eighteen weapons" became widely used since the Song Dynasty. Different authorities designated the "eighteen weapons" differently. During the times of the Song and Yuan Dynasties (10th to 14th centuries), the "eighteen weapons" referred to the following, as illustrated in Fig 16.7:

1. mao (lance); 2. chui (mace); 3. gong (bow); 4. nu (mechanized bow); 5. chong (pipe-like weapon to shoot out darts); 6. bian (whip); 7. jian (rod); 8. jian (sword); 9. chan (spade); 10. zhua (claw); 11. fu (hand axe); 12. yue (battle axe); 13. ge (long sickle); 14. ji (crescent-moon spear) with hook); 15. pai (shield); 16. bang (cudgel); 17. qiang (spear); 18. pa (rake).

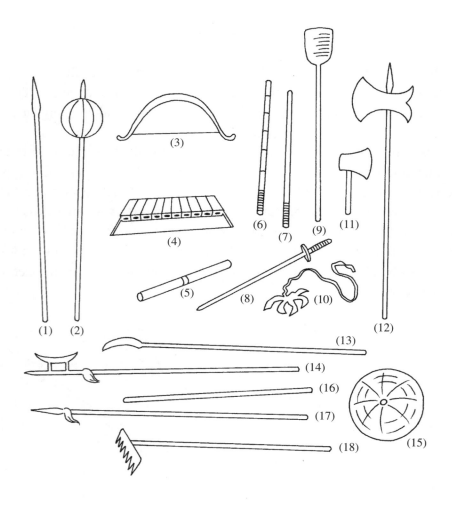

Fig 16.7 Eighteen Weapons (Song and Yuan Dynasties)

During the Ming Dynasty (14th to 17th centuries), the "eighteen weapons" denoted the following, Fig 16.8:

1. gong (bow); 2. nu (mechanized bow); 3. qiang (spear); 4. dao (scimitar); 5. jian (sword); 6. mao (lance); 7. dun (shield); 8. fu (hand axe); 9. yue (battle axe); 10. ji (crescent-moon spear); 11. bian (whip); 12. jian (rod), 13. gao (pole); 14. shu (long weapon with a horn-like structure); 15. cha (fork); 16. pa-tou (rake); 17. mian-sheng (roped weapons); 18. bai-da (empty-hand combat).

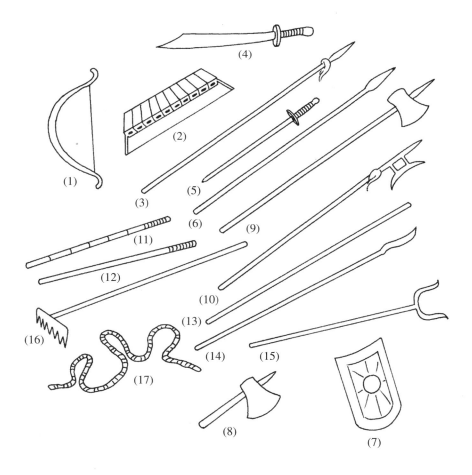

Fig 16.8 Eighteen Weapons (Ming Dynasty)

Although the names of many weapons are the same in both the Song-Yuan list and the Ming list, their illustrations may be different. This is because there were different forms of the same weapon, or because the weapon might have evolved into another form.

In recent times during the Qing Dynasty (17th to 20th centuries), "eighteen weapons" were interpreted variously. One popular interpretation was to classify the "eighteen weapons" into nine long weapons and nine short weapons as follows, Fig 16.9:

1. qiang (spear); 2. ji (crescent-moon spear); 3. gun (staff); 4. yue (battle axe); 5. da-pa (trident); 6. da-dao (halberd); 7. chan (spade); 8. mao (lance); 9. sheng-biao (roped spear); 10. dao (scimitar), 11. jian (sword); 12. fu (hand axe); 13. gou (hook-sword); 14. jian (rod); 15. bian (soft-whip); 16. guai (clutch); 17. chui (round hammer); 18. bi-shou (dagger).

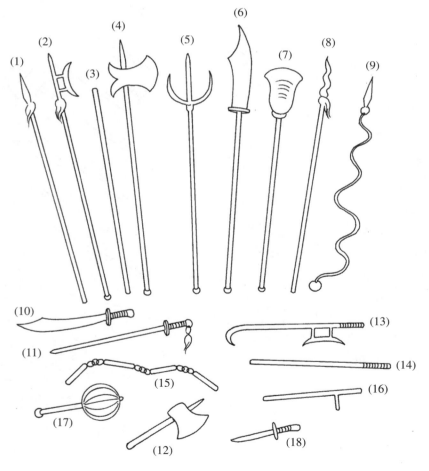

Fig 16.9 Eighteen Weapons (Recent Times)

Besides these regular weapons, there are also "extraordinary weapons", such as butterfly knives, three-sectional staff, big sweeper, wolf-teeth staff, iron-pen, and three-pointed spear, Fig 16.10. There is another class called secret weapons, such as darts, marble missiles, protection-mirror (worn over the chest under clothing), and hidden knives (such as at the tips of shoes), Fig 16.11.

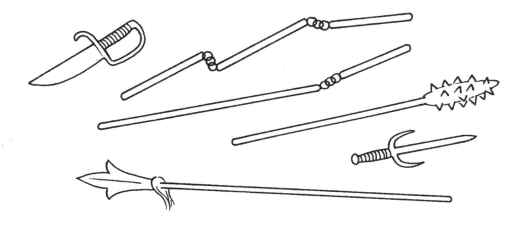

Fig 16.10 Some Extraordinary Weapons

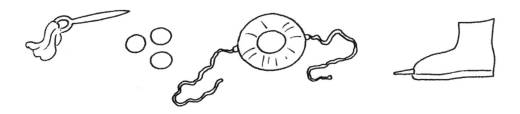

Fig 16.11 Some Secret Weapons

Everyday tools like umbrellas, short benches, stools and walking sticks, Fig 16.12, may also be used effectively as weapons, especially if we understand some basic principles.

If you use an unopened umbrella like a stick to hit an assailant, as many untrained people do, it is unlikely to produce efficacious result, because the springy ribs and folded cloth of the unopened umbrella would cushion off the blows even if you could hit him.

If you wish to hit him, you should use the umbrella handle, especially if it is hard, and you should aim at vulnerable spots like his head, neck, upper arms, elbow, fingers, knees and shins. The most destructive part of an umbrella, however, is its pointed tip. If you use it to poke at an assailant's face, neck, solar plexus or side ribs, you can often hurt him sufficiently for you to escape.

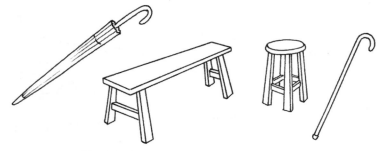

Fig 16.12 Common Tools as Weapons

An obvious weakness of an umbrella poke, unlike a sword thrust, is that the opponent can easily grasp the umbrella. One efficient way to overcome this problem is illustrated in Fig 16.13.

When your opponent grasps your umbrella, use your free hand to hold the tip of the umbrella, move forward slightly (but make sure his front hand could not strike your face), simultaneously pull the umbrella tip towards yourself and strike the umbrella handle at the opponent's temple. Besides striking him, the turning movement of the umbrella acts on a weakness of his grip, thereby releasing his hold on the umbrella. Kick his groin or shin as a coup de grace.

(a)   (b)

Fig 16.13 Using an Umbrella as a Weapon

Ferocious Tigers and Nimble Phoenixes

Among the great variety of kungfu weapons, the four most popular today are the dao (scimitar), the jian (sword), the qiang (spear), and the gun (staff).

The dao (pronounced as "t'ao") is a generic name for a group of different blade weapons with only one sharp edge. The nearest English equivalent is "knife". The most common type of dao or knives is the dan dao, meaning "single knife", which may be translated as "scimitar". Fig 16.14 shows some examples of dao.

Fig 16.14 Some Examples of Dao or Kungfu Knives

Why does the dao or knife use only one sharp edge; isn't it more advantageous to have both edges for cutting? The dao uses only one cutting edge instead of two because both the shape and structure of the weapon (i.e. its form) as well as the application of the dao patterns (its function) are such that using one cutting edge gives the exponent the best technical advantages.

To realize the most destructive functions of the dao, such as chopping, cutting, slashing, and sweeping, Figures 16.15 and 16.16, the blade should be sharp at one edge but thick and heavy on the other so that its destructive power is enhanced. The blade is asymmetrical and convex at the sharp edge so as to increase its cutting effectiveness. Because of these factors, a double-cutting edge would be a hindrance.

Fig 16.15 A Chopping Technique of a Dao

Fig 16.16 A Sweeping Technique of a Dao

The Chinese language makes a clear distinction between a dao, or a kungfu knife like a scimitar, and a jian, or a Chinese sword. A knife has only one cutting edge, whereas a sword, in the Chinese context, is always double-edged.

Hence, what is often called a sword by western readers, such as the Japanese Samurai Sword, is regarded as a knife in Chinese because it uses only one cutting edge. The techniques and skills in using a knife (such as a scimitar) and a sword are vastly different; indeed their difference can easily be suggested in the description of a knife by the Chinese as a ferocious tiger, and a sword as a nimble phoenix.

Thus, the translation of the Chinese "dao" as "broad-sword", as is often done in some kungfu books written in English, is inappropriate in this respect.

If we attach a long handle to a dao, we have a da-dao (pronounced as "t'a t'ao), which literally means "big knife". Fig 16.17 shows some examples of da-dao.

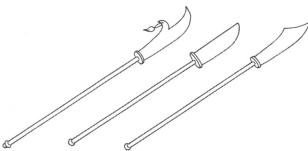

Fig 16.17   Some Examples of Da-Dao

In classical China, da-dao or Big Knives were weapons used by generals on horseback fighting. The famous warrior of the Three Kingdoms period (3rd century), Guan Yu, who is sometimes described in English as the Chinese God of War, but actually it is more appropriate to call him the God of Righteousness, is perhaps the most celebrated exponent of the da-dao. His special da-dao is known by a poetic name, "The Knife with a Green Dragon and the Crescent Moon". This kind of da-dao is commonly called "Guan-dao", meaning the Knife of Guan.

The jian or sword is a good contrast to the dao or knife. A sword exponent seldom uses techniques like chopping, cutting, slashing and sweeping, which are the principal techniques in using a knife; the forte of the sword is thrusting and slicing, which are not suitable techniques for a knife such as a scimitar. Figures 16.18 and 16.19 show the thrusting and slicing techniques of the sword.

Fig 16.18 The Thrust of the Sword

Fig 16.19 The Slice of the Sword

To use a sword like a scimitar, such as clashing the sword with the opponent's weapon or swinging the sword around one's body as is often done with a scimitar, is a sure indication of ignorance in differentiating the principles governing the use of a sword and a knife. A Chinese sword is a light, dainty weapon; clashing it with the opponent's heavy weapon may result in the sword being broken into a few pieces.

When using a scimitar, an exponent often swings it around his own body because such movements give him certain technical advantages. Such circular swinging, known in kungfu term as "covering the head and surrounding the body", provides the exponent with good protective coverage, enables him to maneuver his comparatively heavy scimitar swiftly, and adds power to his attacking patterns.

However, such "covering the head and surrounding the body" is almost never used with a Chinese sword, because as it has double cutting edges such movements would hurt the exponent himself, and because it is comparatively light it does not need the circular swing to aid momentum and power.

As the Chinese sword is light and dainty, how does the exponent block an opponent's attack, especially if the latter uses a heavy weapon? Imagine, for example, that you are using a sword and your opponent chops down with a heavy scimitar; or he sweeps at your waist with a solid staff. If you block the scimitar or the staff with your sword, your sword will be broken into pieces.

Hence, a swordsman almost never blocks! As a good tactician, he avoids the weakness of his weapon and exploits its strong point. Clashing the light sword with a heavy weapon is a weakness; capitalizing its lightness for agile maneuvers is a strong point. Figures 16.20 to 16.25 illustrate an application of the sword against the vertical chop of a scimitar and the horizontal sweep of a staff.

Fig 16.20 shows an opponent moving in to chop me with his scimitar. Instead of blocking or retreating, both of which would be disadvantageous to me, I move forward slightly, slanting my sword to slice at the opponent's wrist, Fig 16.21.

His attack would be unable to hit me because I have moved away from the target, and my sword intercepts his attack at his wrist (not scimitar). As he retreats his arm and body, I follow immediately with a sword thrust, Fig 16.22, but in line with the Shaolin philosophy of compassion, I stop just inches away from his throat.

(16.20)

(16.21)   (16.22)

Fig 16.20 to 16.22 A Sword against a Scimitar

An opponent sweeps his staff at my waist, Fig 16.23. As his staff approaches, I move my back leg a small step backward and lower my body to let his staff sweep past me, Fig 16.24. Immediately I move my body forward and thrust my sword at his throat, Fig 16.25. Again, out of compassion, I stop a few inches from his body.

(16.23)

(16.24)   (16.25)

Fig 16.23 to 16.25 A Sword against a Staff

The King and the Mother

While the scimitar and the sword are short weapons, the spear and the staff are long. Just as the scimitar and the sword offer some interesting contrast — the former is ferocious like a tiger, whereas the latter is gentle like a phoenix; the spear and the staff also illustrate some distinctive difference.

The spear, or qiang in Chinese, is sometimes regarded as the king of weapons, because technically a pierce from a spear is the most difficult to defend against. Hence, throughout Chinese dynastic history, the spear was the choice weapon of most generals. Figures 16.26 and 16.27 show two typical spear patterns.

Fig 16.26 Spear Thrust at Bow-Arrow Stance

Fig 16.27 Reverse Thrust at Unicorn Stance

Why is the spear pierce a superior technique? As a spear is comparatively light, and a piercing attack travels in a straight line, a spear pierce can be extremely fast, almost like an arrow, with the advantage that the spear expert may change the direction of his pierce according to how his opponent moves, whereas an arrow once released maintains a fixed course.

Secondly, the destructive properties of a spearhead are not just its point, but also its sharp sides which act like an extended dagger. So, even when an opponent has dodged the sharp point of the spearhead, the exponent may cut or slice the opponent with its sharp edges.

A spear pierce is made not by holding the spear shaft firmly with both hands and moving both hands forward, like what is done in thrusting with a staff; rather the front hand holds the spear shaft for leverage, and the back hand pushes the spear forward, Fig 16.28.

Hence, not only is the pierce swift, but the recovery of the spear after piercing is also very fast. As soon as the exponent pierces his spear, he pulls it back. In this way he overcomes the two principal counters against a pierce or thrust attack, namely grasping the shaft of the piercing or thrusting weapon, and getting past the attacking point into the exponent. In other words, because the pulling back of the spearhead is so fast, it is difficult for the opponent to grip the spear shaft, or to move past the spearhead.

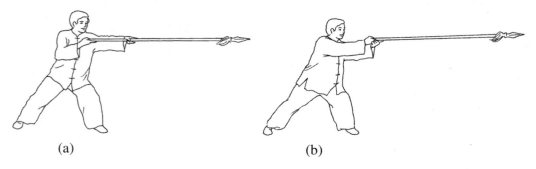

(a)   (b)

Fig 16.28 Thrusting a Staff and Piercing a Spear

Fourthly, even if the opponent can grasp the spear shaft, a skillful exponent can circle his spear in such a way that the sharp point or sides of the spearhead can cut the opponent's wrist or arm.

Fifthly, if the opponent succeeds in moving close to the exponent, thereby overcoming the advantage of the spear's length, the exponent can off-set this weakness by pulling the whole spear shaft behind and use the spear like a dagger.

Thus, if all other things are equal — the only difference being one uses a spear and the other uses another weapon — the spear exponent will defeat his opponent because of technical advantages.

Does this mean that a spear is always better than other weapons? No, because in real life the presumption that all other things are equal, is almost never valid. If you have much strength, you may prefer to use a trident, which is a heavy, massive and long weapon.

By manipulating the three throngs of the trident, you may break the spear, or dislodge the weapon from the opponent. If you are versatile, you may prefer a crescent-moon spear, or the ji, instead of the orthodox spear, or the qiang.

The ji, which is classified as a light, long weapon, has the functions of a spear, a big-knife, a trident, a staff and a hook-sword all in one! By a skillful application of the ji, you may "lock" the spear, and glide down the spear shaft to cut the opponent's hands.

But traditionally, the dan dao or scimitar offers an interesting counter against the qiang or spear. A match between the spear and the scimitar may be described as a match between a dragon and a tiger, which is an idiomatic way of saying a fierce but balanced fight.

Being a short and light weapon (although it is comparatively heavier than the sword), the scimitar is versatile enough to meet the fast and subtle techniques of the spear.

While the spear pierce is deadly, the "trimming" of the scimitar along the spear shaft to cut the spear exponent's hands is a formidable challenge. Further, if the scimitar exponent can master the technique of "weaving flowers" — whereby the scimitar is spun round so swiftly like a fast moving fan — he is able not only to deflect the piercing attack of the spear, but also to slash the opponent with his spinning blade.

While the scimitar, the sword and the spear possess sharp edges to cut the opponent, with threat of possible death, the staff or gun (pronounced as "goon") does not.

Thus, the staff is considered to be a merciful weapon, although if used by an expert it can also be deadly. The staff, understandably, is the most popular weapon amongst Shaolin disciples, whose training pays much attention to the cultivation of compassion.

According to a legend, the monks at the Shaolin Monastery found it cruel to injure their opponents with pointed or blade weapons; so they removed the spear-heads of their qiang (spear) and ji (crescent-moon spear), and the blades of their dao (big knives) and ge (long sickles), to retain only the long handles.

While the spear is sometimes regarded as the king of weapons, the staff is honored as the mother, because the techniques of most weapons, including the spear pierce, the sword thrust and the "weaving flowers" of the scimitar, can be found in the techniques of the staff.

It is quite amazing that a simple looking stick, if applied expertly, can give rise to so many elaborated patterns. In the early 7th century, thirteen monks from the Shaolin Monastery using only plain staffs helped Li Shi Min to subdue oppressive warlords using a wide range of weapons, to set up the famous Tang Dynasty.

Staffs are of two main types, long staffs about seven feet in length and usually taper slightly at the attacking end, and ordinary staffs about five feet and both ends are usually of the same size. Long staffs were formerly used for horseback fighting; they were later shortened for ground combat. Two staff techniques are illustrated in Figures 16.29 and 16.30.

Fig 16.29 The Thrust of a Long Staff

Fig 16.30 The Dot Technique of the Ordinary Staff

There are also other types of staffs, such as the short staff which is like a baton, the small sweeper or small two sectional staff, which spread to Japan where it became known as the nunchaku, the big sweeper or big two sectional staff, and the versatile three sectional staff, Fig 16.31.

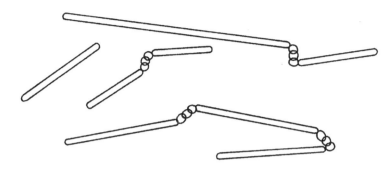

Fig 16.31 Some Other Types of Staffs

According to the Shaolin tradition, the staff was first introduced by Jinnaluo, an Indian Buddhist monk serving as a cook at the monastery. Everyday he used a huge, long stick to stir a gigantic pot of rice in the monastery kitchen. Once a band of bandits wanted to rob the temple. Jinnaluo defeated them single-handed with his staff. After that he taught the fighting art of the staff to the monks. A temple built in his honor still stands in the Shaolin Monastery today.

Numerous generals also contributed much to the development of the Shaolin staff. After his army was defeated by the Tartars, the Song general Yang Wu Lang escaped to Wu Tai Mountain to become a monk.

Influenced by the compassionate teaching of the Buddha, Yang Wu Lang repented his earlier killing, and removed the spearhead of his famous "Yang Family Spear", converting his spear into a long staff. The celebrated staff set of Southern Shaolin Kungfu, known as "Wu Lang Pakua Staff" is reputed to have originated from him.

The great general of the Ming Dynasty, Cheng Da You (also known as Cheng Zong Dou), who repulsed numerous Japanese invasions, was another Shaolin disciple. His "Compendium of Shaolin Staff Techniques" written in 1616, which is one of his many works on military strategy and martial arts, has since remained an authority on the subject. His "Shaolin Knife Techniques" greatly influenced the development of the Samurai Sword in Japan.

17
The Spirit Of Shaolin
(Teaching on Morality, Righteousness and Compassion)

Shaolin disciples are obliged to spread love and happiness to all people, and Shaolin masters are obliged to nurture talents and pass on the Shaolin arts to deserving disciples.

The Ten Shaolin Laws

It is very commonly said amongst those who practice kungfu that the greater aim of their achievement is not superior fighting but moral cultivation. Unfortunately, this noble aim more often hangs on their lips than finds expression in their actions.

Despite their claim to moral cultivation, many kungfu and other martial art exponents are egoistic, intolerant, aggressive and arrogant. This is especially so amongst those whose training is mainly on external techniques and combative skills, with little or no emphasis on internal force and meditation.

Shaolin philosophy has always stressed the moral aspects in its kungfu training. If we recall the origin of Shaolin Kungfu, we shall remember that it was initiated by the great Bodhidharma for strengthening the monks in preparation for spiritual growth.

Morality is the basis of all spirituality; if one is not morally pure, it is impossible to attain the highest spiritual fulfillment. This is not mere polemics, but a timeless universal truth, because the mental imprints of immoral living on the mind, though unconscious to that person, will manifest as rebirth in a lower station of existence in his future life. A mind that is predominated by greed or fear, for example, is likely to result in a rebirth in the animal realm.

A good indication of the moral cultivation as taught in the Shaolin tradition is found in the following Ten Shaolin Laws which we in the Shaolin Wahnam School pledge to uphold and practice. These Shaolin laws transcends all culture, race and religion.

1. Required to respect the master, honor the Moral Way and love fellow disciples as brothers and sisters.
2. Required to train the Shaolin arts diligently, overcoming all hardship, and as a prerequisite, to be physically and mentally healthy.
3. Required to be filial to parents, be respectful to the elderly, and protective of the young.

4. Required to uphold righteousness, and to be both wise and courageous.
5. Forbidden to be ungrateful and unscrupulous; forbidden to ignore the laws of man and heaven.
6. Forbidden to rape, molest, do evil, steal, rob, abduct or cheat.
7. Forbidden to associate with wicked people; forbidden to do any sorts of wickedness.
8. Forbidden to abuse power, be it official or physical; forbidden to oppress the good and bully the kind.
9. Obliged to be humane, compassionate and spread love, and to realize everlasting peace and happiness for all people.
10. Obliged to be chivalrous and generous, to nurture talents and pass on the Shaolin arts to deserving disciples.

Respect for the Master

Respecting the master and honoring the Moral Way, known in Chinese as *zun shi zhong dao*, is the first and foremost moral principle of kungfu exponents of all schools.

In the past, kungfu students treated their master like their father, whose orders would be carried out without question, and whose authority accepted with prostration. Would students carry out orders which appeared unreasonable, such as chopping firewood with their bare hands, or transporting water in containers with holes in the bottom? Shaolin disciples would, without any doubt. They would face a dilemma only if the orders conflicted with the Moral Way, which represents all the written and unwritten moral codes generally accepted by all societies.

If Shaolin disciples were asked, for example, to steal somebody's wife, or to cause grievous hurt to the innocent, the dilemma was not whether they should carry out the orders, but whether the authority they had previously respected, had already ceased to be a master.

Understandably, many modern westerners may consider the students' total obedience to their masters as servile or foolish, and their prostration to their master as ridiculous.

Nevertheless, it was because of such complete compliance to and reverence for their master that the students could derive the best benefits in their training. Their obedience was not due to their dull intelligence or due to an oppressive culture, but due to their complete trust that whatever their master asked them to do was for their benefit, and due to their deeply felt gratitude that their master would teach them secrets that he might not even tell his wife or children. Such a trust and gratitude would be hard to come by in today's societies, east or west.

Kungfu training is a very demanding and exacting process, calling for great self discipline. Someone has said that if you can endure kungfu training, you can attempt anything.

A Shaolin disciple has to practice some kungfu techniques not just many times but thousands of time, not just when he first learnt the techniques but everyday for numerous years, until he has mastered those techniques.

The onus is not to learn techniques after techniques, but to repeat, repeat and repeat selected techniques until accuracy, force and speed in their application are attained. If you wish to master a certain kicking technique, for example, you have to practice this technique tens of thousands of time.

However, before a Shaolin student commences serious kungfu training, he must ensure that he is physically and mentally healthy. This can be achieved through Shaolin Chi Kung, which will be explained in some detail in the next three chapters.

Being filial to parents, and respectful to the elderly, known in Chinese as *xiao ching jing lao*, is a well-established virtue in eastern societies, and is a tradition certainly worth keeping.

In modern western societies where personal freedom is greatly valued, and where some children call their parents by names, their concept of filial piety or of respect to the elderly is understandably different from that of the east.

In eastern societies it is often the norm that whenever the father or an elderly person speaks, the sons and daughters or adults of a younger generation, even if they are public celebrities, merely listen (but not necessarily agree). It is considered rude and unbecoming for them to openly oppose the father or elder although they may hold different opinions.

On a personal note, whenever I was with my master or with an elder, I would not sit unless he was properly seated. In my life so far, which has given me more than fifty years of abundant joy, I have only two regrets: one, I regret that I could have been more kind and loving to my father; and two, I regret that I could have been more kind and loving to my mother.

These regrets are more painful as I realized a bit too late, after my parents had left this world, that such kindness and love can be readily expressed in simple, daily deeds like taking them for a walk in the garden, or taking time to listen and talk to them about their fond memories — simple deeds which all of us can easily do if we want to, but which are probably more meaningful to parents than extravagant gestures like buying them a castle.

Do not be grossly mistaken that being filial to parents or respectful to elders is a sign of weak character. Do not jump into conclusion that if, out of respect, an oriental is not outspoken against an elder's viewpoints, it necessarily means he accepts them gullibly. He may express his different opinions, but when he is in front of elders, he always do so politely, taking care not to hurt their feelings.

Once, when the Buddha came across a pile of dried bones besides a road, he prostrated before it to pay respect. Ananda, the Buddha's attending monk, asked:

The Buddha is the greatest teacher in the three spheres of existence, and the compassionate father of all beings of the four modes of rebirth. He has the deepest respect and reverence of the entire order of monks. Why does he now prostrate to a pile of dried bones?

The Buddha said as he had led countless previous lives, and these bones belonged to beings who also had led countless previous lives, it was probable that the bones were those of his parents and ancestors of his former lives.

The Buddha then described the boundless kindness parents had for their children, and explained that even if a person were to carry his parents on his shoulders for thousands of aeons, or during a famine cut his own flesh to feed his parents as many times as there were dust motes, he still could not have repaid his parents' boundless kindness.

When the Buddha, regarded by many as the greatest teacher of men and gods, could humble himself to prostrate to the bones of his former parents, what traces of vainglory could be left to prevent us to be filial to our parents?

Great Blessings to be Born Human

Just as a Shaolin disciple is respectful to elders, he is protective of the young. Young children, irrespective of who their parents are, should be given every opportunity to laugh and play. Indeed, adults can learn an invaluable philosophical lesson from children: their joy and laughter are not dependent on material wealth at all! But they need to be free from fear and hunger, oppression and adult interference.

Long standing feuds between well known families or different kungfu schools were not uncommon in the kungfu history of old China. Sometimes the head of one family or school would lead his side, usually reinforced with mercenary kungfu experts, for an all-out attack on his enemy.

If the attackers were victorious, the out-come was always barbaric and gruesome, where even small children were not spared. The barbarians reminded themselves of the ignoble saying that "when clearing grasses, eliminate their roots; otherwise, when the wind blows in spring, new grasses will grow", which means that they would not permit any survivor so as to eliminate the possibility of revenge. Any Shaolin disciples involved in such senseless cruelty would be expelled without question.

On the other hand, masters engaged in deadly duels often voluntarily adopted as his own the children of the opponent he killed. These children were very well taken care of, usually given priority over his own children, for the master regarded any sacrifice as some form of repentance for his killing. The dilemma of these children when they had grown up and discovered that their beloved "father" was actually their father's killer, forms a recurrent theme in many kungfu stories.

It is significant to note that at the time of adoption, the master had no doubt that one day his adopted children might be a serious threat to him — he was familiar with the saying about the spring wind and regenerated grasses; yet he would have no hesitation to give the adopted children the best he could, including teaching them the secrets of his kungfu, because to him this was simply the right thing to do.

When the inevitable moment came, the old master often gallantly ask his adopted children to kill him to avenge their father's death. Of course, for those with a different philosophical perspective, the master's belief and action may appear silly or ridiculous; but from the perspective of Chinese kungfu philosophy, such belief and action represent some of the highest expressions of righteousness.

Yet, if the master or his adopted children were familiar with the moral teaching of Shaolin, they would be sparred their mental pain and emotional suffering. In the first place, according to the Shaolin teaching, engaging in a deadly duel is to be avoided. There were many occasions when kungfu experts challenged Shaolin masters, the masters merely walked away.

This, interestingly, is a notable contrast with the thinking found in some other martial arts. For example, many martial artists of the Japanese tradition would consider it a great disgrace if they fail to stand up to an open challenge. Should they be defeated in the challenge, they may commit ritual suicide as an honor.

It is a part of Shaolin philosophy to respect the views of others; hence, I would not comment on the above Japanese tradition, which certainly has its own philosophical justification. But if a Shaolin disciple commits suicide because he has been defeated in a challenge, he will be considered not only stupid but grossly immature.

There is no shame to be defeated by a worthy opponent, especially if one has put up an honest fight to the best of his ability; but if he wins by dishonest means, it would be a disgrace. There is a Chinese saying that "if you come across a high mountain, be reminded that you can come across another mountain that is higher; if you meet an expert fighter, be reminded that you can meet another fighter who is even better."

According to the Buddhist teaching, it is a tremendous blessing to be born a human. We should therefore use this very rare opportunity to make life rewarding for ourselves and for others. It is both silly and immature to take one's own life due to some misplaced pride or glory.

On the other hand, taking someone's life is robbing him of his most precious possession, and the murderer will undo lifetimes of his own accumulated blessings. If the adopted children mentioned above could appreciate this teaching, as well as the teaching on the rare occurrence of their human lives, they would realize, if they could react with calmness and compassion, that as the old master was instrumental in bringing them up, he was the source from which their tremendous blessings flow.

Hence, killing the old master was cutting off their own source of blessings, in exchange for karmic retribution possibly in the form of mental pain and emotional suffering. The first of the five fundamental Buddhist precepts on moral purity is not to kill — others or themselves. The other four are not to steal, not to lie, not to engage in licentious sex, and not to be intoxicated.

Calmness and Compassion

Concerning the need or otherwise of engaging in a duel, and the benefit of a calm and compassionate response, my own experience may serve as an illuminating example.

Many years ago, when chi kung information was not as popularly assessable as it is today, my school and I were concertedly and publicly challenged and ridiculed by some well known kungfu and chi kung masters, because, according to them, we were making arrogant and misleading claims like chi kung could be used to relieve a wide range of diseases, chi kung could enhance kungfu performance, and chi could be transmitted over great distance.

The validity of the above first two claims are now beyond doubt (they were also recorded in classical chi kung and kungfu texts, though these texts were kept as secrets), and a subsequent month-long public experiment conducted by a national newspaper on me confirmed that distance chi transmission is real.

But at that time, I was personally insulted, suggesting that my claim to my Shaolin lineage was spurious, and that my students' demonstrations of chi kung and kungfu were faked.

My inner disciples and I decided to take up a public challenge to a kungfu contest, issued by an instructor from a famous kungfu school. We intended to suggest a three-tier fight, with me as the grandmaster of my school meeting their grandmaster who was undoubtedly a highly accomplished kungfu expert, three masters from our school meeting three of their masters, and our three students meeting their three students.

We fancied it would probably be the fight of the decade, may be of the century, for our school and theirs were the two best known in the region at that time.

Looking back, I am glad that this fight of the century did not take place, because my master, Sifu Ho Fatt Nam, rushed from his retirement to instruct me to stop all preparations for the fight immediately.

"But, Sifu," I tried to reason, "we sincerely believe we have at least 60 percent of winning."

"That is precisely why you must stop. It would be better if you lose, for then that will be the end of the matter. You can be sure that if you win, and I have no doubt you can, there will be no end."

"We are not fighting for any self glory. In fact we know that even if we win, we may be injured, some even badly. But we were ready to sacrifice for the name and honor of our school."

"Do not be silly and immature," my master said. "If an action brings harm to others but not to ourselves, we will not do it. Now we have an action that will bring harm both to others and to ourselves, yet you want to proceed!"

"But our honor is at stake," I said.

"What honor?"

"We have been accused of being fraudulent. We have been insulted publicly."

"Were you really fraudulent?"

"Of course not!"

"Then the question of defending your honor does not arise. As the accusation is false, there is no need for you to defend. What you call 'honor' is just a 'false-name', an attachment to vainglory. Regarding what you call 'insults', you should, as taught by the Buddha, respond with calmness and compassion, and not with anger."

"But, what about the challenge? Should we just ignore it?"

"Did their grandmaster issue a challenge in black and white?"

"No, it was issued orally by one of his instructors in public."

"There you are. If you have responded with calmness and compassion instead of with anger, you would have realized that the instructor does not represent his grandmaster or his school. Besides, he may have made a challenge in a fit of anger, which you should rightly ignore. Even if a challenge is issued, it does not mean you have to accept it."

Then my master gave me some invaluable advice, which may paradoxically appear trite until we take time to investigate into its profundity. He said, "Make friends, not enemies. It is easy to get into animosity, but very difficult to get out of it.

Do not waste your precious Shaolin arts on quarrels which may loom large and important from a narrow spatial or temporal dimension, but which are actually petty if we view them from a wider perspective. Use the Shaolin arts to help people, to relieve suffering and save lives, worldwide and for all times."

Righteousness and Compassion

While Sifu Ho Fatt Nam is well known for his moral consciousness, my other master, Sifu Lai Chin Wah, is famous for his righteousness. He was actually better known by his prestigious nickname, Yi Sook, which means "Uncle Righteousness", than by his own name.

My kungfu and chi kung school, Shaolin Wahnam, is named after them, as a small token of appreciation for their kindness and generosity in passing on the Shaolin arts to me. I also learnt Shaolin Wuzu Kungfu from Sifu Chee Kim Thong, and Shaolin Wing Chun Kungfu from Sifu Chou Hoong Choy. My lineage from the Shaolin Monastery is as follows.

Sifu Lai Chin Wah learnt from three masters, Ng Yew Loong, Chu Khuen and Lu Chan Wai. Ng Yew Loong learnt from Chan Fook, who was reputed to have practiced kungfu at the southern Shaolin Monastery in Fujian.

Sifu Ho Fatt Nam learnt from seven masters, one of whom was Yang Fatt Khuen, the successor of the Venerable Jiang Nan, the Shaolin monk who escaped from the inferno when the Manchurian army razed the southern monastery to the ground. Only the monastery gate remains today, and the Chinese government has erected a stone tablet to indicate the former site of this monastery.

In the spirit of righteousness, many kungfu experts who descended from the southern Shaolin tradition, willingly gave their lives to the noble cause of Dr Sun Yat Sen's revolutionary work to overthrow the Manchurian Dynasty.

Again, viewed from a different cultural background, deeds that were considered righteous by the kungfu community, may seem odd or even foolish by other peoples. If a kungfu exponent promised his mentor that he would do anything for him to repay his kindness, the kungfu exponent literally meant what he said.

For example, if the mentor, for some legitimate reasons, asked the kungfu exponent for his left hand, the latter would just chop it off for the mentor. If the mentor was in trouble, the kungfu exponent would sacrifice even his own family to save the mentor.

The Chinese saying, "once a word drops onto the ground, even a good steed cannot retrieve it", meaning that "once a promise is made, it must be kept no matter what happens", was highly valued and practiced in the kungfu community.

Nevertheless, unscrupulous people may contort the meaning of righteousness for their selfish benefit. Under the pretext of righteousness, many gang leaders demanded their followers to do their bidding, such as extortion, robbery and murder, and to bear the consequences on their behalf if these wicked schemes fail.

Actually, the question of righteousness does not arise here, because the required actions are not right in the first place. Righteousness, including the will and effort to honor one's words, is applicable only when the relevant thoughts and deeds confirm to high moral values. Hence, Shaolin philosophy teaches that what is needed in upholding righteousness in not sheer bravado, but wisdom and courage, mellowed with compassion.

The life story of my master, Uncle Righteousness also provides me with some interesting examples of compassion. Uncle Righteousness was a traumatologist, i.e. one who is trained in "die da" (pronounced as "t'iet t'a") or traumatology, that specialty of Chinese medicine dealing with injuries sustained through "falls and hits" such as dislocation, fractures, muscular pains and internal injuries.

The following represents a typical case. A poor man sustained a fracture from a fall; incidentally rich people, because of their way of life and work, seldom suffer from traumatological injuries.

After receiving treatment (including medicine) from my master for a few months (the time needed for his fracture to heal properly), the patient would say, "Sifu, I am from a poor family. Since the fracture, I have not been working, but I still have to support my large family. Please have mercy on me. Charge as little as you can."

What the patient said was almost always true. The common procedure of requiring the patient to pay a substantial deposit before a modern orthopedic or any specialist would treat him, was never the practice of my master, Uncle Righteousness.

Instead, he would give the patient a kind look, draw out *all* his money from his pocket, and said, "I am sorry this is what little money I have, but take it and buy some good food for yourself and your family. Remember you need good food to replenish your lost chi and blood."

Some of my master's friends often teased him saying that he would never be wealthy. I recall he told me a few times, "If you want to make money from medical practice, do not specialize in traumatology."

Judging from today's standard, it is no surprise if some readers find it hard to differentiate between righteousness and foolishness. It is lamentable that barely half a century after Uncle Righteousness's time, many people are already asking sneeringly, "How much does a `liang' of righteousness cost?" (A `liang' is a Chinese weight measurement of about 50 grams.) However, true Shaolin disciples are determined that righteousness, compassion and other worthy values do not go down to the dogs.

Of course, compassion is more than merely giving money to needy patients. The ideal of compassion is best symbolized in the Bodhisattva, an enlightened being who voluntarily postpones his (or her) entry into Buddhahood so as to return to the phenomenal world to help others.

In the Shaolin Monastery, the principal halls for worship are not dominated by gods or prophets pointing the way to heaven, but are dedicated to two of the most popular Bodhisattvas in Mahayana Buddhism, Guan Yin (or Avalokitesvara) and Di Zang Huang (Ksitigarbha), who have vowed to save suffering humanity on earth and tormented souls in hell.

Compassion in the Shaolin spirit is not limited to any race, culture or religion. Shaolin disciples are obliged to spread love and happiness to all people, and Shaolin masters are obliged to nurture talents and pass on the Shaolin arts to deserving disciples.

18
Wonders Of Shaolin Chi Kung

(The Link between Physical and Spiritual Development)

At a higher level, it helps the practitioner to be in tune with the cosmos, harmonizing his vital energy with cosmic energy, hence linking his physical development to his spiritual development.

Kungfu, Chi Kung and Zen

One of the harder problems I face in my many years of teaching is to convey to my students, including some advanced ones, the tremendous scope and depth of the Shaolin arts.

Some of my students had attained high levels in other styles of martial arts before they practiced Shaolin Kungfu from me. When they learnt Shaolin techniques which they could effectively, and often surprisingly, use to overcome combative situations that they had previously thought to be impregnable, they were certainly very impressed.

Then, after they could perform exotic kungfu weapons in poetic motion, and had achieved fantastic force like "Iron Palm" and "Iron Shirt", they might think they had learnt all there was to be learnt. They would find it so hard to believe it if I told them that what they had attained is actually the beginning of the higher Shaolin arts.

This stage of their development marks a crucial point: if they are proud, they would probably remain at this level as a formidable fighter, and miss the greatest gifts Shaolin can offer them.

If they are humble enough to seek further, they would proceed to the next level, the fascinating world of Shaolin Chi Kung, where they might achieve feats that they would not even have dreamt possible, such as passing energy through walls, astral traveling, seeing into the past or future, and healing others from a great distance!

There is no doubt that these feats, incredible though they may be, are true, for not only they are recorded in authoritative texts, but also they have actually been performed by my disciples and I.

The wonders of Shaolin Chi Kung will be described in this and the following two chapters.

However, those who are ambitious to acquire these abilities should realize that except the first skill in the examples above, i.e. passing energy through walls, and other skills which are comparatively easy to attain, advanced chi kung skills need to be learnt from a master or at least a qualified instructor. Readers are reminded to heed the warnings at the appropriate places in this book where techniques are described for their information, and not for self training.

On the other hand, readers need not be *unduly* worried about such warnings, which are usually concerned with faulty chi kung practice, and which are often given by masters or in books.

It is certainly true that faulty practice may result in harmful side effects — in chi kung as well as in all forms of learning. But practicing chi kung is generally safer than practicing most sports, such as football, jogging and swimming.

This of course does not mean we do not pay attention to the warnings, which often reflect the masters' or authors' sense of responsibility towards their students or readers, but if students follow the relevant instructions and advice with reasonable care, they can be assured that their chi kung practice will be a very rewarding experience.

The division of the most important Shaolin arts into kungfu, chi kung and Zen or meditation is for the sake of convenience. Although many people, including masters, specialize in one of them, sometimes even to the extent of losing sight of the other two outside their specialization, these three arts actually form a continuum of personal development from the physical through the energetic to the spiritual. Chi Kung, the art of energy development, is therefore the link between the physical training of kungfu and the spiritual training of Zen.

While an ideal, but not necessarily the only, approach in the training of the Shaolin arts is to progress from kungfu to chi kung, then to Zen, every one of the three arts is infused in every other.

Even in the most elementary kungfu movements, correct breathing coordination which is an aspect of chi kung, and a focused mind which is an aspect of Zen, are necessary.

Chi kung and Zen are required in the training to acquire the three most advanced arts in Shaolin Kungfu, which are also considered as "the three ultimates of martial art", namely "Shaolin Marvelous Fist" (*Shao Lin Shen Quan*), "Palm of Striking Across Space" (*Pi Kong Zhang*), and "One-Finger Zen" (*Yi Zhi Chan*).

Kungfu literature mentions that a master with "Shaolin Marvelous Fist" can hurt an opponent within a hundred and eight steps without physical contact; with "Palm of Striking Across Space" he can within seventy two steps injure someone behind a wall without damaging the wall; with "One-Finger Zen" he can strike the vital points of an opponent within thirty six steps! By now, hopefully, readers would be already used to incredible feats performed by Shaolin masters; more amazing feats are in store as you read on.

The set of exercises known as "Eighteen Lohan Hands", which was the forerunner of Shaolin Kungfu, forms the basis of Shaolin Chi Kung. Another set of exercises known as "Sinew Metamorphosis", which was the forerunner of Shaolin Chi Kung, forms the basis of internal force training in Shaolin Kungfu.

All these exercises must be performed in a meditative state of mind or Zen. The focus on breathing in and out as a means to achieve a one-pointed mind in Zen practice, is an important aspect of chi kung. All these examples show that kungfu, chi kung and Zen are integrated.

Zen is not necessarily attained in a formal, cross-legged meditation posture; it may be attained while the student is performing a kungfu form or a chi kung exercise. For example, in Spain my disciple Douglas had some interesting Zen experiences while practicing chi kung although he had not started Zen formally.

During a chi kung practice, he first felt an intense separation of his inside and the outside, then, miraculously, this separation disappeared completely.

Zen or meditation is the highest of the Shaolin arts. Just as a highly accomplished kungfu master would find it hard to believe that his accomplishment, in the holistic perspective of the Shaolin teaching, is only a stepping stone to the higher achievement found in the development of energy in chi kung, a chi kung master would find it hard to believe that his fantastic achievement is actually marginal when compared to the greatest attainment in Zen!

If we wish to compare the greatest attainments in kungfu and in chi kung, which are certainly remarkable and even incredible by themselves, with the greatest attainment in Zen, if it is ever attained, it is like comparing a drop of water with the boundless ocean! Why this is so will be explained in later chapters; meanwhile let us have some sound understanding of Shaolin Chi Kung.

The Legacy of Bodhidharma

Like Shaolin Kungfu and Zen, Shaolin Chi Kung was first initiated by the great Bodhidharma, an Indian prince who renounced the throne to teach Zen Buddhism at the Shaolin Monastery in 527 CE. He taught the Eighteen Lohan Hands and the Sinew Metamorphosis to the monks to aid their meditation.

It is said that Bodhidharma also taught another set of chi kung exercises known as "Cleansing Marrow", but while the literature on Eighteen Lohan Hands and the "Classic of Sinew Metamorphosis" have been passed down the generations to us, the "Classic of Cleansing Marrow" is now lost.

From secondary records purported to describe "Cleansing Marrow", these exercises probably resemble a genre of chi kung exercises known as "Self Manifested Chi Movement", which will be described in more details later.

Eighteen Lohan Hands is a set of eighteen dynamic chi kung patterns. "Lohan" is the Chinese term for the Sanskrit "Arahant", who is an enlightened being in Hinayana or Theravada Buddhism. Because of the long history of Eighteen Lohan Hands, during which time it has undergone many modifications and innovations, the individual patterns practiced by different schools may differ. In my Shaolin Wahnam School, the eighteen Lohan patterns are as follows:

1. Lifting the Sky.
2. Shooting Arrows.
3. Plucking Stars.
4. Turning Head.
5. Merry-Go-Round.
6. Angry-Eyed Punches.
7. Carrying the Moon.
8. Nourishing Kidneys.
9. Three Levels to Earth.
10. Dancing Crane.
11. Carrying Mountain.
12. Drawing Knife.
13. Pushing Mountain.
14. Separating Water.
15. Presenting Claws.
16. Windmill Hand.
17. Lift-Heel Squatting.
18. Rotating Knees.

The first eight exercises are similar to the set of exercises known as "Eight Pieces of Brocade" (*Ba Duan Jin*). The original objective of the Eighteen Lohan Hands was "to loosen muscles and bones" so that Shaolin monks could practice meditation for longer periods.

However these exercises have developed in depth and scope, and are now excellent for promoting health, vitality and longevity, as described in Chapter 4 which also explains Pattern 1 (Lifting the Sky) and Pattern 9 (Three Levels to Earth) of the Eighteen Lohan Hands. Aspirants keen to learn Shaolin Kungfu but are too weak for vigorous training, will benefit much if they start with Eighteen Lohan Hands.

Fig 18.1 Eighteen Lohan Hands

While the exercises of Eighteen Lohan Hands are mainly concerned with "external" movements, those of Sinew Metamorphosis are mainly "internal". In Sinew Metamorphosis training, the practitioner stands stationary at twelve postures, and by means of subtle movements, such as of his fingers, toes and wrists, he generates his internal energy to flow harmoniously along various meridians as well as strengthens his internal tissues and sinews. The twelve postures and subtle movements are as follows:

1. Flicking fingers.
2. Flexing fingers.
3. Grasping thumbs.
4. Grasping fists.
5. Stretching up.
6. Pulling body.
7. Jerking elbows.
8. Rotating elbows.
9. Stretching arms.
10. Holding arms.
11. Stretching palms.
12. Holding sun and moon.

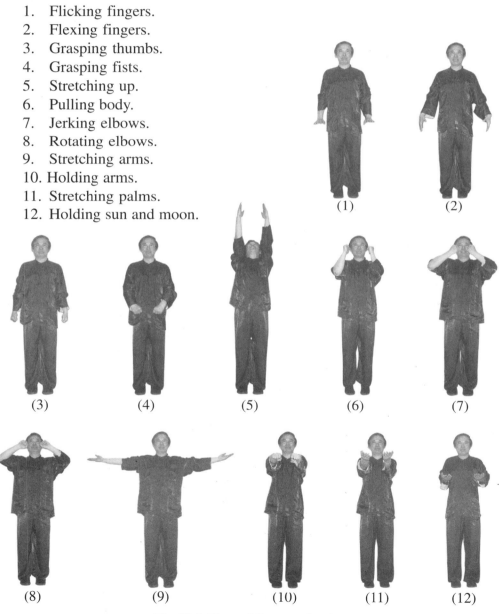

Fig 18.2 Sinew Metamorphosis

Sinew Metamorphosis for Internal Power

The following is a brief description of two of the Sinew Metamorphosis exercises. Stand upright, be relaxed and alert. Close your mouth and clench your teeth firmly. Place the tip of your tongue at your upper gum above the front teeth. (Do not worry if you are wearing denture; perform the exercises the same way as if you were not wearing it.) Fill yourself with chi, or energy — this is done mentally, not physically.

For "Lifting Thumbs" (Pattern 2), drop your two arms, with elbows fairly straight, in front of your thighs. With the fingers clenching in a fist, move both thumbs outward and upward forty nine times, Fig 18.3.

Fig 18.3 Lifting Thumbs

For "Lifting Body" (Pattern 5), raise your arms straight above your head, with the fists loosely clenched and the thumbs facing the back. Your raised arms should be a few inches away from your ears. Raise your heels slightly, about an inch or two above the ground. Next clench both fists firmly, lower your elbows with some strength as if you are pulling your body up, and raise your feet as much as you can to stand on your toes. Then return to the starting position, with arms straight above, and heels slightly above the ground. Repeat forty nine times. See Fig 18.4.

Fig 18.4 Lifting Body

Although these exercises appear simple, they are actually very powerful. If you find tension in your chest after practicing Sinew Metamorphosis, performing "Lifting the Sky" of the Lohan Hands (see Chapter 4) or Self-Manifested Chi Movement (to be explained later) will relieve the tension. If tension persists or pain results, stop praticing the exercises; you probably have been performing the exercises wrongly.

As Sinew Metamorphosis is principally concerned with strengthening, it forms the foundation of many types of force training in Shaolin Kungfu, and later in other styles of martial art. Shaolin Chi Kung for force training has been explained in Chapter 14.

As these Sinew Metamorphosis exercises have undergone various transformations although its fundamental principles remained when they were adapted by martial artists through the centuries for their various needs, many people may not recognize the prototype in the numerous force training methods found in different martial arts today.

For example, the "Golden Bridge" (Fig 18.5) in Shaolin Kungfu, the "Three-Circle Stance" (Fig 18.6) in Taijiquan, and the various "Zhan Zhuang" or Standing at Static Stances (Fig 18.7) in Bagua (Pakua) Kungfu — all of which are meant to develop internal force — owe their origins to the principle of tissue strengthening in Sinew Metamorphosis.

Fig 18.5
Golden Bridge in Shaolin Kungfu

Fig 18.6
Three-Circle Stance in Taijiquan

Fig 18.7
A Zhan Zhuang Pattern in Bagua Kungfu

Later these twelve Sinew Metamorphosis exercises, with some modification, were also performed with the practitioner sitting cross-legged. They are then known as the "Twelve Pieces of Brocade of Shaolin".

While practically all Shaolin masters and students who have dedicated their lives to the Shaolin arts gratefully honor Bodhidharma as their First Patriarch, some scholars, Chinese as well as non-Chinese, most of whom have never practiced any Shaolin arts before but who based their conclusion on often second-hand sources in their ivory towers, eloquently argue that Bodhidharma was only a myth, invented by interested parties to boost their standing — although overwhelming evidence including imperial documents, temple histories and architectural records indicated that Bodhidharma taught at the Shaolin Monastery in the 6th century.

Many of these Shaolin masters and students were highly intelligent and distinguished, like great monks, emperors, generals and state ministers. Hence, it is amazing, if not insulting, that many people tend to accept uncritically the scholars' claim, implying that generations of Shaolin masters and students had been duped.

These scholars say that Sinew Metamorphosis as well as Eighteen Lohan Hands were not taught by Bodhidharma, but were a later invention by the Chinese themselves who might not even belong to the Shaolin tradition.

Shaolin disciples are generally not bothered with this argument; what they are interested is whether the exercises produce the results as claimed; the name for the exercises — Sinew Metamorphosis, Twelve Pieces of Brocade or otherwise — is merely a convenient symbol for reference.

It is of course the readers' privilege to choose between arguing until their chest aches, and practicing them to attain health, vitality and internal power. If you are doubtful whether such seemingly simple exercises can develop internal power, the best is to practice them, such as "Lifting Thumbs" and "Lifting Body" of Sinew Metamorphosis, twice a day for three months to judge for yourself.

A Chance to Test an Incredible Art

Would you believe it if you are told that by practicing some appropriate chi kung exercises, you may move without your volition, such as swaying like a happy willow tree, dancing gracefully and spontaneously, or even making funny noises? Again, in line with the Shaolin philosophy that one should accept the teaching not on faith alone, but on his understanding and experience, you can test the validity of the above statement yourself by practicing the following Self-Manifested Chi Movement exercise.

Before going into the method of the exercise, it is good to understand its philosophy. Self-Manifested Chi Movement, also called Self-Induced Chi Flow, and known as *Zi Fa Dong Gong* in Chinese, is a genre of chi kung exercises. A whole school of chi kung can be built upon just these self-manifested exercises. Probably the most famous set of self-manifested exercises is the "Five-Animal Play" invented by the great 2nd century Chinese physician, Hua Tuo.

The movements spontaneously performed by a practitioner while he is in the midst of the exercise, are "involuntary" in the sense that they are not caused by him consciously, but caused by a "subconscious", enhanced and harmonious flow of his own vital energy inside his body. But at all time, the practitioner is fully aware of his situation, and he can influence or stop his spontaneous movements if he wants. There is definitely nothing occult or religious in this exercise.

Because of various factors — such as his bodily and mental conditions, the nature and site of his illness if any, and the type of exercises used to induce the movements — different people or the same person at different times, will move differently.

Some may hardly move, others may move vigorously, but most sway gracefully, sometimes moving off from their starting position. Sometimes the movements or sounds may be odd or comical; but whatever they are, a beginning student should not be worried, as the movements and sounds are the natural ways your own body and mind react to the working of your own vital energy flow, stimulated by the chi kung exercise, to give you the best benefits. Laughing or crying during the exercise, for example, is a form of emotional catharsis; rolling on the ground or hitting yourself is a form of self healing.

The following four points are very important:

1. You must not be disturbed during the exercise. If someone approaches, for example, indicate to him to wait. Should you be disturbed or affected in any way that causes your chi or vital energy to be deviated in its flow, remedy the situation by performing the whole exercise again at your earliest convenience to bring your chi flow back to proper alignment.

2. You must not resist your energy flow. This means when you feel your energy is moving you, do not attempt to stop the movement. However, at the beginning stage before you have learnt complete control, if your movement starts to become vigorous, gently tell yourself to slow down. You will find that your body always obeys your mind.

3. Never stop abruptly; always bring your movements to a graceful halt whenever you wish to complete the exercise. Remain still for at least a few seconds before moving away from your position.

4. Practice in a safe place, preferably in open space if the weather permits. There must not be any sharp or pointed objects nearby. Do **not** practice near any sharp drop, such as a balcony or an open window of a high building. Though this exercise is excellent, it cannot make you fly should you accidentally drop over the balcony or window.

Self-Manifested Chi Movement

The following is the method to induce self-manifested chi movement. Stand upright and relaxed, with feet slightly apart. Use your middle finger, left for men and right for women (but if you forget, it does not matter much) to press gently on your naval about ten times. Then drop that hand, and use the middle finger of the other hand to massage the crown of your head about three times.

Next perform a series of exercises to induce chi flow. Many different exercises can be used; the five selected below constitute a good combination. As the exercises are means and not ends themselves, you need not worry about performing the form of the exercises exactly.

First, perform "Lifting the Sky" about ten times as follows. Straighten both arms in front, with both palms facing the ground, Fig 18.8 (a). Bring the straightened arms continuously forward and upward, Fig 18.8 (b), simultaneously breathing in gently; then press both palms upward towards the sky, Fig 18.8 (c), gently holding the breath. Next lower the straightened arms to your sides, Fig 18.8 (d), gently breathing out in the process. (Refer to Chapter 4 for detail of this exercise.)

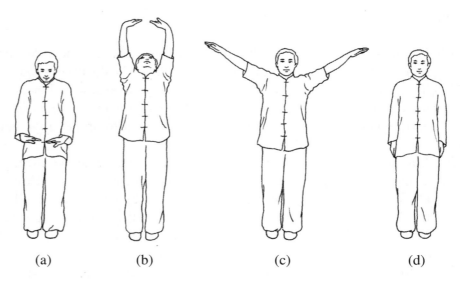

| (a) | (b) | (c) | (d) |

Fig 18.8 Lifting the Sky

Continue with "Windmill Hand" as follows. Bring your righ. continuously forward and upward, Fig 18.9 (a), simultaneously breathing n. gently. Continue the arm movement backward and downward, Fig 18.9 (b), breathing out gently. Repeat with the same hand about ten times. Then repeat with the other hand about ten times. (Note that the "Windmill Hand" here is "soft"; whereas the "Forceful Windmill", as part of the Cosmos Palm training described in Chapter 14, is "hard".)

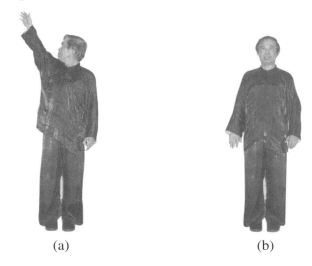

(a)   (b)

Fig 18.9 Windmill Hand

Continue with "Kicking Crane". Turn to your right side, spread out both arms, and kick out your left leg, pointing the toes in front, Fig 18.10. Then lower your left leg, turn left-about to your left side, spread out both arms, and kick out your right leg, pointing the toes in front. Let your breathing be natural. Repeat the procedure about ten times.

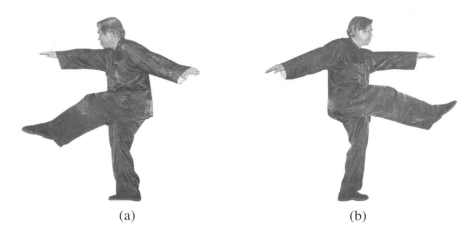

(a)   (b)

Fig 18.10 Kicking Crane

, "Double Dragons". Bring both hands to both sides at breast palms facing the ground. Move the palms, fingers pointing . front by straightening your elbows, bending your body slightly ...reathing out simultaneously. Then bring your palms back to your ..st level, still with fingers pointing in front, bending your body slightly ... and breathing in, Fig 18.11. Repeat the procedure about twenty times.

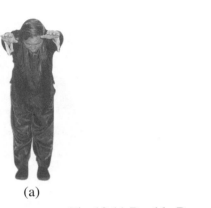

(a)   (b)

Fig 18.11 Double Dragons

Continue with "Fish-Flip". Drop your hands at both sides and do not worry about them throughout this exercise. Continue bending your body forward about 45 degrees and backward about 45 degrees, Fig 18.12, about twenty times. Let your breathing be natural.

(a)   (b)

Fig 18.12 Fish-Flip

After completing this sequence of exercises — Lifting the Sky, Windmill Hand, Kicking Crane, Double Dragons and Fish-Flip — close your eyes (if you have not already closed them), stand upright and be totally relaxed. Follow the momentum as you begin to sway or move in any way; do not resist the movement, but tell yourself to slow down should your movement become too vigorous. Make whatever sound if you feel like it.

Enjoy the self-manifested chi movement for about five to ten minutes. (Later, when you are proficient in this exercise, you may continue for a longer period, but never too long that you become tired; and you may open your eyes during your practice if you wish.)

However, if after the sequence of exercises you are still not moved by your vital energy, stand upright and relaxed with your eyes close. Gently think of a cascade of energy flowing down in all directions from your head to your feet.

Repeat this thought or visualization gently for a few times, and when your body starts to move, follow its momentum and enjoy the self-manifested movements. If there is still no spontaneous movement after a few times of thinking or visualizing the energy cascade, it does not matter; just remain standing in the meditative state for a few minutes, and complete the exercise as described below.

After enjoying the self-manifested chi movement or induced chi flow, gently bring your movement to a graceful stop. Remain still in the standing meditation for a few minutes without any thought or care in the world. Then gently think of your abdomen for a few seconds. Rub your palms together to warm them, and then warm your eyes with your palms as you open your eyes. Gently massage your face and then walk about briskly to complete the whole exercise. You will probably find it one of the best experiences you have ever had for a long time.

This Self-Manifested Chi Movement exercise is very effective for clearing away toxic waste, opening energy blockages, and balancing energy levels, thus curing a wide range of illnesses and promoting physical, emotional, mental and spiritual health. At a higher level, it helps the practitioner to be in tune with the cosmos, harmonizing his vital energy with cosmic energy, hence linking his physical development to his spiritual development.

19
Curing "Incurable" Diseases
(Shaolin Chi Kung and Chinese Medicine)

In case some readers may feel that this hope of recovering from their so-called incurable illness is too good to believe, let me remind them that true Shaolin disciples, in accordance with Buddhist precepts — though true Shaolin disciples need not be Buddhists, and many are not — do not tell lies.

Chi Kung for Curing Illness

Would you believe that people suffering for many years from hypertension, asthma, diabetes, peptic and duodenum ulcers, arthritis, rheumatism, insomnia, migraine, sexual inadequacy, and even cancer, and had been told that these disease were incurable, could be cured by practicing Shaolin Chi Kung?

I myself, who had practiced and taught Shaolin Chi Kung for many years, found it hard to believe that practicing the same set of chi kung exercises could cure such a wide range of different illnesses.

I had read about the wonderful healing effects of chi kung from classical chi kung literature, but at that time I was quite disinterested in these claims because — thanks to Shaolin Kungfu — both my students and I were (and still are) very healthy and fit. We practiced Shaolin Chi Kung not for health or curing illness, but for enhancing our kungfu abilities. Hence we did not have living examples to prove or disprove the chi kung claims of curing so-called incurable diseases.

This was to change when I began teaching Shaolin Chi Kung to the public. All along I knew that Shaolin and other kinds of chi kung were excellent for promoting health, though I was not too sure whether they were equally effective for curing "incurable" diseases, despite the fact that years ago Shaolin Chi Kung cured my migraine, sinus problem and hemorrhoids.

I reasoned to myself that if I were to reserve Shaolin Chi Kung only for selected disciples, who were already fit like fiddles, those who were weakly but for various reasons did not practice kungfu — in other words, those who needed Shaolin Chi Kung most — would be denied the opportunity.

So I selected from Shaolin Chi Kung, patterns that are not too exciting to practice but are effective for promoting health, and taught them to the public without their having to train in Shaolin Kungfu first.

The result was overwhelming. For the first time I actually saw for myself the marvelous effects of chi kung curing so-called incurable diseases, and it gave me the inspiration that one day I would convey this wonderful hope to countless suffering patients.

By now there are literally hundreds of patients who have had their so-called incurable diseases cured after practicing chi kung from me. In case some readers may feel that this hope of recovering from their so-called incurable illness is too good to believe, let me remind them that true Shaolin disciples, in accordance with Buddhist precepts — though true Shaolin disciples need not be Buddhists, and many are not — do not tell lies.

Harmonizing Yin-Yang

How chi kung can cure these so-called "incurable" diseases can be explained by two important principles: "harmonizing yin-yang" and "cleansing meridians". Great Chinese physicians have advised that "if yin-yang is harmonious and the flow of energy in the meridian system is cleansed, illness will not occur."

Those who think that the conventional western medical paradigm is the only correct view, this advice may appear simplistic, if not down-right ridiculous. But if they care, for their own sake, to study it more deeply, they will find that it is, like a most profound mathematical formula, a summation of a tremendous amount of great medical truths expressed in the shortest possible way.

To understand the concept of yin-yang harmony, we must first have a clear picture of what yin-yang means. Yin and yang are not the two primordial forces of the universe, nor the male and female principles in the cosmos, as many western writings on Chinese philosophy misleadingly suggest. Yin and yang are merely symbols, and as symbols they can refer to different things or concepts in different situations. Basically yin and yang symbolize two opposing yet complementary aspects of reality.

In Shaolin Kungfu, for example, we may refer to form as yin, and application as yang. If a student learns only the form of kungfu but does not know how to apply it for combat, he lacks yin-yang harmony in his kungfu training.

In health and medicine, the natural resistance of a person is referred to as yin, and all exo-pathogens as yang. If his resistance is inadequate to meet an attack of gems, expressed in Chinese medical concept as excessive yang, his yin-yang is disharmonious.

Our natural ability to secrete the necessary hormones or chemicals at the right time and place is symbolized as yin, and all the cholesterol, sugar, calcium and other pollutants that get into our systems are symbolized as yang. Even when a person takes food low in cholesterol or sugar, but if his organs or glands (many of which are still unknown to us) are not functioning properly, expressed as insufficient yin, he will be sick due to yin-yang disharmony.

We are, by nature, able to handle stress and other emotional hazards, and this is expressed as yin-yang harmony. But if a person becomes mentally or emotionally unstable, expressed as insufficient yin, or if the stress and hazards become too overbearing, excessive yang, he may have psychiatric problems.

Hence, whether the disease is contagious, organic or psychiatric, it is caused by yin-yang disharmony. Harmonizing yin-yang, therefore, is the logical way of overcoming illness at its root cause.

The premiss in Chinese medical thinking is that health is our natural birthright. We are by nature healthy; if illness occurs, it is only a temporary state when certain systems in our body (and mind, as the Chinese never alienate mind from body) fail to function as they should. According to Chinese medical philosophy, the ultimate cause of illness is internal; therefore, illness can, and should, be relieved by correcting internal faults.

What happens, someone may rightly ask, if an immediate, external factor causing illness is unreasonably excessive? If, for instance, a person drinks an overwhelming amount of liquor, or is exposed to an overwhelming amount of radioactive waste dumped by an inconsiderate manufacturer, would his natural life-sustaining systems be able to neutralize the harmful effects of alcohol or radiation? In such cases, the problem is no longer medical; it becomes a question of suicide or murder.

In contrast, western medical philosophy tacitly presumes that the ultimate cause of illness is external. Hence, in western medicine the onus is to define the external cause — such as bacteria, cholesterol or stress; then to provide an external means to overcome the cause. This crucial philosophical difference between Chinese and western medicine has far-reaching significance, as will be discussed later.

Clearing Energy Blockage

The Chinese go further than curing illnesses; their greater aim is to prevent illnesses from occurring in the first place. From the Chinese perspective, prevention and cure belong to the same continuum of healthcare, and both aims can be realized by clearing the meridians of blockage so that chi or vital energy can flow harmoniously.

If a person is already healthy, ensuring harmonious energy flow will prevent illness from occurring; if he is sick, it will cure him of his illness. Harmonious energy flow can be achieved in many ways, such as physical exercises, taking appropriate herbs, massage and acupuncture, but the best and most direct way is practicing chi kung.

How does harmonious energy flow prevent and cure illnesses? Every part of our body is intimately linked by our elaborate meridian system, through which our chi or vital energy flows.

In western medical terms, this meridian system incorporates our feed-back system, immune system, transport system, disposal system, self-defense system, and self-regenerative system.

If disease-causing agents enter a certain part of our body, such as through a cut into our blood, through breathing into our lungs, or through eating into our digestive tract, our whole body is alerted by our meridian system to this new situation of temporary yin-yang disharmony.

Our whole body is then mobilized to meet this new challenge, like channeling "defense energy", known as *wei chi* in Chinese medical terminology and which probably corresponds to antibodies in western terms, to overcome the foreign invaders, and activating the disposal system to clear away any resultant dead cells. If the foreign invaders are substantial, our body will call up reserve energy from the "great spleen collaterals", and if needed from the "eight wondrous meridians".

All these necessary activities to overcome the foreign invaders, such as alerting the whole body and mobilizing the required forces, are possible if our chi is flowing harmoniously. If there is a blockage, for example, between the invaded site and the "great spleen collaterals", reserve forces may not be adequately channeled to restore the yin-yang balance.

If you think that all this description is merely speculation, be assured that the overcoming of foreign invaders by our body systems is happening all the time in everyone of us, usually we are not consciously aware that this is happening.

If you think one must take antibiotics to overcome contagious diseases, you will be amazed that the number of diseases all the antibiotics in the world today can cure is miserably small. Some western experts believe that if not for our own wonderful defense and other systems, no one can be alive for more than ten minutes!

Not only are we daily invaded by countless deadly microorganisms, many of which are still unknown to medical scientists, we are also constantly polluted by harmful substances and bombarded by lethal radiation. Yet, we remain alive and healthy — thanks to our yin-yang balance and harmonious energy flow.

All the time, cholesterol is clogging our blood vessels, sugar flowing into our blood stream, acid pouring into our stomach, pollutants chocking our lungs, calcium solidifying in our kidneys, and other harmful substances blocking cells, tissues and other organs.

Yet we are not sick, because as soon as the accumulation of these harmful substances reaches a critical level, as soon as excessive yang is registered by our meridian system, chi in the form of electric impulses will instruct the respective parts of our body to produce the right chemicals in the right amounts at the right places to neutralize the harmful substances so as to restore our yin-yang harmony. Only when chi flow is blocked, when yin-yang is disharmonious, illnesses like high blood pressure, diabetes, peptic ulcers, asthma, kidney stones and other organic diseases occur.

Similarly our wonderful body systems prevent and cure us of cancer, thousands of times without our knowing, despite the lethal radiation and sea of carcinogens all around us. In fact, curing degenerative diseases, including cancer, is the hallmark of chi kung therapy; I have hundreds of cases to substantiate my claim.

Another remarkable achievement of chi kung is preventing and curing psychiatric disorders, which are referred to as "illness of the heart" in Chinese terminology. According to Chinese medical philosophy, the cause of psychiatric disorders, like that of somatic diseases, is ultimately internal; that is why the same external situation, like anxiety in work or disappointment in failure, may be psychotic to one person but not to another.

The yin-yang disharmony in emotional health which causes psychiatric illness is related to various *zang chi*, or energy of the various organ systems, which also causes organic diseases.

If the chi at the lung meridian system is disharmonious, that person's ability to bear grief is affected; if it is at the kidney meridian system, he is prone to fear; at the liver meridian system, prone to anger; at the heart meridian system, he may be unable to accept joy; and at the spleen meridian system, he tends to worry excessively.

A person whose lung energy is blocked, for example, feels depressed easily, whereas one who lacks kidney energy would be in a state of shock and nervousness. Chinese medical scientists summarized such knowledge from their years of empirical studies into the principles of the five elementary processes of metal, water, wood, fire and earth, which some scholars merely reading these terms at their surface meaning, ignorantly but arrogantly say are metaphysical or superstitious.

Instead of persuading a patient who suffers from depression to believe that the world is a laughing stage, or reasoning with a nervous patient that his fear is unfounded, we can teach them chi kung exercises to promote smooth flow of their lung energy and kidney energy respectively. When they have achieved harmonious energy flow at their respective organ systems, they would improve their emotional balance, with the result that they can, on their own, become more cheerful and realize their fear is actually unwarranted.

If you have wondered why a chi kung master can be so relaxed even when he faces a situation which will be stressful to most other people, you can have a good guess at the answer now.

As the meridian system of the master is clear, whatever stressful emotions like grief, fear, anger, joy and worry that most other people with energy blockage would succumb into, will be flushed out by his harmonious energy flow.

This also explains why a person who is anxious, worried or angry would feel better after letting out his pent-up emotions on a dummy, or after some vigorous sport; and a grief-stricken person would experience some relief after a good cry. Vigorous sports, crying, laughing and shouting are indirect ways of generating energy flow; practicing chi kung is direct and methodical.

Chi Kung for Curing Cancer

The first time I saw Maria, she looked old, haggard and depressed; she suffered from breast cancer, and already had three surgical operations to remove her tumor. Despite her operations which were "technically successful", her cancer kept coming back. She was also on a powerful course of chemotherapy, which made her weak, nauseous and bald.

I opened some relevant vital points on her body, transmitted some chi into her, and helped her to experience self-manifested chi movement. At first she swayed gently, then she performed some spontaneous dance-like movements. But the most memorable part was when I asked her to smile from her heart. I said, "Do not worry how you do it, but do it. Smile from your heart." And she did that.

Douglas, my disciple who was with me throughout the therapy session, and I were amazed to find the smile from her heart transformed Maria from an old-looking, depressed patient to a young, beautiful woman she really is. At the end of that therapy session, I asked Maria to give a blessing to anyone she liked.

Maria practiced at home the self-manifested chi movement exercise I taught her. A few days later she came for her second therapy session. At first Douglas and I almost could not recognize her. She had changed so much just over a few days: she was no longer the haggard, depressed Maria we first saw; she was young, cheerful and even bouncing with energy!

She did her self-manifested chi movement exercise beautifully. Her spontaneous movements resembled a graceful dance, and she wore a smile on her face most of the time. Half way through the therapy session, she asked me if it was all right for her to sing while in her self-manifested chi movement, for she simply felt like singing. I felt very happy for her, for I knew very well that she was on the sure path of recovery. She concluded the session with a blessing for someone she liked.

After the practice she told Douglas and me that the chi kung experience was fantastic. She confessed she was skeptical at first, but soon discovered the benefits were just unbelievable. She said that even after the first session, the pain in her head and upper body which she had suffered for some time disappeared as if by magic.

All these happened only two weeks ago. Hence, at the time of writing, Maria has not recovered, but from her response and from my experience with cancer patients I can safely predict that her recovery is a matter of time. Probably six months later when she goes for a medical test for cancer, the result will be negative.

I chose her case for illustration here, instead of others who have been proven to have recovered from cancer, partly because her case is very remarkable, and mainly because it readily comes to mind as I write.

Cancer can be cured, and many have been cured. This is a serious claim, made earnestly, for it pains my heart to know that, for some reasons, while millions are suffering in dehumanizing agony, a proven cure for cancer that is cheap and should be easily available, is still unknown to those who need it.

I will be happy and ready to work with sincere organizations desirous to test my claim, and to share the knowledge and skill of curing cancer with others.

Cancer is only frightening if we view it from the western medical perspective. The renowned oncologist, Dr D. W. Smithers, explains that cancer is "just a shortened way of saying something that cannot be simply defined." Because western experts fail to pin-point the cause or causes of cancer, they are quite helpless in providing a cure.

However, if we view what the west call cancer from the Chinese perspective, immediately its morbidity vanishes, because according to Chinese medical philosophy there is no such thing as an incurable disease.

In fact cancer is unknown in traditional Chinese medical literature; the nearest term to it is "poisonous growth", which the Chinese has never considered to be fatal or incurable. The term *ai*, which modern Chinese use to refer to cancer, is a translation from English, and is not a traditional Chinese medical concept.

How, then, would a traditional Chinese physician describe a patient who suffers from a condition (or conditions) which the west would conveniently call cancer? The Chinese physician will not call it "cancer", or by any word with a similar meaning, simply because the concept of cancer does not exist in Chinese medicine.

The physician will, as in all other diseases, describe the condition of the patient, not the condition of the disease. He may, for instance, describe the patient as "having poisonous heat at the liver meridian".

Another patient whom a western doctor would similarly describe as suffering from cancer, may be described differently by the Chinese physician, according to the patient's pathological condition, like "having false-fire at the intermediate level".

Interestingly this phenomenon of the same "stuff" appearing as different "reality" falls perfectly in line with Buddhist philosophy. What appears as water to us, for example, is fire to ghosts and spirits, and as crystals to gods. (Please ignore the previous sentence if you do not believe that beings other than what we can see, exist in other dimensions on our puny earth or in other parts of our boundless universe.)

This difference of perspective means the difference between life and death for the patient. If he is described as suffering from cancer, it is tantamount to saying he is going to die, usually painfully.

According to the western medical paradigm, as the cause of illness is unknown, the cure is unknown too. Cancer is "incurable" not because there is no cure available, but because it is not known what actually is to be cured.

If the same patient is described as "having poisonous heat at the liver meridian", or "having false-fire at the intermediate level", it is telling him that the cause of his temporary state of ill-health has been defined, and the logical step in restoring him to his natural state of good health is to overcome the cause of his ill-health.

According to the Chinese medical paradigm, all illnesses can be cured because it is natural and normal to be healthy. If the patient's "poisonous heat at the liver meridian" or "false-fire at the intermediate level" is eliminated, then his disease, irrespective of what label it may be called, will be relieved.

Thematic and Holistic Approaches

If the patient can remedy the temporary faults in his own body systems, thus restoring them to their natural functions, cancer or any disease can be cured. In Chinese medicine many approaches can be used to restore the patient's natural functions, such as acupuncture, massage therapy, physiotherapy, external medicine, herbalism and chi kung therapy.

For diseases like cancer where the external causes are unknown and the internal causes hard to define, practicing chi kung is the best approach. This is because while the other approaches are generally thematic, i.e. diagnosing the causes, then prescribing the appropriate therapeutics to correct them, chi kung is generally holistic, i.e. treating the patient as a whole person, without the need to address the particular cause of the illness directly.

For example, if an acupuncturist diagnoses a patient as having "poisonous heat at the liver meridian", he would manipulate appropriate acu-points to release the "poisonous heat" at the liver meridian.

He will also manipulate other acu-points to detoxify and flush out the "poison" that has spread to other parts of the body, to strengthen the kidney system so that its effect can benefit the liver, and to stimulate the gall bladder meridian and clear the lung meridian so that energy at the liver meridian can flow smoothly. Should the causes of the disease be different, he would use different therapeutic principles and methods. His approach is therefore thematic.

A herbalist treating the same patient would employ the same therapeutic principles, such as eliminating the "poisonous heat" at the liver meridian, detoxifying and flushing out the "poison", strengthening the kidney system, and promoting smooth energy flow. But his method would be different.

Instead of using needles, the herbalist would use appropriate herbs to achieve the same therapeutic objectives. His approach is also thematic; he prescribes the therapeutics according to the causes of illness.

Chi kung therapy is generally holistic, although thematic treatment is also possible. Indeed many cancer patients have their so-called incurable disease cured by practicing from me the same chi kung course which also cures others of a wide range of disorders, like asthma, diabetes, gall stone, high blood pressure, heart problems, kidney failure, peptic ulcers, rheumatism, insomnia, depression, nervousness, sexual inadequacy, and infertility.

How Does Chi Kung Cure Illness

How is it possible that the same chi kung exercises can cure different diseases? If we view it from the western medical paradigm, such as from chemotherapy, probably the most representative of western medical practice today, which dictates that a particular drug is prescribed for a particular disease, or from surgery, considered by many as the most advanced of wes-ern medical technology, which conveniently cuts off the diseased parts, this concept of chi kung as a panacea for all ills would appear ludicrous as well as primitive.

But if we remember that the western medical paradigm is not the only way we can use to view health and medicine, and if we examine the topic from a different perspective using the Chinese medical paradigm, which actually has successfully and continuously served the world's largest population for the longest period of history, we shall find this holistic effect of chi kung in curing illness logical and scientific.

Put in a nutshell, chi kung therapy can achieve holistic healing of the patient because its principal function is cleansing meridians and harmonizing yin-yang. It can achieve this purpose excellently because of the natural characteristic of chi to flow to where it is needed most. Chi flows from high energy levels to low energy levels, just like water flows from high to low places.

Where energy levels are lowest are sites of illness, irrespective of whether the illness is contagious, organic or psychiatric. For example, if there is insufficient energy to overcome pathogens at an infected site, a contagious disease like influenza develops; if an organ does not have sufficient energy to function naturally, an organic disorder like kidney failure occurs; if the "heart", which is generally translated as the mind in English, lacks the energy to accommodate stressful situations, a psychiatric problem like intra-personal loneliness happens.

Often the low energy level occurs at a site not because there is insufficient overall energy in the body, but because of energy blockage that hampers smooth flow of energy to where it is needed.

The blockage may occur at different scales, such as at the cellular scale at certain nerves which may cause hormonal imbalance, or at an organic scale at the coronary artery which may cause a heart attack.

Almost always the root cause of a blockage at the organic scale which eventually results in a structural defect such as arteriosclerosis (hardening of arteries), has its origin as a functional disorder caused by energy blockage at the cellular level.

Practicing chi kung clears energy blockage, especially at the cellular and sub-atomic levels, with the beneficial effects gradually spreading to the levels of tissues, organs and the whole body including the mind. When vital energy is increased and its flow harmonious, yin-yang balance is achieved.

Thus, if there is an infection, symbolized as excessive yang, reserved energy, symbolized as yin, will overcome it. If there is insufficient energy at a particular organ for its normal functioning, or inadequate yang, energy tapped from the cosmos and transformed into vital energy of the body will be channeled through a better system of energy flow to that organ to overcome its lack.

If the mind is inadequate in handling stress, which may be expressed as mental yin insufficiency, the mind is expanded, expressed as increasing mental yin, so that now it can cope with stress effectively.

Similarly, cleansing meridians and harmonizing yin-yang can cure cancer. It is sickening but true that cancer has made some people very rich, and these people, wittingly or unwittingly, have vested interest to ridicule any claim to cancer cure, while cancer patients and their families suffer helplessly, often unnecessarily!

On the other hand, it is heartening to note that everyone literally has cancer thousands of times in his lifetime, but the very same thousands of times, the cancer is cured by his own body systems without him knowing.

Generally, everyone is exposed to the same cancer-causing agents, but only in a comparatively small proportion of people, whose yin-yang is disharmonious and energy flow impeded, cancer surfaces as a clinically recognizable disease.

Of the many schools of chi kung that can overcome cancer and other so-called incurable diseases, Shaolin Chi Kung, in my opinion, is the best because of the following five reasons.

While some schools make use of only one or two categories of chi kung exercises, Shaolin Chi Kung uses all; its comprehensive repertoire therefore provides a wider scope to meet the different needs of patients.

Secondly, Shaolin Chi Kung is very powerful; it produces effects in fifteen minutes what it may take an hour in other types of chi kung. Often the benefits are immediate; although it needs a few months of daily practice before cancer or other diseases can be cured, the patient can feel immediately after a Shaolin chi kung session beneficial effects like deep relaxation, joy and elimination of pain. It is certain that his (or her) quality of life will improve.

Fourthly, Shaolin Chi Kung involves the mind, whereas many other types of chi kung are only physical; this allows the patient to reach heightened states of consciousness which can be rewardingly employed to speed up his recovery.

Finally, Shaolin Chi Kung touches on the spiritual, irrespective of one's religion; many of my patients who were dejected and lost because of their suffering, found new hope and meaning in living.

What are the suitable chi kung exercises for curing cancer and other so-called incurable diseases? Appropriately selected exercises from Eighteen Lohan Hands and Self-Manifested Chi Movement, like those described in the previous chapter, are suitable; but exercises from Sinew Metamorphosis and most other martial art chi kung or "hard" chi kung are not. Quiescent breathing and meditation, to be explained in the next chapter, are also suitable for patients with some chi kung experience, but not for beginners.

20
The Internal Cosmos

(A Marvelous Art called the Small Universe)

An exponent of the Small Universe is a living example of radiant health: he is physically fit, emotionally stable, mentally alert and spiritually peaceful.

Man as Miniature of Cosmos

Many people have heard of the Chinese concept, which is also found in many other great civilizations, that man (including woman, of course) is a miniature of the cosmos, but not many know why this is so. This concept may be explained at three levels -- physical, energetic and spiritual — which are actually closely related.

At the physical level, the ingredient that makes us is the same as the ingredient that makes the universe. Centuries before modern scientists, great chi kung masters since ancient times have mentioned that both we and the universe are made of the same chi or energy. The following story by Chuang Tzu (Zhuang Zi), the great 4th century Taoist master, is illustrative of the physical unity between man and the cosmos.

When Hui Zi visited Chuang Tzu to pay his last respect to the his (Chuang Tzu's) wife who had just died, he found Chuang Tzu drumming on a basin and singing.

"Your wife had lived with you and reared your children. Now that she had passed away, it is not enough you do not weep but you even beat music and sing! Isn't it too much?"

Chuang Tzu replied, "Of course I feel for my wife. But then I thought: man originally had no life; not only that, he had no form or spirit. From the midst of formlessness, spirit is born, then form and then life. Now my wife is transformed back from life to form to spirit and to formlessness, like the passing of spring, summer, autumn and winter, and she is now the same as the cosmos. If I wail and weep, it only shows that I am ignorant of this great cosmic truth."

At the energetic level, ancient Chinese scientists and philosophers discovered that there are different types of energy in the universe, and they used various ways to classify them.

Irrespective of the manner of classification, there is a direct relationship between cosmic energy in the universe and vital energy in man. Numerous terms have been used to describe this cosmos-man correspondence, such as "cosmos-man unity" (tian ren he yi), "one body of formlessness" (hun ran yi ti), "myriad things are one" (wan wu wei yi), and "one energy throughout the universe" (tong tian xia yi qi).

The various different types of cosmic energy may be divided into two main groups known as zenith energy (su tian) and nadir energy (zai quan), which correspond to man's vital energy flowing in the conceptual and the governing meridians, or ren mai and du mai.

In other words, the flow and interaction of zenith energy and nadir energy in the cosmos, are similar to those of the governing energy and conceptual energy in man. Hence, the famous art of chi kung that connects the energy flow in these two meridians is known as the Small Universe, or the Micro-Cosmic Flow.

Cosmic energy is often classified into five types according to their characteristic behavior, and they are symbolized by the five elemental processes of metal, water, wood, fire and earth.

These five types of cosmic energy correspond to the five types of vital energy found in man's internal yin organs, namely lungs, kidney, liver, heart and spleen, and their related yang organs, namely colon, urinary bladder, gall bladder, intestines and stomach.

If an alignment of heavenly bodies, for example, generates good metal energy in the cosmos, it will also be propitious for water energy. Similarly, an increase of lung energy in man will also nurture his kidney energy.

Chinese scientists have also classified the different natures of cosmic energy into six types, known figuratively as cold energy, hot energy, dry energy, damp energy, windy energy and fiery energy.

Chinese physicians have found that while the positive effects of these energy types are good for man, their negative effects correspond to the six external causes of illness, which are figuratively termed as cold, heat, dryness, dampness, wind and fire.

At the mind or spiritual level, man is not just a miniature of the cosmos; if he attains enlightenment, which is the highest attainment any being can achieve, he realizes and directly experiences that he IS the cosmos!

In his cultivation to achieve this supreme achievement, he may have glimpses of this ultimate reality, and he realizes in his moment of beauty and inspiration that the skin which presumably separates him from the rest of the cosmos is actually illusory, that there is in ultimate reality no difference between him and the universe!

The actualization of cosmic reality is taught in all off the world's great religions, and is specially emphasized in Buddhism. The Heart Sutra, which is one of the most important scriptures in Mahayana and Vajrayana Buddhism, says:

Form is not different from emptiness; and emptiness is not different from form. Form is emptiness; and emptiness is form.

These famous lines, often quoted but not understood, teaches that in his spiritual cultivation, when an aspirant expands or transcends what he previously and ignorantly thought was his personal mind, he attains Universal Mind where he and the cosmos IS one.

The Small Universe

If you wish to experience the internal cosmos in you, practicing an advanced art of chi kung called the Small Universe, or the Micro-Cosmic Flow, is a good move.

It is prefixed "small" for two reasons: to differentiate from the real universe, and to differentiate it from a more advanced art of chi kung called the Big Universe, or the Macro-Cosmic Flow, where vital energy is cultivated to flow continuously through all the twelve primary meridians directly related to the internal organs. Do not be misled by the adjective "small"; the Small Universe is actually one of the greatest arts of energy known to humanity.

The Small Universe was originally developed by Taoists long before Bodhidharma introduced chi kung in the Shaolin Monastery. Because it is a marvelous art, Shaolin monks, who are Buddhist, learnt it from the Taoists and have valued it very highly.

Hence, in Shaolin Chi Kung there are also many typical Taoist terms and concepts like cosmos (hun yuan), spirit (shen) and will (yi); in Buddhist terms these concepts would normally be called void (kong), mind (xin) and consciousness (shi), although there are some differences in connotation.

The Small Universe is highly appreciated by all the three groups of chi kung practitioners: those who practice chi kung for health, for martial art and for spiritual training.

Summing up the beneficial effects derived from practicing this art, past masters have said, without exaggeration, that "if one attains the breakthrough of the Small Universe, he will eliminate all illness."

The truth of this statement has been time-tested, and has been amply substantiated by my students who have achieved the Small Universe. Radiant health is achieved with the Small Universe because it is a comprehensive and in-depth way of cleansing meridians and harmonizing yin-yang, as explained in the previous chapter.

In the past when a kungfu master achieved the Small Universe, he often gave a banquet to celebrate his success. The ability in maintaining a continuous flow of vital energy throughout the conceptual (ren) and governing (du) meridians when the breakthrough of the Small Universe is attained, enables the practitioner to have tremendous power and stamina.

Moreover, the Small Universe not only acts as a safety precaution against possible harmful effects due to faulty training, but also speeds up the developmental process in advanced martial art chi kung such as Iron Shirt, Golden Bell and Diamond Palm.

In spiritual cultivation, the Small Universe enables the aspirant to merge his personal spirit with the Cosmic Spirit, or in Buddhist terms to transcend his individual mind to realize the Universal Mind.

Taoist masters use the Small Universe as one of their chief methods of cultivation. Chi or vital energy is first circulated round the "small universe", then accumulated as a pearl of elixir in the "dan tian", or field of elixir, at the abdomen. This pearl of elixir, figuratively called the "divine foetus" in Taoism, is imbued with the aspirant's spirit, gradually nurtured and eventually released from the crown of his head as an immortal.

In Zen Buddhism, this pearl of elixir, known as "inner illumination", is cultivated until it expands beyond the illusory boundary of the skin so that inner and outer illumination becomes one or the void in ultimate reality.

Achieving the Small Universal Flow

Obviously such an advanced and fantastic art as the Small Universe should be practiced with the personal supervision of a master. Self practice without proper guidance often results in serious harmful effects.

During one stage of my Small Universe training, I felt solid and stable like a rock. Eager to test my attainment, I asked my wife to push me. She did so at a wrong time, and my chi deviated. Except for some yellowish tint in my otherwise bright eyes, there were no visible signs at all to indicate anything was wrong, but I felt feverish and unsettled. It took me a few months of remedial exercise and medication to recover.

The important point is that if an informed person like me, training with a master's supervision, could develop such serious harmful effect due to a comparatively minor mistake, it is not difficult to imagine what risk a beginner would face if he is stubborn enough to attempt self-training despite clear-cut warning. Thus, the description below is meant for knowledge, **not** for self-practice.

There are different methods employed by different schools to achieve the Small Universe. The method used by us in our Shaolin Wahnam School is as follows.

There are five stages: Abdominal Breathing, Submerged Breathing, Long Breathing, Forceful Small Universe Breathing, and Gentle Small Universe Breathing. Each stage must be attained before progressing to the next one.

Stand upright and relaxed. Smile from the heart and keep the mouth slightly and comfortably open. Place both palms gently above the abdominal dan tian or field of elixir.

Use the palms to deflate the abdomen, and breathe out gently through the mouth, simultaneously visualizing (or thinking) that negative energy or stale air flow up from the body and out through the mouth, Fig 20.1. Pause for a short while. Then release your palms on your abdomen, breathe in gently through the nose, and visualize good cosmic energy flowing into you. Pause for a short while.

Repeat the breathing out, pause, breathing in, pause for a suit-able number of times, the number depending on the nature and progress of the practitioner.

At the end of the Abdominal Breathing exercise, close your eyes (if they are not already close) and stand relaxed at Standing Mediation. Gently think of a pearl of energy at the "qihai" energy field at your abdomen. "Qihai" means "sea of energy".

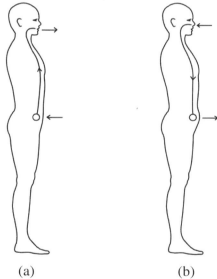

(a)   (b)

Fig 20.1 Abdominal Breathing

At the second stage of Submerged Breathing, the outward form is similar to that at the first stage. But as you deflate your abdomen to breathe out through your mouth, visualize a stream of vital energy flowing from the qihai energy field at the abdomen to the "huiying" energy field between the anus and the end of the spinal column, Fig 20.2. "Huiying" means "meeting of two yings". And as you breathe in gently through your nose, visualize a stream of cosmic energy flowing into your qihai energy field. Repeat for a suitable number of times.

At the end of the Submerged Breathing exercise, stand at Standing Meditation, close your eyes and gently think of a pearl of energy like a silvery moon at your huiying energy field.

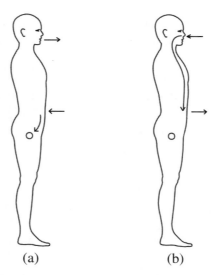

(a)   (b)

Fig 20.2 Submerged Breathing

At the third stage, stand relaxed as before, but as you breathe in gently through your nose, visualize a stream of cosmic energy flowing down right to your huiying energy field.

As you breathe out through your mouth, visualize a stream of your vital energy flowing from the huiying energy field near the coccyx up the whole spine to the "baihui" energy field at the crown of the head, Fig 20.3. "Bai-hui" means "meeting of hundreds of meridians". Repeat for a suitable number of times. After the Long Breathing exercise, remain at Standing Meditation and visualize a pearl of energy like a golden sun at the crown of your head.

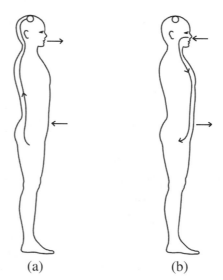

(a)   (b)

Fig 20.3 Long Breathing

In the fourth stage of Forceful Small Universe, breathe in using your chest, instead of using your abdomen as in the earlier breathing methods. As you breathe in cosmic energy gently through your nose, your chest rises and your abdomen falls, Fig 20.4. Place the tip of your tongue at your upper gum just above your front teeth. Simultaneously visualize a stream of vital energy flowing from your huiying energy field near your anus up the spine to your baihui energy field at the top of your head.

Then breathe out about 70 percent of your chi (or breath) gently through your mouth, placing the tip of your tongue at your lower gum just below your front teeth; your chest falls and your abdomen rises.

Simultaneously visualize a stream of vital energy flowing from your baihui energy field down the front part of your head and body to your qihai energy at your abdomen. Then gently swallow the remaining 30 percent of your chi with your saliva into your abdomen, and visualize a stream of vital energy flowing from your abdomen to your huiyin energy field, thus completing the continuous stream of vital energy round your body in the ren mai and du mai, or the conceptual and governing meridians. Repeat for a suitable number of times.

After this, close your eyes at Standing Meditation, and visualize your vital energy flowing continuously in the Small Universe.

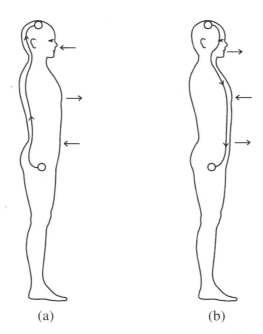

(a)   (b)

Fig 20.4 Forceful Small Universe at Standing Upright

When you can perform the Forceful Small Universe fairly well while standing upright, progress to practicing the art at the Cosmos Stance, Fig 20.5. The procedure is the same, except the stance is different. But at Standing Meditation at the end of the practice, the feet are together as before.

Fig 20.5 Forceful Small Universe at Cosmos Stance

In the final stage of Gentle Small Universe, revert to abdominal breathing, but remain at the Cosmos Stance. As you breathe in gently through your nose, your abdomen rises; place the tip of your tongue at your upper gum and visualize a stream of cosmic energy flowing into your qihai energy field at your abdomen.

As you breathe out gently through your mouth, your abdomen falls; place the tip of your tongue at your lower gum and visualize a stream of vital energy flow from your qihai down to your huiyin at your anus, up the spine to baihui at the head, then down again to your mouth, thus completing the micro-cosmic flow of the Small Universe. Repeat for a suitable number of times. Then bring your feet together to stand upright at Standing Meditation, and visualize the continuous flow of the Small Universe.

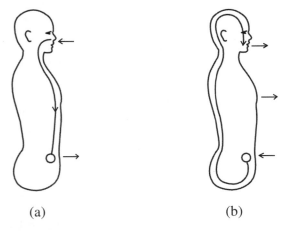

(a)   (b)

Fig 20.6 Gentle Small Universe

Breakthrough and Time Difference

The aim of the Small Universe is to attain what is called a "real" breakthrough of the ren and du meridians, in contrast to a "false" breakthrough.

In a "real" breakthrough, the ren and du meridians are continuously filled with chi flowing in a never-ending circuit; there is no gaps in the stream of energy through the two principal meridians round the body.

In a "false" breakthrough, the two meridians are not continuously filled; there is only a "bubble" or some "bubbles" of energy going through the two meridians round the body, and there are wide gaps in between where there is no energy flow.

The breakthrough is termed "false" because the energy flow is not an never-ending stream, and the "bubbles" of energy may be diffused to other parts of the body resulting in energy blockage again.

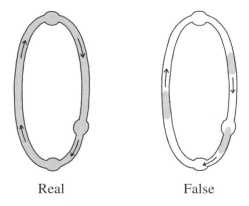

Real   False

Fig 20.7 Real and False Breakthroughs

A false breakthrough, which is also beneficial although its benefits are far, far behind those of a real breakthrough, may be attained in a few days with appropriate chi kung exercises, such as those from Self-Manifested Chi Movement. A master with relevant techniques may induce a false breakthrough in a practitioner in a matter of minutes.

A real breakthrough obviously needs a much longer time to achieve. In the past when conditions were different and the standard demanded of chi kung was very high, practitioners might take more than ten years to achieve a real breakthrough. Now in my chi kung school if all the three factors of methodology, teacher and student are ideal, students take only about six months to accomplish a real breakthrough in the Small Universe!

Why is there such a big difference in the time needed to attain the Small Universe? It is due to the big difference in the three factors of methodology, teacher and student. I myself took three years to accomplish the Small Universe, and in my times it was considered a very remarkable achievement.

In the past when chi kung information was scarce (as it was the norm for masters to keep their secrets), the methods used by many past practitioners might not be the best available for achieving the Small Universe. Naturally, if the methods were inferior, even if they led to the Small Universe, it would take a much longer time.

As evident from chi kung literature, two commonly used methods in the past were "Abdominal Breathing" and "Visualization at Silent Sitting". The practitioner performed Abdominal Breathing for such an extended time that his vital energy "overflowed" and ultimately completed the Small Universe. In Visualization at Silent Sitting, the practitioner sat cross-legged in meditation and used his mind power to will his vital energy to accomplish the small universal chi flow.

The set-backs of these classical methods when compared to the modern methods described earlier are easily discernible. If the practitioner had not cleared that part of his ren meridian between his naval and his anus, prolonged abdominal breathing might result in a "bloated" abdomen. If the other practitioner in the Visualization at Silent Sitting did not have sufficient vital energy to start with, and did not know how to tap cosmic energy to increase his energy volume, his visualization alone was unlikely to produce the small universal chi flow.

The second factor in the training of any art involves the teacher. In the past masters purposely tested the patience and suitability of students, especially in learning such an advanced art as the Small Universe.

When my master taught me the Small Universe, he did not tell me it was the Small Universe; he merely showed me a seemingly simple posture and told me to practice it daily without further explanation. He left me at that for a few weeks — though he secretly supervised me — until he found I had developed sufficient foundation for the next stage of the training.

Many of my classmates could not continue simply because they had not practiced enough for the required foundation, and they missed this fantastic art without even being aware of it.

But the most important factor in the training of any art is the student himself. Even if he has the best method and the best teacher, but if he himself is not willing or not ready to practice, there will be little or no accomplishment.

The modern student compares very favorably with his olden counterpart in this respect. A student who has easy access to chi kung knowledge, knows exactly what he is aiming at, has his training program methodologically set up by a sympathetic teacher, is inspired by the proven success of his fellow classmates, is more willing and ready to put in daily effort to acquire the Small Universe than his counterpart in the past who might not even know what art he was training.

But there is definitely a significant difference in the standard of the art between a practitioner in the past who had spent ten years on it, and a modern student who has trained for only six months.

Although the breakthrough of the Small Universe in both persons are real, the energy flow of the past practitioner was a huge column, whereas that of the modern student is only a tiny stream.

What we had gain in time, we have to sacrifice in standard, but if the modern student continues to practice, he too can acquire a huge column of energy flow. Yet, for our modern purposes, even a tiny stream of energy flowing continuously in the ren and du meridians provides us with tremendous benefits, which can be confirmed by signs indicative of the Small Universe.

Signs of a Real Breakthrough

What are the signs to tell us that we have attained a real breakthrough of the Small Universe?

Firstly, if you have attained the Small Universe, you will have eliminated all illness if you have any, and will be spared all illness in all your future life! This is guaranteed by generations of past masters. An exponent of the Small Universe is a living example of radiant health: he is physically fit, emotionally stable, mentally alert and spiritually peaceful.

So if you still suffer from any pains or disease, you have not achieved a real breakthrough of the Small Universe; if you have practiced the art before yet you are still not healthy, you have merely learnt the techniques but not acquired the "force".

Secondly, attaining a real breakthrough in the Small Universe provides you with a never-ending supply of energy. As soon as some energy from your small universal flow is used up, it can be readily replenished from the cosmos.

Hence you have tremendous power and stamina for martial art, sports and work. Shaolin masters could spar for hours without becoming tired because they made use of their Small Universe. For Lao Ker Yew, my student about seventy years old, the Small Universe not only cured him of about a dozen diseases including kidney problem, arthritis, rheumatism and hernia, but also enables him to out-last opponents three times younger than him in games like badminton!

There are also many signs that frequently show up during the Small Universe practice. Some students actually feel a stream of energy flowing round their conceptual and governing meridians; others experience sensations of electric sparks or warmth.

Feelings like pain, sour sensations and of needles prickling at diseased sites are common; these are indications that their vital energy is working to relieve the practitioners of their illness. An almost certain sign is a pulsation at the anus, and later a quivering effect at the lips when the lower and then the upper gaps between the ren and du meridians are bridged. Pulsation at the crown of their head, and a sensation like shampooing the hair are also frequent.

During meditation in the Small Universe, many students have interesting and extraordinary experiences, such as feeling as if part or whole of their body is missing, and psychicaly seeing their pearl of energy in their abdomen or their energy flow in various parts of their body.

As their mind has expanded, many practitioners are surprised that many problems which puzzled them before now appear to be very clear. The physical world also looks more beautiful. Some feel that they have merged with the void. All these beautiful experiences are expression of their spiritual development.

Yet, all these achievements of the Small Universe, and all other arts of Shaolin Chi Kung including the more advanced Big Universe, as well as all the fantastic accomplishments in Shaolin Kungfu like Cosmos Palm, Golden Bell and the arts of lightness are like a drop of water in a boundless ocean when compared to the highest attainment in Zen, if it is ever attained!

This is because however great or marvelous the achievements in chi kung or kungfu may be, they are concerned with our present *one* life, whereas the highest achievement in Zen solves for us here and now the myriad problems of life and death, liberating us from the endless cycle of *countless* births and rebirths to attain everlasting bliss.

That was why the Buddha, Bodhidharma and many other great minds willingly gave up their throne to seek, and help others to seek, this greatest achievement. Of course, for those who are not ready, this endeavor does not make sense.

Nevertheless, the last six chapters, which are to me the most important chapters of this book, provide the philosophy and methods for this spiritual quest, irrespective of one's religion. But before that, let us study in the next two chapters, two other worldly Shaolin arts, namely traumatology and poetry.

21
Do Not Worry If You Have Broken Your Bones

(An Introduction to Shaolin Traumatology)

In Chinese traumatology, of which the Shaolin tradition is the most famous, treating a patient injured with a fracture is not merely setting the bone, dressing it in a plaster cast, and leaving God do the healing.

A Unique System to Treat Injury

What would you do if you accidentally sustain a powerful punch or kick from your sparring partner? I was appalled to learn that many instructors routinely ignore such injuries sustained during sparring, or similar injuries from sports like football and gymnastics.

This is probably one reason why many students and even instructors are not healthy as evident from their dull eyes and complexion, although they are physically fit, because the untreated injuries accumulated in their sparring have insidiously weakened their body systems.

A student once told me that when he was hard of breathing after sustaining a kick, his instructor merely asked him to bend his body a few times them jump about to let his blood flow! If an injury is serious, the victim is rushed to a hospital, but often doctors are unsure of how to treat the injury except checking and ensuring that the victim's heart and other essential systems are functioning properly.

Such injuries, however, are always treated competently by kungfu masters. It is usual for kungfu masters to know traumatology, which is a branch of Chinese medicine specializing in the treatment of injury.

Shaolin traumatology is the best known in China, and probably the best system for treating injury in the world, as will be substantiated in this chapter. All my four kungfu masters were traumatology experts. Traumatology belongs to kungfu as well as to Chinese medicine, and is unique in the world. As far as I know, no other martial arts or medical systems, do we find a specialized discipline dealing with injury.

The Chinese make a distinction between sickness (*bing*) and injury (*shang*): sickness is caused by the internal failure of the body to harmonize with the environment, whereas an injury is inflicted externally.

For example, if gems enter your body and you fail to overcome them due to certain internal failure of your body systems, you suffer a sickness. If you fall and have a cut, despite your healthy bodily functions, you sustain an injury. Normally your body is able to harmonize with the new environment of excess gems entering through the cut, but if it fails to do so then a sickness may follow.

The formal term for traumatology in Chinese medicine is *shang ke*, which literally means the knowledge of injury; but it is better known by its colloquial kungfu term of "die da" (pronounced as "t'iet t'a") in Mandarin, or "tit ta" in Cantonese.

"Die da" or "Tit ta" literally means "falls and hits", which are two principal causes for the types of injury treated in traumatology, such as bruises, sprains, cuts, dislocations, fractures, internal blood clot, energy blockage, and damage to internal organs. As traumatology is a wide and deep subject, its description in this chapter is necessarily a brief introduction.

Various Types of Injuries

Injuries may be conveniently divided into two classes: external injuries of skin, muscles and bones; and internal injuries of blood, energy and internal organs.

Skin injuries may be open such as a cut where the skin is broken, or close such as a bruise where the skin is intact. An open skin injury may be simple, like a wound caused be a sharp weapon; or complex, like the skin and flesh being smashed up by an Iron Palm strike or by a motor accident.

Similarly, a close skin injury may be simple, like a blood clot in the flesh; or complex, like serious internal hemorrhage affecting internal organs. An open, simple skin injury may not necessarily be less serious or urgent than a close, complex one. For example if an open, simple cut is deep enough, the resultant loss of blood can be immediately life threatening.

Injury to muscles is very common amongst adults, whether during martial art training or in daily life. Most patients who consult traumatologists today complain of muscle injuries like twisted necks, sprained ankles, or back pains often caused by blood blockage due to damaged muscles. Muscle injuries may be caused by a direct, impact force, or by a spiral, turning force. Simple muscle injuries restrict bodily movements, while serious muscle injuries interrupt energy flow and affect internal organs.

Bone injuries are classified as external because bones are outside body tissues, in contrast to injuries to blood, energy and internal organs which are within the body tissues.

If an injury affects only the bone surface, it is classified as minor; if it involves joint dislocation or fracture, it is regarded as major. Simple dislocation and fracture usually do not present much problem, but complex bone injuries like when a dislocation has affected the nervous system, or a fracture has pierced an internal organ, must always be left to a competent specialist.

While injuries to the skin, muscles and bones are considered external, injuries to blood, vital energy and internal organs are internal. However one must bear in mind that the classification is meant for convenience. Blood flow and energy flow are always affected, or "injured" in Chinese medical terms, in any form of injuries.

There are two main kinds of internal blood injuries, namely irregular blood flood and internal blood blockage. Irregular blood floor, figuratively called "angry blood", refers to blood flowing outside its proper places, i.e. blood vessels.

It can be caused by a violent impact, such as from a powerful blow of a martial artist, a fall from a high place, or a motor accident, with symptoms like the patient vomiting blood or blood oozing out from various orifices.

The injury could be more serious, though less frightening outwardly, if the "injured" blood does not flow out "irregularly" but lodged in the patient's body as internal blood blockage. Although such injuries pose a great problem to conventional doctors, they can be readily treated in Shaolin traumatology.

Another area where the west can learn much from Shaolin traumatology and Chinese medicine, involves injury of chi or vital energy. In fact, according to Chinese medical philosophy all sickness is ultimately caused by disharmonious energy flow, or "energy injury", which can result in a breakdown of the body's natural defense system against contagious diseases, disruption of the functions of internal organs causing organic illness, and blockage of emotional energy bringing about psychiatric problems. In traumatology, the term "energy injury" generally refers to deviated flow and blockage of vital energy in the body.

Deviated energy flow can be caused by intense negative emotion or a sudden distraction to mental concentration. An intense fright, for example, may cause energy to flow wildly, resulting in loss of urinary or excretory control. Prolong deviated energy flow makes the patient fidgety and nervous. Taking tranquilizers, as is common in western medicine, is merely attending to the symptoms, but not the cause of the disorder.

Blocked energy can be inflicted by a kungfu master using "soft" or internal force to strike an opponent without leaving any external mark. It can also be caused by the person himself in faulty training of advanced kungfu. Such injuries of vital energy can lead to serious complications, such as disorientation of motor nerves, weakening of the feedback system, or dysfunction of internal organs.

Unless the physician or therapist is well versed in Chinese medical philosophy or a medical system with rich knowledge of energy connections, it may be difficult to discern the relationship between these serious disorders and energy blockage. Hence doctors trained in conventional medicine are quite helpless when faced with such disorders, because chi or vital energy is not in their medical vocabulary.

When patients with serious energy injury submit themselves to elaborate and expensive medical tests, the machines often say there is nothing clinically wrong with them. I have had many patients with such an experience; this is because western medical instruments at present do not measure vital energy.

However if the same patients consult kungfu masters or Chinese physicians, just by looking at the patients' face or listening to the way they speak, even before feeling their pulse and attempting other means of diagnosis, the masters and physicians can easily tell that the patients' energy flow is seriously blocked or deviated.

Injury to internal organs can be directly caused, such as by a kick to the liver, or indirectly caused like a strike to a vital point by a kungfu master who knows "dian xue" ("dim mak" in Cantonese") whereby the energy blockage at the vital point affects its related internal organ. A direct injury is usually structurally damaged, whereas the damage of an indirect injury is usually functional.

By "dotting" or striking the "qimen" vital point below the opponent's ribs, for example, a master can interrupt the function of the opponent's liver, resulting in serious but insidious injury.

If a western specialist examines the liver, he will find nothing structurally wrong with it; if he tries to increase the function of the malfunctioning liver by injecting hormones or by other medical means, he would aggravate the injury, because the fault lies not in the liver but at the qimen vital point.

As a rough analogy, the specialist's action is like charging more electricity directly to a bulb (and thus may damage it) when the fault is an interruption of the flow of electric current at a major intersection. A Shaolin master could restore his liver function by releasing the energy blockage at the qimen vital point.

Faulty training of kungfu force or a sudden influx of tremendous negative emotion can also injure an organ. For example, striking a palm on a sandbag unremittingly and without proper medication or chi kung cleansing exercises, may harm meridians that affect the heart or the eyes.

Tremendous grief injures a person's lungs, making him vulnerable to pulmonary diseases. Taking vitamins to strengthen the injured organ or its system, or taking antibiotics to kill the micro-organisms that attack the organ, is only an ad hoc means to treating the symptoms. A traumatologist would first eliminate the cause that injured the organs; then use appropriate means to restore the damaged function and structure of the organs.

Therapeutic Principles in Traumatology

After a brief survey of various types of common injuries in traumatology, let us examine some essential therapeutic principles before studying the therapeutic methods. The following three principles are very important.

1. Balance between local and holistic treatment.
2. Attention to both external and internal injury.
3. Coordination between static and dynamic approaches.

Suppose a student broke his arm in a sparring practice. Setting the fracture properly, which is the local treatment, is only part of the traumatologist's task. He must bear in mind that the local fracture will have repercussion over the whole body; thus, holistic treatment is also necessary.

The traumatologist should ensure, for example, that the patient's blood flow and energy flow are back to normal, his defense system is strengthened to prevent possible exploitation by external as well as internal disease causing agents, and all organs carry on their normal functions. In other words, he must ensure balance of local and holistic treatment; and he must remember that he is treating not a fracture but a patient.

A fracture is considered an external injury, but the traumatologist must remember the internal damage caused by this external injury. For example, the fracture results in blood flowing out of its blood vessels, and as the skin is not broken, the disorderly blood flow will cause internal blood clot.

The blood clot, together with tiny bone fragments not only affect a proper setting of the fractured bone, but also interrupt smooth flow of blood and energy urgently needed at the injured site. Thus appropriate measures, like external application of herbs and the taking of internal medicinal concoction, must be taken to clear the internal blockage.

Moreover, the traumatologist must strengthen the patient's liver and kidneys, the two organs particularly affected by a fracture, as they have to work extra hard to regulate and produce blood and bones respectively. The traumatologist does not want his patient to recover from his fractured arm at the expense of weakening his kidney or liver. All this represents paying attention to both external and internal injury.

While it is important to immobilize a fractured bone after it is properly set, it is also essential to maintain its normal dynamism as a living organ, and not relegate it as a superfluous limb temporary cast aside during the period of its healing. This is the principle of coordination between static and dynamic approaches.

Comparing the standard approaches between western orthopedists and Chinese traumatologists is illuminating. A western orthopedist usually casts the arm in plaster of Paris to immobilize it. The cast is broken only after a few months when the fracture has been healed.

This breaking open of the plaster cast is often of much trepidation, with the patient and often the orthopedist hoping that the arm which they have not seen for a few months would turn out satisfactorily. The orthopedist routinely accepts a small margin of displacement so long as the function of the arm is restored.

On the other hand, a Chinese traumatologist uses splints and bandages to immobilize the fractured arm. Some people may think this method primitive, but they are unaware that the traumatologist prefers this to the plaster cast (which he could use if he wants to), because of its many advantages.

Firstly it spares the patient the agony of scratching the surface of the plaster of Paris when the real itch is the arm below it. Secondly the splints and bandages can be replaced easily, thus permitting the traumatologist to apply and change appropriate medication on the fractured bone for various important purposes like easing pain and itch, clearing blockage, draining away dead cells, and promoting energy and blood flow to speed up recovery. Thirdly, within reasonable limits, this splints and bandages method enables the patient to move his arm close to normal conditions so that his arm would not be shriveled after a few months of unuse, and he would not have to perform follow-up physiotherapy exercises to use his arm again.

But the most important advantage of using splints and bandages instead of plaster of Paris for immobilization is that it allows the traumatologist to check the alignment of the fractured arm at all times, and to correct the slightest misalignment as soon as it occurs, so that perfect alignment is expected, instead of being left to chance as often is the case in western treatment.

Chinese traumatologists regard immobilization by means of plaster of Paris as unsatisfactory because although the arm is fixed externally, internal movements like blood flow, muscle twitching and tendon jerking do affect bone alignment.

Treating a Broken Bone

With an understanding of its therapeutic principles, we are now ready to study how a traumatologist treats a patient with a simple fractured arm. For convenience, the treatment may be divided into three stages: initial, middle and concluding.

First the traumatologist tells the patient not to worry, and assures him that his injury is under control, which is the truth for if the traumatologist feels that any case is beyond his ability he must not treat it. It is a basic ethical principle that a healer treats his patients only within his confidence and ability. Of course if a case beyond his ability is immediately life threatening, he should provide first aid as best as he can to sustain life, and redirect the case to proper professionals.

If there is swelling at the fracture site, the traumatologist will reduce swelling and stop pain before treating the broken bone. As patients are usually anxious to have their broken bones mended immediately, the traumatologist should explain that it is better to reduce pain and swelling first, and that fractured bones can be left unattended even for a few days if they are properly immobilized by bandages.

Reducing swelling and pain, as well as clearing blockage and promoting blood and energy flood can be easily achieved by applying stuck-on medication of appropriate medical mixtures with herbs like *pu huang* (Typha latifolia), *da huang* (Rheum officinale), *mo yao* (Commiphoria myriha) and *ru xiang* (Pistacia lentiscus).

When swelling has subsided, the affected part is gently massaged with medicinal wine possessing local anesthetic effect, and then the fractured bone is carefully set using appropriate manipulative methods. In Shaolin traumatology, these manipulative methods to set dislocations and fractures are given poetic names like "Across the Plain into the Cave" (for dislocation of a spinal vertebra), "Playing with the Unicorn" (for dislocation of the femur), and "Drawing the Precious Sword" (for fracture of the ulna).

This setting of the fractured bone is the most crucial part in the treatment of fractures, and it demands great manipulative skills and experience. If the bone is not properly set, the arm will be deformed when healed.

A deformed arm, such as the arm is slightly shorter or its functions are restricted, is probably the worst thing that can happen to a conscientious traumatologist, for the patient would carry the deformity for life. Any ethical traumatologist will therefore make doubly sure that both the function and the normal appearance of the fractured limb are restored.

The traumatologist also prescribes for internal consumption medical recipes such as "Tou Ren (Semen Perisae) Decoction" and "Xi Jiao Di Huang (Cornu Rhinoceri and Radix Rehmanniae) Decoction" to clear internal hemorrhage and correct disorderly flow of blood.

Clearing internal hemorrhage and correcting "disordered" blood, two aspects often neglected in western treatment, are very important; otherwise it will affect the production of new blood and its harmonious flow, thus hindering speedy recovery.

At the middle stage of treatment, the main objective is to restore the natural functions and abilities of the patient. In Chinese medical terms, this is known as "restoring good", as compared to the initial stage of "eliminating evil", i.e. eliminating all pathogenetic factors like swelling, pain, blood and energy blockage, and the fracture itself.

In "restoring good" the traumatologist is guided by the following three techniques: "harmonizing nutrients and stopping pain", "joining bones, muscles and tendons", and "loosening muscles and cleansing meridians".

When "harmonizing nutrients and stopping pain", the traumatologist restores the natural self-curative and self-regenerative abilities of the patient, and at the same time removes whatever pain his injury may cause him.

The pain may be local or general, at the fracture site or elsewhere. Localized pain, for example, may be experienced in the arm due to a resultant energy blockage, or spread over the whole body in the form of anxiety. Restoring the patient's natural abilities and eliminating pain can be achieved by means of external or internal medication, or both.

The principle of "joining bones, muscles and tendons" is to ensure that the set bones are properly aligned, dead cells are cleared away, blood and energy flow is harmonized, bone production is increased, and muscle and tendon functions are improved.

Medicinal recipes like "Decoction for Correcting Bones and Creating Blood" and "Powder for Comforting Muscles and Activating Meridians" are prescribed. If the traumatologist is also well versed in chi kung, he can transmit vital energy to the patient to stimulate better blood and chi flow. If needed, appropriate physiotherapy exercises may be recommended.

The principle of "loosening muscles and cleansing meridians" is for overcoming pathogenetic conditions like energy and blood stagnation, residue of blood clot, stiffness of muscles and joints, and rheumatic pains. "Bolus for Comforting and Strengthening Tendons" and "Decoction for Joining Bones and Activating Blood" are helpful medicinal recipes. Any chi transmitted to the patient will be a great help.

At the concluding stage, the main objective is to nourish the patient so that he becomes as healthy and fit, or even healthier and fitter, as he was before his injury. Four fundamental principles to achieve this objective are "invigorating energy and nurturing blood", "nourishing spleen and stomach", "nourishing liver and kidneys", and "warming and clearing meridians".

As the patient has used up much of his vital energy and blood for his recuperation, and has not been doing regular exercises, it is necessary to replenish his energy and blood to restore his natural resistance to diseases. The "Eight Precious Herbs Decoction" is an excellent recommendation. It is also necessary to restore his appetite by strengthening his spleen and stomach systems. The "Strengthening Spleen Nurturing Stomach Decoction" is a good choice.

During recuperation, the liver and the kidney systems work extra hard to replenish injured muscles and bones. Nourishing the liver and kidneys, like taking the "Six Herbs with Da Huang Pills", is helpful.

A patient undergoing long period of treatment often suffer from stagnation of vital energy and blood, as well as from external pathogenic causes like "wind", "dampness" and "cold". These problems can be overcome by "warming and clearing meridians" with such medicinal recipes like "Ginseng Purple Gold Pills" and "Ma Gui Warming Meridians Decoction". Remedial chi kung exercises, like appropriate selections from the Eighteen Lohan Hands, are very helpful.

Hence, in Chinese traumatology, of which the Shaolin tradition is the most famous, treating a patient who has a fracture is not merely setting the bone, dressing it in a plaster cast, and leaving God do the healing.

The traumatologist, equipped with a comprehensive framework of therapeutic principles and making use of all the main approaches in Chinese medicine, including massage therapy, herbalism, external medicine and chi kung therapy, treats the patient holistically, and not just the injury.

22

The Songs And Poetry Of Shaolin

(Describing the Grandeur in Rhythm and Rhyme)

Jade mountains and fragrant clouds start the spiritual realm. Pearl forests and rains of flowers still the heart of Zen.

Emperor's Praise and Master's Advice

The above poetic couplet was written by the famous Emperor Qian Long of the Qing Dynasty for the Bodhidharma Chamber of Shaolin Monastery. Poetic couplets, which follow certain literary rules like tonal values and mutually matching meanings, are a unique form of Chinese literature. The two lines of a poetic couplet are frequently hung one line at each side of an important portal.

"Jade mountains" in the top line of the above poetic couplet, harmonizes with "pearl forests" in the bottom line in both tonal values and matching meanings. The two Chinese words *yu xiu* for "jade mountains" spoken in a "falling" tone, harmonize with *zhu lin* for "pearl forests" spoken in an "even" tone; "jade" and "mountains" harmonize with "pearl" and "forests" in meaning respectively.

Other expressions like "silver streams" or "golden pavilions" will be inappropriate because they are not congruous in tone or meaning. Similarly, "fragrant clouds", "start" and "spiritual realm" harmonize with "rains of flowers" (written as "flower rains" in Chinese), "still" and "heart of Zen" ("Zen heart") respectively. "And" and "the" in the English translation are not necessary in original Chinese. The poetic couplet in the Chinese language reads elegantly yet majestically as follows:

Yu xiu xiang yun kai fa jie
zhu lin hua yu jing chan xin

The beauty of the couplet, however, lies not merely in its harmonious music created by certain literary rules, or the fact that it was composed by an emperor, but in the subtleness and depth of meaning. Jade mountains and pearl forests aptly describe the marvelous environment of the Shaolin Monastery, with five summits known as "Five Bosom Peaks" in the background, and surrounding trees which blossom as if with pearls.

"Fragrant clouds" is a familiar term in the opening praises in Buddhist scriptures which are chanted daily in the monastery. "Spiritual realm" is a gentle reminder that the aim of the Shaolin Monastery is for dedicated aspirants to seek spiritual fulfillment.

"Rains of flowers", besides portraying the blossoming scene in spring, is another familiar Buddhist term indicative of the coming of enlightenment. "Still the heart of Zen" suggests that Zen, or the highest spiritual fulfillment, is transmitted from heart to heart, and its attainment reveals the undifferentiated tranquility of cosmic reality.

Another interesting and profound poetic couplet of Shaolin is as follows, with its English translation below it:

Miao fa fa zhong sheng miao fa
Qi gong gong shang jian qi gong

In wonderful techniques are created more wonderful techniques
Upon marvelous force is revealed further marvelous force

This poetic couplet, written not on doorways or walls but in the hearts of many Shaolin disciples, is a guiding principle in my Shaolin Wahnam School. Its teaching has been illustrated many times in this book.

For example, in the chapters on kungfu techniques, there are many situations where it appears as if the exponent simply has no way to get himself out of the opponent's wonderful technique, such as being locked in a seemingly unbreakable manner, or being kicked at while both hands are held.

Yet, in the nick of time, the Shaolin exponent not only neutralizes the opponent's wonderful technique, but reverses the situation more wonderfully that the opponent even in his defeat cannot help a feeling of awe and respect.

To many people breaking a brick with a palm strike is a marvelous feat. It is more marvelous when they find that the palm is not rough and tough, but soft and gentle. If the master puts one brick on top of another, and by striking the top brick with the Shaolin Cosmos Palm he breaks the bottom brick while the top brick is intact, it is even more marvelous.

Upon such marvelous force, further marvelous force is revealed when the master uses his Cosmos Palm to heal people, in an incredible but seemingly simple way, of so-called incurable diseases.

The above poetic couplet was composed by a great master of Southern Shaolin Kungfu in the Qing Dynasty, the Venerable Xing Yin, who was the most senior disciple of the First Patriarch of Southern Shaolin Kungfu, the Venerable Zhi Shan.

Their names, like the names of all great monks, are meaningful and poetic too, showing that the Chinese choose names with deep thought and care. "Zhi Shan" means "Extreme Kindness", and "Xing Yin" means "Retreat to Cultivate Amidst the Almond Grove."

"Almond grove" is a figurative term in Chinese meaning "circles of scholars", indicating that the Venerable Xing Yin, like many other Shaolin masters, are expert in both the martial as well as the scholarly arts. Being well versed in both literature and kungfu, known as *wen wu shuang quan*, is the ideal of a cultured person.

Breadth of Kungfu in a Song

Shaolin Monastery is rich in poetry. Not only emperors, poets and scholars have written beautiful poetry to praise it, much of the Shaolin arts are also recorded in poetic writings called "songs of secrets", or *ge que*. It is quite amazing that virtually all the main points of such an extensive field like Shaolin Kungfu are summarized in the following poetic song.

> Shaolin Kungfu includes eighteen different arts
> The fist is the source of fighting techniques
> Unarmed combat lays the foundation for weapon sets
> Force training is superior to punches and kicks
> Vital energy to be channeled, applied and tapped
> Train the hands, legs, body, footwork, and eyes
> Strengthen bones and muscles and other body parts
> Tell real from false, separate front from behind
> Employ the palm, the fingers, and the punch
> Comprehend principles besides developing skills
> Let the mind be fresh and the heart relaxed
> The art of breathing can be dynamic or still
> When alone it is suitable to develop force
> With partners train how to spar and fight
> The secret of success is diligent practice
> Mastering the arts use both brain and might

The meaning of the above *ke que* or song of secrets is self explanatory; yet the following comments are helpful. Shaolin Kungfu is extensive, and includes all the eighteen classes of kungfu weapons. Any person who wishes to use any weapon well must first put in some time and effort in unarmed combat, as it provides the foundation for all weapon sets.

It is important to develop force and skills, not just learn kungfu form; otherwise what is accomplished is not real kungfu but some form of demonstrative art disparagingly called "flowery fists and embroidery kicks". Chi kung provides the basis energy for force training, and includes the art of channeling energy to wherever we want, applying energy for effective combat, and taping energy from the cosmos.

In Shaolin Kungfu, not just the hands or legs are trained; it includes training all parts of the body, footwork and eyesight. Not only the external body parts are strengthened, but also the bones, muscles and internal cells, tissues and organs.

In this training, as well as in all other aspects of the Shaolin arts, the student must be able to differentiate real benefits from apparent ones, and progress systematically from elementary to advanced levels. For example, merely striking the fist or kicking the leg brutally onto some hard training material gives only false or apparent benefits, because not only the power developed is limited as it is mechanical, but such superficial training may cause irreversible damage to the form, function and other aspects of the hand or leg. In contrast, training that brings real benefits involves strengthening the hand or leg intrinsically, and enhancing their natural functions.

In combat, all aspects of the factor in question should be fully used. For example, in using the hand, the Shaolin exponent does not limit himself to only one particular manner such as punching, but includes other hand forms such as various types of palm and finger attacks. When he employs punching, he does not limit himself to only one form of punching, such as the level punch, but includes other forms of punching like the cup-punch, phoenix-eye punch, leopard punch and elephant punch.

The Shaolin exponent does not only develop force and skills, but also understands the underlying principles of the techniques he uses as well as overall combative principles. For example, he does not merely learn a certain defensive technique against some attack situations, but he also understands why this particular technique is preferred to other techniques, what necessary force or skill he should have to execute it competently, and in what situations this technique would not be suitable. Mental freshness, emotional stability and breath control are also studied.

Shaolin Kungfu training can be carried out alone or with partners, and both ways should be practiced. Yet, the most important single factor of becoming a master is diligent practice, without which all these priceless guidelines become useless. A Shaolin master is not one who merely has might; he also has brain.

Songs of Energy and Compassion

The following verse, or song of secrets, highlights the crucial points in chi or energy training, which as mentioned in the preceding verse is the basis of force development, which in turn is superior to practicing kungfu form.

Circulation of chi is graceful and gentle
Application of chi is forceful and fast
Moving forward the breath shoots out
Moving back in comes the breath at last
In rolling momentum the body moves
In the midst of movements come the strikes
Being so fast their forms unseen
Hitting the opponent without respite
What's the secret of this marvelous skill
Correct breathing and being inwardly still

The above song advises that if the aim in chi kung training is to circulate chi or vital energy, the breathing and bodily movements are graceful and gentle. But if the aim is to apply vital energy, as in combat, the breathing and bodily movements are forceful and fast.

For example, when practicing Cosmos Palm, the exponent breathes in and out gently, and moves his arms gracefully to build up internal force. But if he uses the Cosmos Palm to strike an opponent during combat, he would do so forcefully and fast, breathing out explosively at the same time.

Generally, when movements are forward, such as in executing a punch or a kick, the exponent breathes out; but when the movements are inward, like pulling back a punch or retreating his body to "swallow" an attack, he breathes in.

During combat, breathing is coordinated with momentum so that bodily movements are like huge waves overwhelming the opponent. In the midst of these overwhelming movements the Shaolin exponent shoots out his attacks so fast that the opponent cannot even see their forms properly, and thus the opponent is hit before he even realizes what has happened! What is the secret of this marvelous skill? It lies in correct breathing and in being inwardly still.

Sometimes a verse or a song of secrets can be very concise. The whole art of Shaolin *qin-na*, or holding and gripping the opponent's vital points, can be crystallized into the following stanza of only twenty eight words!

This song of secrets is my own composition, drawing inspiration from the teachings of past Shaolin master, to help me have a clearer perspective of *qin-na*, which happens to be one of my favorite arts. The song is listed below in Romanized Chinese, first in its original sound in Cantonese (my native tongue), then in Mandarin (which is used for all other verses and poems in this book) to give readers a feel of its rhymes and rhythms, which unfortunately are lost in its English translation that follows.

Chet sap yi pa kam na sau
Sim lam wai hsin pa cheng lau
Fen khen chor jit na yuit fatt

Shen hei fai chuk keng kong yau
Qi shi er ba qin na shou
Shao lin huai shan ba qing liu
Fen jin cuo jie na xue fa
Shen qi kuai su jing kang rou

Seventy two techniques of holds and grips
Compassion is shown in this Shaolin art
Tear muscles, dislodge joints, grip vital points
Spirit and energy, speed, force, soft and hard.

Most people, including those who practice kungfu and understand Chinese, may not understand the verse, because it is purposely written in such a way that even if readers know all the words in the verse, they still will not know its meaning unless they have been initiated.

The first line of the verse reminds the initiated, i.e. one who has practiced and understood the art, of all the seventy two techniques of the Shaolin art of qin-na which he has learnt. The second line reminds him of the Shaolin philosophical teaching on compassion, which dictates that the art of qin-na is specially meant to subdue an opponent without maiming or killing him. How this can be done is summarized in the third line, listing the three main areas of applying qin-na to combat, namely tearing the opponent's muscles, dislocating his joints or gripping his vital points.

All these tactics effectively put the opponent out of action, but without hurting him seriously so that he can later seek a traumatologist to relieve the temporary inhibiting injury. If you strike an opponent's heart or kick his liver, you may maim or kill him.

If you lock his arms and legs, or throw him onto the ground (unless this breaks his bones), he will fight again once you release the lock, or he gets up from the fall. But if you tear his muscles, dislocate his joints (but not break his bones), or grip his vital points, he will be temporarily inactivated.

The fourth line indicates that to achieve this objective of effectively subduing the opponent without hurting him permanently, the exponent must be mentally alert, full of energy, fast and able to use both hard and soft force competently.

In other words, if he merely knows the gripping techniques and may even be successful in applying them, but if he lacks the mental freshness, intrinsic energy, speed and internal force, he will still be unable to subdue the opponent effectively.

This song of secrets therefore describes all the four aspects of qin-na, namely:

1. Form — the seventy two techniques.
2. Philosophy — compassionate fighting; effectively subduing an opponent without permanently hurting him.

3. Application — tearing muscles, dislocating joints, gripping vital points.
4. Force — mental freshness, abundant energy, speed, hard and soft force.

Exquisite Charm of Shaolin

There is no lack of poetry about Shaolin. Among the many poets and scholars who have sung poems to praise Shaolin Monastery in every dynasty, are some of China's best. Due to space constrain, only three poems from the classical period, and one poem from our modern time are illustrated below.

All the poems and verses in this chapter, as well as elsewhere in this book, are taken from Chinese originals, and are translated by me, always keeping to the original meaning and spirit. If readers do not find any poetic beauty in them, the fault lies in my translation.

The earlier "songs of secrets" in this chapter are termed "verses", rather than "poems" because although, at least in their Chinese original, they have metre and rhymes, and often insight (into kungfu), they are usually devoid of personal emotion, which is considered by many literary critics as an essential feature of poetry.

The following poem is by Shen Quan Qi (656-714), who greatly influenced the form and development of the famous *lu shi* of Tang poetry. *Wu yen lu shi*, a poem of four or eight lines with five words to each line, was the most popular poetic genre from the Tang Dynasty.

A Visit to Shaolin Monastery

This accompanying song to visit the precious site
Strolling many times along the forests of pearls
The frost on the pagoda of flying ducks is old
The dragons' pond deep with many years unfurled
Oh the magnificence of the temple after rain
With the great hall glowing in the autumn shade
The returning road shrouded in evening mist
With mountain cicadas chanting in leafy cascade

The beauty of this poem, as typical of the romanticism of Tang poetry, lies in its saying little yet saying a lot. Unlike the verses quoted earlier which supply invaluable advice concerning the Shaolin arts, Shen Quan Qi's poem says nothing substantial on physical matters.

Its description of the picturesque Shaolin Monastery environment with its "forest of pearls", magnificent temple, glowing hall, autumn mist and chanting cicadas, though elegant by itself, does not add much to factual knowledge. The "pagoda of flying ducks" and the "dragons' pond" were past landmarks on the mountain, but had not been preserved to the present days.

But its beauty lies in its poetic music and the delicate outflow of emotions aroused by the exquisite charm of the rustic scene, and conveyed to us by the poet to enrich our emotional experience. For Shen Quan Qi, usually preoccupied with imperial duties, like many of us busy with hectic modern living, the delicate balance of calm and grandeur of the Shaolin environment as revealed in the poem would be both soothing and exhilarating.

Symbolism in Shaolin Poetry

One of the most famous poets of Chinese literature is Bai Ju Yi (Po Chu-i, 772-846), also of the Tang Dynasty, which is regarded by many people as the golden age of Chinese poetry. Despite his demanding job as the Minister of Internal Security, he often visited the Shaolin Monastery and left many poems in its praise.

Bai Ju Yi was a keen student of Zen, but was also much influenced by Taoist philosophy. In his retirement he dedicated his life to poetry and wine, and was known to his friends as the "Recluse of the Fragrant Mountain". The following poem praising the Shaolin Monastery was written in a poetic genre known as *qi yen lu shi*. It is made up of eight lines consisting of seven words each, and is also a very popular form of Tang poetry.

Visit to Shaolin Monastery from Longtan Monastery, dedicated to fellow travelers.

Six or seven fellow travelers wearing peasant cloths and shoes

Flowers in hand, stepping over green grass towards a rippling stream

The moon at Nine Dragons' Lakes is reflected in a glass of wine

Three drafts of cypress breeze vibrate musical strings of dreams

While strong and healthy one should visit this scenic and sacred place

The freshness and coolness make us forget the heat of the summer air

Previously I knew only of riding a crane to fly beyond the clouds

But now I know of becoming a saint here free from worldly cares

The romanticism of Tang poetry is evident here as in the previous poem, but while the former is purely hedonistic, with Shen Quan Qi pouring out his exquisite emotion spontaneously, this poem is also symbolic, suggesting that Bai Ju Yi here is a master craftsman besides being an artist. His craftsmanship is seen in his subtle, perhaps unconscious, exposition of Zen and Taoist philosophy.

"Longtan" (pronounced as "loong th'an") means "Dragons' Lakes". Longtan Monastery in Shanxi Province was related to Shaolin Monastery. Situated near nine lakes, where according to legends dragons came down to frolic, it was a favorite retreat of the famous Empress Wu Ze Tian and her daughter Princess Peace. (In Chinese culture, dragons are majestic divine creatures bringing peace and prosperity.)

Although Bai Ju Yi was an imperial minister, he preferred wearing peasant clothing like his fellow travelers when he visited the Shaolin Monastery, suggesting the simplicity of Zen.

On the other hand, his liking for wine is indicative of his Taoist influence, as drinking wine in cheerful company is a typical Taoist practice. Three drafts of breeze coming from a cypress tree is a symbolic way of saying three experiences of Zen as taught in the Shaolin tradition, and these experiences awaken in him aspirations towards spiritual development.

"Freshness and coolness", while describing the actual pleasant weather conditions at Shaolin, is a symbol for Buddhist wisdom; hence it can be interpreted that Bai Ju Yi found his attainment of Buddhist wisdom helped him to cope with the demands of his ministerial duties.

Previously he aspired to ride a crane to fly beyond the clouds, which means to practice Taoist cultivation to become an immortal. But having practiced Zen and found refuge at the Shaolin Monastery, he discovered he could attain enlightenment here and now.

Legends Recalled in Poetic Beauty

The next poem is by Li Yun Zhong, a professor of the Imperial University in the Song Dynasty. Besides its poetic value, it contains historical interest as it mentions some famous legends in Zen Buddhism.

Staying a Night in Shaolin Monastery

Meeting Ambassador Song Yun at Pamir Heights
Holding one shoe going west, without knowing why
In the mountain attain the art of calming heart
He severed his arm while snow fell from the sky
Striking the ground, clouds reflected in streams
Flower of five petals blossoms from this place
No need to stare at image of the shadow rock
Spiritual body is all over the mountain face

This poem, like Bai Ju Yi's poem above, was written in the poetic genre called *qi yen lu shi*, meaning "poetry of seven words to a line composed according to some special rules of metre and rhyme patterns". But unlike Bai Ju Yi's poem, which can be understood by readers at least at the surface meaning, even without being aware of their underlying symbols, Li Yun Zhong's poem would be incomprehensible if readers do not know the significance of the legends involved. Both poems are of course a contrast to Shen Quan Ji's poem which captivates us not by its contextual meaning but by its exquisite feeling.

Staying in Shaolin Monastery stimulated in Li Yun Zhong nostalgic reflections on some important Shaolin legends about Bodhidharma spreading Zen Buddhism in China. First the poet recalls the miracle about the Ambassador of Northern Wei Dynasty, Song Yun, meeting Bodhidharma at the Pamir Heights, holding only one shoe in his hand, and going westward.

"Where are you going, Master?" the Ambassador asked.

"I am going home."

"But why are you holding only one shoe?"

"You will know when you get to Shaolin Monastery," Bodhidharma replied.

When Song Yun arrived at Shaolin Monastery he learnt to his great surprise that Bodhidharma had passed away. The monks were more surprised when Song Yun told them that he had met Bodhidharma at the Pamir Heights going westward. "That's impossible," they exclaimed. "In fact we buried his body in the hill behind the monastery."

When they dug up the coffin and opened it, they found nothing inside except the other shoe. "Our master have gone home," they said, "and he has left one shoe as evidence of this seemingly impossible happening." They all prostrated three times in the direction of the west in honor of Bodhidharma, the First Patriarch of the Shaolin arts.

Then the poet reflects on how Hui Ke, the Second Patriarch, attained "the art of calming heart" from Bodhidharma, as described earlier in Chapter 2. To show his determination in Zen cultivation, Hui Ke severed his arm in the snow. Later when Bodhidharma visited Hui Ke recuperating in a cave behind the Monastery, the master found that there was no water supply nearby. So he struck the ground with his monk's staff, and hey presto, water flowed out forming four streams, each with a different taste of sweetness, sourness, bitterness and tartness!

Bodhidharma transmitted the "heart of Zen" to Hui Ke, who transmitted it through three generations of Patriarchs to Hui Neng, the Sixth Patriarch. From Hui Neng, regarded by many as the Chinese Buddha, Zen later developed into five schools.

In the last two lines of the poem, Li Yun Zhong says that Zen is found not just by staring at the Bodhidharma's image imprinted in the "shadow rock" (please see Chapter 2); he says that wherever one looks, he can see Zen because the Spiritual Body of the Buddha, which is the Buddhist term for the Supreme Reality, is everywhere. This last line shows the poet's profound understanding of Buddhism. He suggests that spiritual fulfillment is realized not just by orthodox methods like worshipping a divine presence, or faithfully accepting the teaching of a past master, although these methods may be suitable for many people, but the highest spiritual fulfillment can be realized directly now and here if we are spiritually awakened.

A Modern Poem on Shaolin

The modern poem below is by Yan Chen (b. 1911), who is one of the best known poets of modern China. His poetic works have been translated into English, Russian, Japanese, Persian and Korean.

The Road to Shaolin

The road to Shaolin is long, very long,
    Rubbing shoulders and continuing heels along
    the way, with dust flying high.
For what reasons do you go there?
With what curiosity, and what dreams?

The famous Pagoda Forest is now tranquil.
    Eternal life does not necessarily come
    to those who yearn for it.
Only Songshan remains evergreen,
And the mountain stream still flows clear.

The road to Shaolin is tortuous and steep.
    Along the way are found men and women
    who have come from four directions.
What do you seek by going there?
Do you go with faith or go with doubt?

Great masters are sparse like morning stars.
    To accomplish great attainments
    necessitates great sacrifice.
Look at the foot impressions at the training hall,
A deep imprint every step has made.

The returning road is very long and also short.
  The returning road from Shaolin is tortuous
  and also even.
What are you thinking all along the way?
The breeze is so gentle, the sky so blue.
A drop of water will not dry in a river.
  Creativity and success, all start
  with your first step.
Cleanse the dirt from your heart, the whole
  body becomes light and happy,
Only in the happiness of other people can
  you find your greatest happiness.

A modern poem is often open to different interpretations, and readers may like to attempt their own. Explaining some terms, and providing some guiding questions may be helpful.

Pagoda Forest refers to the large collection of pagodas or stupas a few hundred meters from the monastery proper, where the "crystals" or relics of past great monks were kept. Songshan is the mountain system which includes the Shaoshi Mountain where Shaolin Monastery is situated. Deep foot impressions are left in the Shaolin Kungfu training hall today as a result of continuous stamping of monks' feet in the past.

The general theme of the poem that different people have different aspirations as well as different approaches and results in their pursue of the Shaolin arts, is quite clear. What is the significance of the lines in the poem that goes; the famous Pagoda Forest is now tranquil, Songshan remains evergreen, and the mountain stream still flows clear? Why does the poet say that the breeze is so gentle, and the sky so blue? What is the intention of saying a drop of water will not dry in a river? Perhaps most importantly, how would you cleanse the dirt from your heart? What strong emotions or hopes has the poet aroused in you?

For me, the four concluding lines of the poem are most inspiring, and the Shaolin arts have provided me both the philosophy and methods to find my greatest happiness. Different people, understandably, will interpret the dirt in their heart differently, according to their own level of personal understanding and development.

The Shaolin arts provide the principles and practice for our physical, emotional, mental and spiritual development, irrespective of our religious profession or even the lack of it. Describing the same progress in different terms, the Shaolin arts enable us to actualize fully our physical body, energy body and spiritual body, through kungfu, chi kung and Zen.

Hence, from the Shaolin perspective, at the highest level cleansing the dirt from our heart is clearing the phenomenal illusion that has been shrouding our mind, so that we can, as mentioned in an earlier poem, see transcendental reality everywhere. In Zen terms, it is "going home" or "seeing our original face".

The attainment of this highest spiritual fulfillment, known as Zen in the highest Shaolin arts, can be achieved by people of any race, culture or religion. To have a clear understanding of transcendental reality, called variously by different peoples such as God, Allah, Brahman, Tao and the Tathagata, is an intelligent step towards this highest attainment, and will be explained in the next few chapters.

23
The Divine And The Cosmos

(The Magnificence and Universality of All Religions)

Despite our superficial differences, we are all fellow travellers along similar spiritual paths aspiring to the same cosmic reality.

Meeting Place of Many Religions

Many readers must be surprised to discover that throughout history people of different religions — Taoists, Confucianists, Christians, Muslims and others — have voluntarily stayed and practiced the Shaolin arts in the Shaolin Monastery, though it is regarded as a Buddhist monastery. There are three good reasons for this happy situation.

Buddhists have never regarded Buddhism as a religion as the west knows it; they regard Buddhism as the highest teaching open to all people. In other words, Buddhism is not exclusive only to professed followers, nor the followers prevented from accepting other religious teachings. Also, there is nothing whatsoever in the Buddhist teaching that belittles the beliefs of other religions.

Secondly, Shaolin masters have never attempted to convert any students into Buddhism. In fact, those who wished to be ordained as Buddhist monks literally had to beg to be admitted. Many Buddhists believe that converting a pious believer in any religion into Buddhism, may slow down his path to spiritual fulfilment because he is already on his way in his chosen religion.

The third reason is most heart warming. Despite their outward differences in ritualistic practice by the populace, all the major world religions, as revealed by the greatest of their respective masters and scriptures, are similar in their aims and aspirations.

Even the methods the high priests and the adepts employ in seeking spiritual fulfillment, as well as the spiritual ecstasy they experience during the fulfillment, are similar. Perhaps, this has to be so, if Reality or Truth is one, though it can be interpreted in different languages and cultures, and at different levels.

Universality of World's Religions

This fundamental universality of the world's great religions can be readily verified if we examine their highest teachings. In Hinduism, the supreme aim is to unite Atman, the spirit in man, with Brahman, the Universal Reality. The way to achieve this unity, or yoga, is through meditation. The Upanishads, the holy books of the Hindus, teach that:

Brahman is all. From Brahman come appearances, sensations, desires, deeds. But all these are merely name and form. To know Brahman one must experience the identity between Him and the Self, or Brahman dwelling within the lotus of the heart. Only by so doing can man escape from sorrow and death and become one with the subtle essence beyond all knowledge.

Taoism is amazingly similar to Hinduism. In fact, in the above quotation if we replace the term "Brahman" with "Tao", it can readily express the essence of Taoist philosophy. The supreme aim of Taoists is to be united with the cosmos or Tao. The way is also through meditation. What is Tao? Lao Tzu, the Patriarch of Taoism, said:

It is nebulous
Before the existence of heaven and earth
Soundless, formless, independent and eternal
Forever evolving, forever transforming
Can be said to be the mother of everything
I don't know its name, therefore call it Tao
If forced to describe, will say it's great
Great until there's no limit
Limitless until it's infinite
Infinite until it returns to its original point

The supreme aim of Buddhism is attaining nirvana, and the essential path is meditation. Nirvana is a state of enlightenment when we experience reality as it really is, when, as illusion has been dispersed, we become one with Reality. The great second century Buddhist master, Nagarjuna, whose writing forms the core of Mahayana Buddhism, says in his classic Madhya-maka Karika (Treatise of the Mean):

Coordinated here or caused are separate things,
We call this world phenomenal.
But just the same is called Nirvana,
When view without Causality, without Coordination.

What Nagarjuna means is that in our normal waking consciousness, we see the world of phenomena existing as separate entities, which are dependent upon a complexity of causes and coordinates. For example, we regard a thing or event as real because it is caused by another thing or event, or because it is compared to a man-made coordinate. However, when our mind is purified so that we can see Reality, when there are neither causality or coordination, the same world as undifferentiated and eternal is called nirvana.

Jaideva Singh summarizes the essence of Nagarjuna's philosophy succinctly:

> The Absolute and the world are not two different sets of reality posited against each other. Phenomena viewed as relative, as governed by causes and conditions constitute the world, and viewed as free of all conditions are the Absolute. The Absolute is always of uniform nature. Nirvana or the Absolute Reality is not something produced or achieved. Nirvana only means the disappearance of the fabrications of discursive thought.

In different words, Hinduism, Taoism and Buddhism expound the same spiritual fulfillment: going beyond the illusionary phenomenal world to be merged with the Absolute Reality, where duality has disappeared, where there is no difference between the subject and the object, between the knower and the known. When this is attained, the personal self dissolves itself into the timeless, spaceless Absolute, breaking away from its countless cycles of births and rebirths, rising from its mundane human level to that of the divine, and accomplishing eternal life. John Blofeld, who is a Buddhist, describes this aim beautifully. Although he was referring to the Taoists' quest for immortality, his description can be applied to any religion:

> The aim is to return to the Source by undergoing an apotheosis that can be best be hinted at in words. The illusory ego falls away, yet nothing real is lost. Spirit, freed from its bonds, returns to Spirit, not as a dew-drop destined to form an insignificant particle of a vast ocean, but as the boundless returning to the boundless. The liberated consciousness expands to contain — to be — the entire universe! Could there ever, ever be a more glorious endeavour?

Divine Manifestations of Supreme Reality

Not all people, understandably, can reach a stage of mental and spiritual development to comprehend and appreciate fully this returning to our eternal Source, this realization of our innate immortality.

Hence, great teachers of the respective religions have to present to the common people this profound universal Truth in simpler, picturesque form, or even initially to teach them moral values in the form of parables as a preparation for their later spiritual development.

A universal approach is to personify the abstract Absolute Reality into a Divine Being or Beings, such as Lord Vishnu, Lord Krishna and Lord Ganesa in Hinduism; Primordial Lord of Heaven, God of the Earth, and the Eight Immortals in Taoism; Amitabha Buddha, Manjusri Bodhisattva, and Guan Yin Bod Satt (Avalokitesvara Bodhisattva) in Mahayana Buddhism.

It is a gross mistake to think that these Divine Beings are mere concepts or symbols. These Divine Beings are more real and meaningful to their followers than the philosophical abstraction of Absolute Reality; and have helped the followers in countless, concrete ways.

However, even with divine help, one must put in personal effort if he wants to achieve the highest spiritual fulfillment. The Divine Beings, who are necessary for those devotees who may not yet have attained the required development for understanding the profound truth, are manifestations of the Supreme Reality. In the Bhagavad-Gita, the Supreme Reality speaks through Sri Krishna:

> Men whose discrimination has been blunted by worldly desires, establish this or that ritual or cult and resort to various deities, according to the impulses of their inborn natures. But it does not matter what deity a devotee chooses to worship. If he has faith, I make his faith unwavering. Endowed with the faith I give him, he worships that deity, and gets from it everything he prays for. In reality I alone am the giver.

The main methods to achieve the highest spiritual fulfillment are similar in all these religions. Thus, a typical method in one particular religion, may be easily mistaken for that in another religion. As you read the methods taught by some of their greatest teachers, see whether you can tell which one is Hindu, Taoist or Buddhist. Some technical names which may give the clue away, have been replaced by more general terms.

Listening to Soundlessness

When you meditate, your mind may be in your body, may be outside your body. You cannot touch the mind to open it. You could only cultivate it patiently and sincerely.

Place your mind at your third eye. Gradually, an internal light will shine forth. Then, your physical body may disappear. You will feel that there is another body besides your physical body. You will find another world besides this world. The most marvelous part is when the internal light coalesce to form your spiritual body. This is the secret that has been kept for millennia.

Your mind must be still and alert. If thoughts arise, your mind will be scattered. If you are sleepy, your mind will become unclear. How to prevent dullness and keep your mind still? Regulate your breathing, which must be gentle and soft. Place your mind on your breath, and reflect on and listen to it.

How to reflect? This is using your eyes to view your breath internally. How to listen? This is listening to your breath internally. When you listen, you hear the soundlessness of your breath. When you reflect, you view the formlessness of your breath.

Wisdom and Enlightenment

Be seated in a position that is firm and comfortable. The most famous posture is the lotus posture. The aim is to achieve an effortless alertness, which may be accomplished by thinking of the limitless expanse of the sky.

After mastering posture, the next step is to regulate cosmic energy by means of breath control. This can be done in numerous ways: by stopping the breath externally, or internally, or placing it at appropriate energy centers in our body.

When breath control is accomplished, the breath may stop on its own accord at any time the meditator concentrates upon an external or an internal object, like a flower or an energy center in his body. Then the covering of the Inner Light is removed, resulting in dispersing ignorance and gaining control over the senses. The mind becomes purified and accomplishes the power of concentration.

Concentration is holding the mind within a center of spiritual consciousness in the body, such as the naval, the heart or the middle of the forehead, or fixing the mind on your chosen Divine Ideal within your body or outside it. Prolonged concentration leads to meditation, which will result in wisdom. When, in meditation, the true nature of reality shines forth, undistorted by the mind, that is enlightenment. All these must be practiced regularly and gradually, and stage by stage.

Looking At The Stilled Mind

When you meditate, you must make sure that your posture is correct and comfortable. You may adopt the double lotus or single lotus position. Make sure that your nose and your naval are in line. Sit motionlessly. This is regulating the body.

Count your breaths in sets of ten. Your breathing may be controlled or spontaneous. Place your mind on your breathing as you count.

When your breathing has become very soft, or when your mind cannot focus on the counting, then change to following the breath. Again, the breathing can be controlled or spontaneous. Gently focus the mind on breathing in and breathing out. This is regulating the breath.

When the body and the breathing are well regulated, the next stage is regulating the mind. This is attained by keeping the mind still, and you may experience vital energy inside your body and cosmic energy outside mingling freely through your skin.

To still the mind is accomplished in two ways: subduing any thought from arising; and overcoming the four common problems in meditation, namely sinking, floating, slacking and hurrying mind.

When the mind becomes sleepy, that is the sinking symptom. To overcome it, focus at the tip of your nose. When extraneous thoughts arise in your mind, that is the floating symptom. It can be overcome by focusing your mind at your naval. When your mind is neither sinking nor floating, that is regulating the mind.

Regulating the mind may be accomplished too fast or too slowly. When the mind was full of thoughts before it was stilled, this is the hurrying symptom, and the stilling of the mind is said to be too fast. This can be remedied by letting go of the thoughts so that the mental energy flows downward. The slacking symptom is when the will is lazy or mental reaction is too slow. This can be remedied by quickly placing the mind on counting or following the breath. This is controlling the mind.

What you have just read are three of the most famous methods, although more often heard than known, in the respective religions in seeking spiritual fulfillment. These methods are advanced, and are not meant for beginners unless they are supervised by masters or competent instructors.

The first method is from a sacred text, "Teachings of the Pristine Golden Flower from Saint Lu", reprinted from the secret collections of the Dragon Gate School of Taoism, and explaining a Taoist approach to immortality.

The second method is from the authoritative "Yoga Sutra" of Patanjali, the father of yoga, teaching the union of the human spirit with the Universal Spirit.

The third method is from "Six Wondrous Gateways" of Venerable Zhi Yi, the founder of Tiantai school of Buddhism, expounding six steps to tranquility and insight meditation for attaining nirvana.

The Spiritual Aspect of Confucianism

Readers expecting Confucianism to be a way of virtuous living instead of a religion worshipping some divinities, will be surprised that its spiritual aspect is similar to that of Hinduism, Taoism and Buddhism! Besides ancestor-worship and Confucius-worship, which are traditional rites performed because of respect, not because of any shamanistic benefits, Confucianists are generally unconcerned about the after-life. (This does not necessarily imply they do not believe in an after-life.)

Although Confucianism refers to one of the three major religions of the Chinese, many people of other races and culture are actually Confucianistic in their beliefs and way of life. If you happen to be well educated, interested in sports and games, well versed in culture and arts, conscientious in the welfare of the community, concern about a comfortable, righteous life in the present, and not bothered about lives in the past or future, if any, then you, irrespective of the religion you may profess or even claim not to profess, are aptly qualified to be called a Confucianist.

The supreme aim of a Confucianist is to become an "ideal person", or jun zi, who is well versed in both the scholastic as well as the martial arts. Nevertheless, many Confucianists today have neglected the martial aspect of a cultured man, concentrating only on intellectual pursuit. To enhance their mental faculties, Confucian masters advocate meditation. The Confucian master Chu Hsi (Zhu Xi in romanized Chinese) advised, "Spend half the day on meditation, and the other half on study."

The intellectual achievements of the Confucianists are outstanding. If you think that their achievements are only in arts and literature, you will be in for some surprise. Expressing the intuitive wisdom that he gathered from meditation, Zhang Dai explained:

> The cosmos is a body of chi. Chi has yin and yang. When it disperses it permeates all things; when it unites it becomes nebulous. When this settles into form it becomes matter. When it disintegrates it returns to its original state.

We cannot help wondering that had our modern physicists and astronomers read about such ancient writings, their rediscoveries might have happened decades earlier. Zhang Dai's intuitive wisdom was not a rare exception; it was quite common among many ancient masters, Confucian or otherwise. The records of Confucian masters described below, illustrate that although they seldom deliberated on metaphysics or mysticism, their intuitive experience of the cosmos is transcendental and spiritual, similar to those of Hindu, Taoist and Buddhist masters.

> Hu Zhi: One day, suddenly my mind was enlightened; there are no irrelevant thoughts. I saw all the myriad things in the world inside me, making me exclaim that the whole cosmos is me.

> Jiang Xin: Since meditating at the Daolin Temple, I have lost my fear of death and my grieve for my dead mother. Suddenly one day I experienced the great Nature. The whole cosmos and I become one. There is no difference between the outside and the inside of me. The whole phenomenal world and my body become undifferentiated.

> Lu Kun: In stillness, my mind is as big as the universe. It is void and silent: there is nothing inside. But when I ask my mind, it is full of life; everything is there.

These experiences verify the profound truth emphasized by the great Confucian master, Mencius: "Everything in the cosmos is me; I am everything in the cosmos."

Entering God's Kingdom

It is heartening — or disheartening, depending on one's attitude — that while there are great differences at the ritualistic level of the populace, at the philosophical and spiritual level, Christianity and Islam are similar to Hinduism, Taoism, Buddhism and Confucianism.

Because of cultural and linguistic differences, the Supreme Being is known by different names, such as God, Allah, Brahman, Primordial Lord or Buddha; and is frequently personified as a Provider and Saviour, Who will reward pious followers in heaven. But for the adepts at the highest level, salvation or enlightenment is attainable here and now, with the absorption of world in mind, and the fusion of subject and object, when the adepts merge into the immanent, omnipotent, omnipresent Supreme Reality.

In Christianity, the immanence, omnipotence and omnipresence of God is clearly stated in the Bible:

For all things were created by Him, and all things exist through Him and for Him. (Romans 11:36)

There is one God and Father of all mankind, who is Lord of all, works through all, and is in all. (Ephesians 4:6)

The aim of Christianity is to return to God's kingdom, to be united with Him. Where is God's kingdom? Jesus himself explained:

Some Pharisees asked Jesus when the Kingdom of God would come. His answer was, "The Kingdom of God does not come in such a way as to be seen. No one will say, 'Look, here it is!' or, 'There it is'; because the Kingdom of God is within you."
(Luke, 17.20)

Let us find out from Christian masters how they realized this highest spiritual aim. The great 14th century Christian theologian, Meister Eckhart, emphasized that God is Being, and that this true Being becomes manifest in man in an inward journey.

William James, the father of American psychology, said:

The basis of the (Christian mystic) system is *orison* or meditation, the methodical elevation of the soul towards God. ... The first thing to be aimed at in orison is the mind's detachment from outer sensations, for these interfere with its concentration upon ideal things. Such manuals as Saint Ignatius's Spiritual Exercises recommended the disciple to expel sensation by a gradual series of efforts to imagine holy scenes. The acme of this kind of discipline would be a semi-hallucinatory mono-ideism — an imaginary figure of Christ, for example, coming to occupy the mind.

Not only are the methods of the Christians masters similar to those of other masters, their experiences during their spiritual ecstasy are also similar.

Saint Teresa: In the orison of union, the soul is fully awake as regards God, but wholly asleep as regards things of the world and in respect of herself. During the short time the orison lasts, she is as it were deprived of every feeling, and even if she would, she could not think of any single thing. ... God establishes himself in the interior of this soul in such a way, that when she returns to herself, it is wholly impossible for her to doubt that she has been in God, and God in her. ... All that I know is that I tell the truth; and I shall never believe that any soul who does not possess this certainty has ever been really united to God.

Saint Benedict: He saw a light which banished away the darkness of the night — upon this sight a marvelous strange thing followed. The whole world gathered — as it were — under one beam of the sun, was presented before his eyes. For by that supernatural light, the capacity of the inward soul was enlarged. But albeit the world was gathered before his eyes, yet were not the heaven and earth drawn into any lesser form than they be of themselves, but the soul or the beholder was more enlarged.

As the knowledge reported here is not commonly available to ordinary people, many readers may find the information revealed on these pages startling or even disagreeable. It is worthwhile to bear in mind that such information is neither my invention nor opinion; it is a report of the teachings and experiences of established masters in their respective religions.

Returning to God

Fundamentally, Islam is similar to Christianity and Judaism, except that Muslims regard Mohammed, not Jesus nor Moses, as the final prophet. Some readers may be pleasantly surprised that Islamic sciences, especially medicine, astronomy and mathematics, have contributed greatly to the welfare of all humanity.

In Islam, God or Allah is beneficent and merciful, as well as immanent, omnipotent and omnipresent. Their holy book, Koran, begins with singing praises to God:

Praise be to Allah, Lord of the Worlds,
The Beneficent, the Merciful,
Owner of the Day of Judgement,
Thee we worship; Thee we ask for help.
Show us the straight path,
The path of those whom Thou hast favored,
Not of those who earn Thine anger nor of those who go astray.

As in most, if not all, religions, the faithful are rewarded in the everlasting after-life. The aim of Islam is the return to God. An Islamic master, Shaykh Hakim Moinuddin Chishti, says:

Every scripture and every prophet from the first have said the same thing: that we are created by a wise and loving Creator, and that the special purpose of our existence is to endeavor to work our way back to Him. Our objective in life is to regain union with God.

How do Muslims regain union with God? Let us learn from their masters. Dr Mir Valiuddin says that this is achieved by "muraqaba" or contemplation:

Muraqaba is to fix firmly in the mind that God ever watches over you. *Muraqaba* operates at two levels: external and internal. External contemplation means "the turning away of the five emotional senses from the world and all its creatures; and disengaging from them both in society, and from vainglorious and meaningless thoughts when alone." ... And internal contemplation is nothing but the "guarding of the heart" (*muraat al-qalb*). "It is the preventing the heart from thinking of anything whatsoever, keeping it free from all vain thoughts, while sitting or reclining in public or in private, and disengaging from it cogitating on the past or the future. While engaged in contemplation if the thought of even prayer or worship comes, it should be negated at once, because this will bring contemplation from a higher to a lower level."

Hence, while the common devotees wait for the next life, the masters can attain union with God here and now. The similarity between Islam and the other religions discussed earlier — both regarding the beliefs of the populace as well as the aspirations and methods of the highest adepts — is remarkable.

The Muslim master gives us an illuminating account of spiritual fulfillment:

Tajliya-i-Ruh or the "illumination of the Spirit" implies the filling of
the human spirit with the effulgence of the Vision of God, and the fervor
of His love. ... In all individual human souls the same Universal Spirit
has manifested Itself according to the aptitudes of the individual essences.
... For the illumination of the spirit it is necessary that every relationship
that the spirit has formed, after entering the body, with this world through
sense of perception and knowledge, should be gradually severed, for it
is their relations and attachments with this world that form a veil and
keep the spirit remote from God. Anything to which the spirit is attached,
and in whose love it is imprisoned makes it its bondsman.

As in any religion, shallow understanding can be dangerous. Dr Mir
Valiuddin clarifies the following crucial point. Of course, "love", below, refers
to spiritual love.

According to the *Sharia, ittihad* or "oneness with God", if understood
in the literal sense, is sheer unbelief and blasphemy ... For those who
look behind the veil, other than God does not exist. God is the only
Being, and none exists besides Him. ... In the terminology of the Sufis,
what is meant by *ittihad* is the state of the lover in which he is absorbed
completely in the contemplation of his beloved, and in that state he does
not behold anybody except his beloved (*halat-i-istighraq*). This is the
highest reach of love's journey.

This important point has been explained by the famous 12th century master,
Muhyyuddin Mohammed Ibn al-Arabi, who also emphasized the universality of
God. Commenting on him, Najib Ullah says:

The fundamental principle of his system is the "unity of being." He
says that there is no real difference between the Essence and its attributes,
or, in other words, between God and the universe created by Him. ...
Al-Arabi believed that the primary function of men is to reveal his divine
nature, and those among men who reach perfection are the prophets and
saints. Muhammed, the Seal of Prophet, was the most perfect of men.
But, Ibn al-Arabi recognized the divine manifestation in other men, and
the divine truth in other religions.

Describing his union with God, another master, Mansur al-Hallaj, ecstatically
exclaimed:

I am He whom I love and He whom I love is I.

Although many followers of the religions may be surprised at the conclusion, when we carefully examine the teachings of their highest masters, we can clearly find that not only the aims, but also the principal methods and spiritual fulfillment of the world's major religions — Hinduism, Taoism, Buddhism, Confucianism, Christianity and Islam — are basically similar.

This does not merely explain why disciples from different religious background could train together happily in the Shaolin Monastery, but more significantly it rightly reminds us that, despite our superficial differences, we are all fellow travellers along similar spiritual paths aspiring to the same cosmic reality.

24
Various Vehicles Of Enlightenment

(The Beauty and Wisdom of Buddhism)

When he attains liberation, it is not because his teacher says so or it is described in the scriptures, but because he really knows and personally experiences it.

An Amazing and Inspiring Religion

If we ask people what they would like to become, should they be given a wish, many would want to be a king or a prince, especially in classical times. What, then, do you think of real kings and princes voluntarily forgoing their luxurious lifestyles and power to become monks so as to lead, and help others to lead, more rewarding and meaningful lives? There are many such cases in the history of Buddhism. These princes and kings were not deranged in thoughts nor forced by circumstances; they were in fact some of the finest minds the world has ever produced, making historic decisions at the prime of their lives that have greatly benefited humanity.

Besides Gautama Buddha and Bodhidharma, other great royal personages in Buddhist history include An Shih Kao, a Parthian prince who declined the throne; Kumarajiva, son of a Kucheaan princess; and Subhakarasinha, King of Orissa — all these were Buddhist monks who had sacrificed luxurious lives in the palace to brave deserts and snowy mountains to bring Buddhism from India to China. What is so great or beautiful about Buddhism, for which the Shaolin Monastery was built, and which inspired these great monks, and other important people, like Emperor Liang Wu Di of China who entered a monastery three separate times during his reign as a menial worker, or Emperor Harsha of India who publicly and proudly kissed the feet of Xuan Zang (Hsuan Tsang) as a form of highest respect when this Chinese pilgrim was in India in his quest for Buddhist scriptures? Many people, including Buddhists who have not yet studied the philosophy adequately, will be amazed at the depth and wealth of the Buddhist teaching.

The Historical Buddha

Millions of years ago, a poor man and his mother were crossing the sea when their ship sank. As he was dying, he wished some day to be able to ferry safely countless beings on the perilous journeys from life to life. This was born the thought, which grew stronger and stronger with each succeeding life, until Dipankara Buddha declared, for the first time, that the extraordinary ascetic then living as Sumedha would be born as Gautama Buddha, our historical Buddha, the twenty fourth in the long line of Buddhas from Dipankara.

Siddhartha Gautama Sakyamuni (623-543 BC) was born as the only prince to King Suddhodana and Queen Maya of Kapilavastu in today's Nepal. He was a prince of great courage, strength and beauty, and lived his early life in abundant luxury. At twenty nine, after the birth of his only son, Rahula, by his wife, Princess Yasodhara, Siddhartha made the Great Renunciation, leaving his family and worldly pleasures to seek salvation for suffering humanity.

He first learnt from the most renowned ascetic teachers of that time, such as Arada Kalama and Udraka Ramaputra. But after six years of the most austere practice which weakened him physically, he still could not find the answers he sought. After recovering his strength from taking milk provided by a female cowherd, Sujata, and realizing the futility of the two extremes, asceticism and worldly pleasures, he chose the middle path, and meditated under a bodhi tree. On the forty ninth day, he vowed that unless he attained complete perfect enlightenment, he would not come out of his meditation.

He meditated throughout the night, and attained four dhyana, or levels of consciousness. At the first level, he witnessed all his previous lives; at the second, he understood the rebirth cycles of all sentient beings; at the third, he eliminated all sensual desires and achieved the highest wisdom; and at the fourth level at dawn, he saw the "original face of reality". Gautama, therefore, attained samma samadhi, or supreme enlightenment, and was henceforth known as the Buddha, or the Enlightened One.

Soon after Gautama Buddha's enlightenment, Brahma leading a host of gods, devas, dragon kings and other heavenly beings requested the Buddha to teach the dharma, or the spiritual law. The Buddha preached the Avatamsaka Sutra (the Flower Adornment Sutra), but it was so profound that very few understood it. Hence, for the early part of his teaching, the Buddha taught a simplified form of the scriptures, the Agamas, to prepare common people for the later advanced dharma. Two merchants, Trapusa and Bhallika, who provided the Buddha with food, and Sujata the cowherd became the Buddha's first male and female lay disciples, or upasakas and upasikas respectively.

Three weeks later, the Buddha went to Sarnath where he gave his first public sermon on the Middle Path and the Four Noble Truths, and established the sangha, or the order of monks. His earlier teachers became his first clerical disciples, or bhiksus. Some of the influential people of the time who became the Buddha's early bhiksus were Sariputra, Maudgalyayana, Upali and Ananda. Later, the Buddha accepted female clerical disciples, or bhiksunis.

For the next forty five years, the Buddha spread his dharma to liberated people from suffering. Records show that he had never uttered a harsh word, and he treated all people, kings or paupers, equally and respectfully. He practiced what he preached, and no one could find a fault with which to condemn him. His hallmarks were compassion and wisdom. He taught not only humans, but also gods; in fact the number of heavenly beings who attained deliverance from his teaching was larger than that of humans!

One day at Vaisali, at eighty, a devotee unknowingly offered him some contaminated food. The Buddha knew the food was poisonous, but rather than hurting the unwitting devotee, he ate it. Then he went into meditation, and passed away serenely, entering parinirvana, or the final nirvana. Many kings attended his cremation and brought back his relics to their kingdoms as national treasures. The Buddha's parting words to his disciples were: "Life is transient; work hard for liberation."

Main Features of Buddhism

The Buddha's teaching was initially transmitted by words of mouth; it was written down only a few hundred years later. The huge body of Buddhist religious and philosophic literature is collectively known as the Tripitaka, or the Three Baskets of sutras (scriptures), vinaya (monastic rules) and sastras (treatises), which, more than seven hundred times the size of the Bible, is the most extensive collection of religious works in the world. Hence, it is no surprise that even the majority of Buddhists have only a superficial knowledge of Buddhist philosophy.

If you ask conscientious Buddhists how do they work for liberation, some may say they follow a highly virtuous way of living, as prescribed in the Noble Eightfold Path; some become lost to the outside world in their daily recitation of scriptures in front of a statue of a Buddha; some totally immerse themselves in answering an illogical question known as *gong-an* (*koan* in Japanese), like what is the sound of clapping with only one hand; while others focus their mind on an elaborate, esoteric design of circles and triangles known as a mandala.

All these are established Buddhist methods, and if the devotees work hard enough, they will one day attain liberation. Yet, they are so different from one another that those devotees who are familiar only with their own chosen method, may vehemently protest that the others are non-Buddhist!

This apparent confusion can be cleared when we realize that there are three traditions of Buddhism, namely Theravada, Mahayana and Vajrayana; and in each tradition there are different sects or schools which may appear to contradict one another — hence adding to the richness and depth of Buddhist philosophy.

All the sects of Buddhism, however, follow the same common basic precepts and doctrines, which are characteristically Buddhist, and aim to attain nirvana. The variations are actually the result of historical, geographical, cultural and developmental differences.

Before we study the three traditions of Buddhism, let us look at their common factors. All of them honor Siddhartha Gautama Sakyamuni as the historical Buddha, and accept his teaching as the foundation of their philosophy and practice. The Buddha's teaching is beautifully summarized in his own words:

Avoid doing evil,
Do good,
And purify the mind.

The most outstanding features of Buddhism, exemplified in the life of the Buddha himself, are compassion and wisdom. A true Buddhist is always loving and kind to other people, respective of their culture, race or religion. In the spread of Buddhism throughout the ages, not a drop of blood has been shed nor a harsh word said against another religion.

Manifesting wisdom, a Buddhist disciple is frequently asked not to accept Buddhism on faith alone, but evaluate it according to the best of his knowledge and experience. This does not necessarily mean that faith is irrelevant in Buddhism, nor decision based on one's knowledge and experience is always correct. But it means, at the highest level, that when he attains liberation, it is not because his teacher says so or it is described in the scriptures, but because he really knows and personally experiences it. Purifying the mind is the pathway to such attainment.

Two fundamental concepts in Buddhism are karma and the illusion of the phenomenal world. Karma means that whatever we are now, is the result of our past thoughts, speech and actions. We are, therefore, responsible for our own destiny. If we do good, we will be rewarded in future, not by God nor any external power, but as an inevitable unfolding of forces or happenings issuing from our good effort. Buddhism, therefore, does not believe in fatalism nor determinism.

Buddhism does not depend on Grace. A Buddhist achieves liberation due to his own effort, not because of divine charity. This principle is particularly important in Theravada Buddhism; while in Mahayana and Vajrayana Buddhism, Bodhisattvas and other enlightened beings may help the devotee in his efforts.

Buddhists believe that our phenomenal world is illusory, and we are deluded because of our ignorance. This does not mean that our everyday things and events are not real. The chair I am sitting on is solid, and the being I call me has been me since I was born — that is, if we experience the phenomenal world at our ordinary consciousness. But when we are enlightened, we know that there is vast expanse of "empty space" amidst the atomic particles that make up the chair, and that literally millions of individual cells in our body are destroyed and created each time we breathe in and out. We appreciate these truths not because modern science tells us so, but because we realize them when we are in deep meditation.

Buddhism is often divided into two main approaches, Hinayana and Mahayana, from which Vajrayana is derived. As Hinayana, meaning the Small Vehicle, may sound disrespectful, a more polite term, Theravada, which means the Council of Elders, is now commonly used, although historically Theravada was one of the Hinayana schools.

At the second Grand Buddhist Council at Vaisali, about a hundred years after Gautama Buddha entered parinirvana, philosophical differences between the Sthaviras, or the Elders, and the Mahasanghikas, who reflected the majority opinion, led to a split into two branches of Buddhism. The Mahasanghikas coined the term Mahayana, meaning the Great Vehicle, to represent their system; and called the Sthaviras, Hinayana.

Today, Theravada Buddhism is prominent in Sri Lanka, Burma, Thailand, Laos and Cambodia; Mahayana Buddhism in China, Japan, Korea and Vietnam; and Vajrayana Buddhism in Tibet and Mongolia. Theravada Buddhism is sometimes called Buddhism of the Southern Transmission; whereas Mahayana Buddhism, the Northern Transmission.

Theravada — Buddhism of the Elders

The principles and practices of Theravada Buddhism can be expressed through the Four Noble Truths and the Eightfold Path. The Four Noble Truths propound that life is full of suffering; the cause of suffering is carving; to eliminate suffering, we have to eliminate carving; and the way to accomplish this is to follow the Noble Eightfold Path.

The Noble Eightfold Path includes the following eight precepts: right speech, right action, right livelihood, right views, right intention, right concentration, right effort, and right mindfulness.

The eight steps can be classed into three groups, known in Theravada scripture written in Pali as Tividha Sikha, or Threefold Training: right speech, action and livelihood as Sila, or moral purity; right views and intention as Panna, or full knowledge; and right concentration, effort and mindfulness as Samadhi, or enlightenment.

Sila and Panna are preparation for Samadhi, which is realized through meditation. This means that unless a person practices meditation, which may be in various forms, he cannot attain the spiritual goal in Buddhism. It is indeed astonishing that many Buddhists are not aware of this important fact. The Venerable Paravahera explicitly says:

In all time and at all places it (meditation) is the only means to the attainment of final deliverance, the eternal happiness taught by the Buddha as Nirvana.

Some people who understand the Theravada teaching superficially, especially the first noble truth, often comment that Buddhism is pessimistic. Deeper understanding readily shows otherwise.

To say that life is full of suffering is courageously and succinctly stating a universal truth. Very few people throughout the whole history of humanity can even dream of a life more luxurious and glamorous than Gautama's. His father, King Suddhodana, forewarned by a prophecy that his only son would one day leave the palace to seek an answer to mankind's suffering, went to the extent of prohibiting anyone mentioning a sorrowful word or displaying a sorrowful gesture in front of the prince.

Gautama was so well looked after that he hardly had any worldly need which could not be fulfilled. Yet, when he secretly went out of the palace to meet his people, the sight of birth, old age, sickness and death manifested to him human suffering that no one could avoid. But such suffering was nothing, as he was to learn later when he inflicted torture upon himself in his ascetic practice, if compared to the suffering of samsara, the endless cycle of births and deaths.

Buddhism does not merely reveal life's suffering; it is mainly concerned with providing a practical way to overcome suffering and attain everlasting joy in nirvana. Nirvana is not annihilation, as some people erroneously believe; nirvana is a pristine state when the mind, free from mundane desires and attachment, experiences the Supreme Reality.

If you ask people what they consider as the most pleasurable experience in life, if they are normal and honest, many will say it is sexual fulfillment. Yet, many great spiritual teachers, who undoubtedly had experienced sexual fulfillment before, explicitly stressed that sexual pleasures are simply incomparable to spiritual bliss, which is hundreds, even thousands of times, more joyous than carnal delights.

Of course such bliss cannot be described; if you wish to experience it, work hard along the proven methods suggested in this book, or along the religious paths of your choice.

Mahayana — Buddhism of the Great Vehicle

Mahayana Buddhists accept all the teachings of Theravada Buddhism, which they regard as preparation for more profound knowledge and wisdom. The knowledge and wisdom of Mahayana Buddhism, as recorded in their voluminous literature, are startling, and they concern not only arts and religion, but also philosophy and science.

One of the greatest Buddhist masters of all time was Nagarjuna, who lived in India in the second century, and whose earthly appearance and contribution to Buddhism had been predicted by the Buddha himself. Among his many works, Madhyamaka-Karika, or Treatise on the Mean, which provided much foundation for Mahayana philosophy, illustrates some crucial, though little known, differences with Theravada philosophy. Modern scientists who care to study his work, will be amazed that this great master expounded the void and relativity — two of the greatest discoveries of modern science — more than 18 centuries ago.

By the time of Nagarjuna, both the Theravadins and the Mahayanists had analyzed all physical, emotional and mental phenomena in the universe into dharmas, or subatomic particles or forces; and they classified these dharmas in ways more profound than what our chemists and physicists do today to elements or particles!

The Theravadins explained that according to the principle of pratityasamutpada, or the principle of dependent origination, there is a causal relation between the temporal sequences of real entities. However, the Mahayanists said that the very nature of pratityasamutpada explains that all dharmas are relative; hence all phenomena, which owe their apparent reality to dharmas, are devoid of objective existence. Nagarjuna said:

> Since there is no element of existence (*dharma*) which comes into manifestation without conditions, therefore there is no *dharma* which is not *sunya* (devoid of real independent existence).

Another delicate difference between Mahayana and Theravada expounded by Nagarjuna concerns nirvana. Both Theravadins and Mahayanists have questioned whether nirvana is a transformed state of mind or another dimension of being.

Although there are statements to show that nirvana has a metaphysical basis, the emphasis in Buddhist literature is on nirvana as a transformed mental state.

Theravadins say that nirvana is eternal (nitya), blissful (sukha), and the opposite of phenomena (samsara). On the other hand, Nagarjuna says:

> Nirvana is that which is neither abandoned nor acquired, it is neither a thing annihilated, nor a thing eternal; it is nether destroyed nor produced.
> ... Nothing of phenomenal existence (samsara) is different from nirvana, nothing of nirvana is different from phenomenal existence.

Mahayana Buddhists belief that attaining nirvana does not involve a change of objective order, but is a subjective transformation. If defilements and phenomenal existence were ultimately real, nothing could change them.

The change, therefore, is in our outlook: the transformation is psychological not ontological. When we understand the Buddhist concept of nirvana — either from the Mahayanist or the Theravadin viewpoint — it becomes obvious that those who think Buddhism is nihilistic are grossly mistaken.

Another philosophical difference between Mahayana and Theravada Buddhism is their spiritual ideal. A Theravadin aspires to be an Arahant, that is a worthy being who has perfected himself and won enlightenment. However, an Arahant does not feel any responsibility to help others to gain enlightenment, because he believes that since liberation is a personal affair, everyone has to work for it himself.

A Mahayanist's ideal is a Bodhisattva, one who has attained bodhi, or perfect wisdom, and become a Buddha, but he postpones entering Buddhahood so as to help other sentient beings to achieve enlightenment.

To a Bodhisattva, liberation is a universal aspiration, not just a personal accomplishment. The most outstanding characteristic of a Bodhisattva is bodhicitta, or universal love resulting from transcendental wisdom. Hence, while the attainment of nirvana is the supreme aim in Theravada Buddhism, in Mahayana it is the realization of Buddhahood for all humanity, as everyone has Buddha-nature in him.

Perhaps the most decisive difference between Theravada and Mahayana is their concept of Buddha. Contrary to popular belief, even Theravadins do not accept the concept that the Buddha is all that Siddhartha Gautama represents. Hence, the statement that Siddhartha Gautama is the founder of Buddhism is incorrect, as there have been many Buddhas before him.

According to Buddhist philosophy, the Buddha has three bodies, namely the transformation body (nirmana-kaya), the reward body (sambhogakaya), and the spiritual body (dharmakaya).

Both Theravada and Mahayana hold similar views regarding the transformation body, like the visible human body of Gautama, and the reward body, which the Buddha may use to appear in different forms and at different times in different dimensions. But there is vital difference in their views regarding the spiritual body.

In Theravada Buddhism, the dharmakaya or spiritual body of Buddha represents the sum of all qualities and teachings of all Buddhas. When a devotee takes refuge in the Buddha, for example, he takes refuge in the dharmakaya, not in the person of Gautama.

In Mahayana Buddhism, the dharmakaya of the Buddha is the omniscient, omnipotent and omnipresent Supreme Reality, of which Siddhartha Gautama is a manifestation in our historical time to save suffering humanity.

In the Lotus Sutra, one of the most important scriptures in Mahayana Buddhism, the Eternal Buddha, personified for the comprehension of ordinary people, explains that:

All Buddhas take the one vow:
"The Buddha-way which I walk,
I will universally cause all the living
To attain this same Way with me."
Though Buddhas in future ages
Proclaim hundreds, thousands, kotis,
Countless ways into the doctrine,
In reality there is but the One-Vehicle.

Hui Neng, the Sixth Patriarch of Chan (Zen) Buddhism, mentioned this point explicitly:

The pure nature of Supreme Reality is the real Buddha.

There are many schools of Mahayana Buddhism. Though their practical approaches to achieve enlightenment may be different, even seemingly contradictory at times, their philosophy is similar. The major Mahayana schools, their philosophy and methods will be discussed in the next chapter, with special reference to Chan (or Zen) Buddhism, of which the Shaolin Monastery was the fountain-head.

Vajrayana — Buddhism of the Mystics

It is inspiring to note that the great missionaries instrumental in the spread of Buddhism were princes and princesses. While Mahinda and Sanghamitta, the prince and the princess of Asoka the Great, brought Theravada Buddhism to Sri Lanka in the third century BCE, from where it blossomed to other places, Padmasambhava, the prince of Udyana who declined the throne to become a monk, was mainly responsible for the development of Vajrayana Buddhism in Tibet in the eighth century, and later spread to Mongolia.

An interesting prediction by Padmasambhava which has come true is that "When iron birds fly in the sky, Tibetans will bring Buddhism to the land of the white people."

Earlier in about CE 640 Mahayana Buddhism was brought to Tibet with the marriage of Princess Khrican of Nepal and Princess Wen Cheng of the Chinese Tang Dynasty to the famous Tibetan King Song-Btsang-Sgam-Po. However there was strong opposition from other nobles who followed Bon-po, the native religion.

In CE 741 epidemic and flood devastated Tibet, and lightning and thunder struck the palace. According to legend, these were caused by hostile spirits of the Bon religion.

The king invited the scholar-warrior Padmasambhava to Tibet to subdue these Bon spirits. The compassionate Padmasambhava, who possessed tremendous Tantric magical powers, did not destroy these spirits, but converted them into Buddhism.

Hence, Tibetan Buddhism became a blend of Mahayana Buddhism, Tantrism and Bon religion, to be known as Vajrayana Buddhism. "Vajra" means diamond, and also the void. Vajrayana means the Diamond Vehicle, suggesting the many facets of the Void in Buddhism.

From Mahayana Buddhism, the Vajrayanists derive the concepts of sunyata (void), karma, impermanence, and the rare opportunity of being human. The universe is void; we regard phenomena as absolute reality because of our ignorance, which results in samsara, the endless suffering of births and rebirths.

The cause of samsara is karma, which manifests the effect of past thought. Our past karma leads us to our present life, which is impermanent, a split second in the long painful cycle of births and rebirths. But, to be born a human is an extremely rare opportunity, an effect of meritorious deeds done in past lives. So we, as humans, must make precious use of this rare opportunity to liberate ourselves from karma and samsara, to attain nirvana, which is everlasting bliss.

From Tantrism, the Vajrayanist inherits some practical tools, like mudra, mantra and mandala, to help him attain nirvana. A mudra is a particular position of the body, especially the way of holding the fingers, and is mystically related to one's consciousness in meditation.

A mantra is a special way of intoning, silently or aloud, a particular combination of sounds with mystical powers. The most famous mantra is "Om Mani Padme Hum", which means "Hail to the jewel in the lotus."

A mandala is a mystic design, usually of geometrical shapes, symbolizing certain cosmic forces. The mudra, mantra and mandala correspond to the bodily, pranic (or breathing) and visualizing aspects of meditation. Skillful application of mudra, mantra or mandala may produce psychic abilities; a true Buddhist, for his own sake as well as others', will never abuse these abilities for unethical purposes.

Tantrism also provides the Vajrayanist the technique of visualizing spiritual beings for redirecting his emotional energies. These mental images may be beautiful or horrendous, depending on the emotions. This explains why you may see wrathful deities in Tibetan religious art. A controversial influence of Indian Tantrism on Vajrayana Buddhism is sex. In Tantric belief, sexual copulation symbolizes the union of male and female energies of the cosmos. Hence, while celibacy is strictly followed by monks of Theravada and Mahayana Buddhism, some sects of Vajrayana Buddhism allow their monks to have wives and possess properties.

The third important influence that gives Vajrayana Buddhism a typical Tibetan color and outlook is the native Bon religion. In Bon belief, there are heavenly and earthly spirits that guard the treasures of the cosmos.

Shamans and Bon priests are required to mediate with these spirits concerning various human affairs, like birth, death, marriage, sickness, agriculture, warfare and any important national activities. Elaborate rituals are involved.

These spirits, however, were subdued by Padmasambhava, and together with Bon rituals were incorporated into Tibetan Buddhism. The great liberation through hearing in the Bardo, popularly but misleadingly known in the west as recitation of the Tibetan Book of the Dead — which is a series of attempts to remind the consciousness (or soul) of the dead that he is actually an integral part of Reality, thereby helping him to attain immediate liberation — is much influenced by the Bon religion.

The path to enlightenment in Vajrayana Buddhism, as in Theravada and Mahayana Buddhism, can be divided into three stages: ethics, meditative stabilization and wisdom. The following is a brief description of Vajrayanist cultivation as explained by the Dalai Lama Tenzin Gyatso.

The Vajrayana ethics consists of avoiding non-virtues — like killing, stealing, sexual misconduct, lying, divisive speech, harsh speech, senseless talk, covetousness, harmful intent and wrong view; and fulfilling vows — such as vows of personal liberation, of Bodhisattvahood or of Secret Mantra.

Meditative stabilization is abiding the mind one-pointedly, without distraction, on any virtuous object. The meditator must initially create calm abiding in the mental continuum, and then create special insight. To cultivate calm abiding, he must abandon the five faults of laziness, forgetfulness, laxity or excitement, failure to apply "the eight antidotes" when needed, and failure to concentrate even when laxity and excitement are absent. The eight antidotes are faith, aspiration, effort, pliancy, mindfulness, introspection, intention of application, and equanimity.

When calm abiding is achieved, the meditator cultivates insight by progressing from the Desire Realm through the Form Realm to the Formless Realm, and from the Desire Level through seven other levels to the Peak of Cyclic Existence Level.

When meditating progressively on these nine levels, the meditator passes through four concentration stages, and then contemplates on limitless space, limitless consciousness, nothingness, and the peak of cyclic existence. The effect of this attainment is that the meditator, if he wishes, may be reborn as a god in the form or formless realms.

Rebirth as a god, however, is only an intermediate stage of spiritual development. The highest stage is to attain Buddhahood, which is accomplished by training in special wisdom. The meditator, in his human form, investigates and analyses the suchness of selflessness of persons and of phenomena.

In other words, he cultivates the special wisdom of realizing that in ultimate reality both he and phenomena are void. A principal method to accomplish this is the esoteric practice of Secret Mantra, taught only to specially initiated disciples. The Dalai Lama summarizes the approach as follows:

> Through becoming skilled in the techniques of putting concentrative emphasis on internal winds or energies (*rlung, prana*), channels (*rtsa, nadi*), essential constituents (*khams, dhatu*), and so forth, the mind enters into the sphere of the Great Seal (*phyag rgya chen po, mahamudra*) of clear light devoid of dualistic elaboration. Through being absorbed in this yoga, the resultant Wisdom Truth Body of a Buddha is achieved.

Hence, the practice of Secret Mantra is a form of chi kung, similar to the Shaolin art of Big Universe. It is quite clear that "concentrative emphasis", "energies" and "channels" in the above quotation correspond to "meditation", "chi" and "meridians" in the Shaolin arts, and "essential constituents" probably refers to "dan tian" or energy fields.

In both Theravada and Vajrayana Buddhism, as well as in Mahayana Buddhism which will be further described in the next chapter, meditation is the essential path to enlightenment. Meditation is called "Dhyana" in Sanskrit, transcribed into Chinese as "Chana", which is usually shortened to "Chan", from which the Japanese term "Zen" derives. That school of Buddhism which emphasizes meditation is Chan or Zen Buddhism, of which the Shaolin Monastery is the fountainhead.

25
Ancient Wisdom On Modern Science

(A Survey of Various Chinese Schools of Buddhism)

You will be amazed at the Buddhist wisdom which the latest physicists, astronomers, biologists, psychologists and other modern experts are only now rediscovering.

Was Mahayana Buddhism taught by the Buddha?

If you think that practicing Buddhism is merely praying to the Buddha, you will be in for a big surprise. If you read Buddhist scriptures, provided you understand their deeper meanings, it is like reading an encyclopedia of modern science. You will be amazed at the Buddhist wisdom which the latest physicists, astronomers, biologists, psychologists and other modern experts are only now rediscovering.

Some people who think that Buddhism is only a moral way of living, claim that Mahayana Buddhism is not the original teaching of the Buddha, but a later development based on Nagarjuna's teaching. Consequently they say that all Mahayana sutras, including famous ones like the Amitabha Sutra and the Heart Sutra that are recited daily by literally millions of Buddhists throughout the world, are forgeries!

One of the most admirable statements countering this claim is made by the Venerable Hsuan Hua, the famous Buddhist master in America, who says that if the Mahayana sutras he is translating and spreading are not the true teachings of the Buddha, he is willing to go to hell to atone for false teaching.

The courage and confidence shown by the Venerable Hsuan Hua are of the highest order, for any master at his level knows that thoughts and words are reality, a concept modern scientists are beginning to investigate. The Venerable Hsuan Hua clarifies that his statement is not made rashly, but as a result of deep understanding and experience.

Virtually all the important teachings characteristic of Mahayana Buddhism are found in Theravada sutras, which recorded the earliest teachings of Gautama Buddha. Typical Mahayanist concepts such as numerous Buddhas and Bodhisattvas, various heavens where pious followers may go to, creation of the universe and life in other world systems, and nirvana as the direct experience of transcendental cosmic reality are mentioned in various Theravada texts, although Theravada Buddhism generally pays little emphasis on them. Because of space constraint, only a few examples, all taken from Theravada sources, are illustrated below.

The Buddha says in the Udana Sutta that "There is an Unborn, an Unbecome, an Unmade, an Uncompounded. If there were not this Unborn, Unbecome, Unmade, Uncompounded, there would be no escape from the born, the become, the made, the compounded."

This is a description of what scientists would call the unified energy field. Buddhists call the realization of this Unborn, nirvana, i.e. the direct experience of transcendental cosmic reality.

The Buddhavamsa Pali, or the History of the Buddhas, gives a historical account of Gautama Buddha and many Buddhas before him. At the start of this important Theravada work, the Buddha explains that he was Sumedha Bodhisattva in a previous life, and he went through the necessary *paramitas*, which form a typical feature of Mahayana training, in his cultivation to attain Buddhahood. Gautama Buddha also says that Ajita Bodhisattva, who is now residing in Tusita Heaven, will appear as the next Buddha.

Professor Edward Thomas reports that "it is in these (Sarvastivada) documents that we find the earliest form of the bodhisattva doctrine." Sarvastivada is an early school of Hinayana Buddhism, from which Theravada evolved. The Bodhisattva doctrine is a Mahayana teaching that characteristically differentiates Mahayana from present day Theravada Buddhism.

Another common misconception which many people think is a later Mahayana invention, is that metaphysics and cosmology are absent in original Buddhism. They must be very surprised to find that Theravada works describe the twenty four heavens of our world system, known as the Saha world, in details.

Astrophysicists investigating into the multidimensional universe theory, may get some helpful ideas from these Buddhist scriptures, which describe, among many other things, that just above our human realm is the Catu-maharajika Heaven, or Heaven of the Four Great Kings, who are Dhataratha, Virupakkha, Virulhaka and Vessavana.

The next time you see huge statues or images of these four heavenly kings, like the ones found in the Hall of Heavenly Kings in the Shaolin Monastery and in other large Mahayana temples, remember they were originally taught by the Buddha in Theravada scriptures, although Theravadins today are generally unaware of them.

The Buddha also mentioned in Theravada suttas that in his previous lives he was the all-powerful Brahma, the God of the Brahma heavens, as well as Sakka, the ruler of gods.

Some readers, having been conditioned by the so-called objectivity and empirical facts of Newtonian science for the last three centuries, may think such Buddhist teaching as illusory and superstitious. They must be surprised to find out that according to the Buddha's teaching, what they consider as objects and facts are equally illusory. But they will probably be more surprised that many leading scientists today lament "the echoless, empty caverns of Newtonian space." An associate professor of physics, Roger Jones, says:

Bare empty space is a relative new conception — one that would be alien, unfamiliar, and incomprehensible to people of primal and ancient cultures. If we think of these earlier views of space and time as naive, misinformed, and anthropomorphic, we must at least recognize the sense of home, security, and support the earlier conceptions of space gave to those who believed and dwelt in them. We have given up this nourishing quality of space — of our abode — at our peril.

He also says:

There are indications that we may be filling space once again with meaning and substance, as in earlier times. In Einstein's general theory of relativity, space-time becomes equated with matter and energy themselves, and even with gravity. In modern quantum theory it is the empty vacuum of space itself that is seen as the source of all matter and energy in the physical universe.

Theravada scriptures describe Buddhist cosmology in some detail, with accounts on the universe expanding, and thousands and thousands of galactic systems with thousands and thousands of suns and moons. In the Digha Nikaya, written fifteen centuries before our astrophysicists suggest that life on earth might be seeded from outer space, the Buddha gave an interesting description on how life originated in our world:

There they dwell, made of mind, feeding on joy, self-luminous, moving through the air and glorious, and there they abide for a long, long time. During that period the world was one mass of water and all was utter darkness. No moon, no sun, no constellations or stars could be seen, there were no months or fortnights, no years or seasons, nor was there male or female — beings were just beings. And after a long, long time, a savory scum formed over the surface of the waters where those beings were. It looked like the skin that forms on hot milk as it cools. It had the color of quality ghee or butter, and it was sweet like the taste of pure white honey. Then some being of a greedy nature said: 'I say, what can this be?' and tasted the scum with its finger. When it did this, it liked the taste, and a craving arose. Then other beings did the same thing, and craving arose in them too. So they began to break off pieces and eat them. And as a result of this, their self-luminosity disappeared, and as a result of that, the moon and the sun, night and day, months and fortnights, years and seasons all came into being.

All these teachings which are now considered to be characteristically Mahayanist are of course familiar to Mahayana Buddhists and are common in Mahayana literature. The important point is that although they are not normally taught in Theravada Buddhism, claimed by some as the original Buddhism, they are found in Theravada scriptures extant today.

Nevertheless, Mahayanists are generally not too worried over whether Mahayana or Theravada or any other form is the original Buddhism. This is probably the reason why that despite so many points — historical, philosophical, psychological, and canonical — to their favor, Mahayana masters have not come forward in any organized manner to settle such scholarly disputes, which they would reckon as squabbling over who the archer was instead of attending to the victim shot with the arrow.

In other words, they are more concerned with whether the methods they practice help them and others to attain enlightenment, rather than whether the methods were really taught by Gautama Buddha. Basing on records, the number of adepts achieving enlightenment through Zen far exceeds that in any other school.

The Buddha is of course honored as the greatest teacher in all Buddhist schools, but if there are other teachers who can also contribute to the enlightenment process, it would be sheer arrogance if not folly for neglecting them.

Thus, in Zen Buddhism for example, there are two main categories of meditation to attain enlightenment, known as Tathagata Zen and Patriarch Zen. Tathagata Zen refers to the type of meditation taught by the Buddha, and Patriarch Zen by Bodhidharma. Most Zen disciples in the Shaolin Monastery as well as in other Zen monasteries use Patriarch Zen because it is most direct and, from experience, more effective.

This does not mean that Patriarch Zen is superior. Because of their different nature and needs, other people may find Tathagata Zen better, still others may need other methods. Of all the world's great religions, Buddhism has the widest range of cultivation methods, and of the three Buddhist traditions Mahayana Buddhism offers the most number of approaches.

Mahayana literature says there are 84,000 gates to the spiritual realm, which is a figurative way of saying there are different methods or expedient means to meet the varied needs and development stages of aspirants.

Various Schools of Buddhism

Because of differences in interpretation, emphasis, local needs and other factors, there were already numerous schools of Buddhism in India before the Buddha's teachings were first written as sutras around the beginning of the Common Era.

Traditionally there were eighteen schools, but different authorities list these eighteen schools differently. The following list, adapted from Professor Edward Conze, is useful. The ten Mahayana schools were Mahasanghika, Ekaryavaharika, Lokottaravada, Bahusrutiya, Prajnaptivada, Caitriya, Purvasaila, Aparasaila, Rajagirika and Siddharthika. The eight Hinayana schools were Sthavira, Pudgalavada, Sammitiya, Dharmottariya, Bhadrayaniya, Sannagarika, Vibhajyavada and Sarvastivada. Theravada, which is now the most prominent if not the only existing Hinayana school, is derived from the Vibhajyavada.

When Buddhism spread to China in the first few centuries of the Common Era, both Mahayana and Hinayana were well represented. There were at first ten major schools, six of which were Mahayana — San Lun (Madhyamika), Nie Pan (Nirvana), Di Lun (Dasabhumi), Jing Tu (Sukhavati), Chan or Zen (Dhyana) and She Lun (Samparigraha); and the other four were Hinayana — Pi Tan (Abhidharma), Cheng Shi (Satyasiddhi), Lu Zong (Vinaya), and Ju She (Abhidharmakosa).

However by the 7th century when Chinese Buddhism experienced its golden age during the Tang Dynasty, there remained only one Hinayana school, the Lu Zong or Vinaya School, among the eight famous Chinese Buddhist schools existing then. The other seven Mahayana schools were San Lun, Jing Tu, Zen, Tian Tai (Lotus School, developed from Nie Pan School), Hua Yen (Avatamsaka, developed from Di Lun School), Fa Xiang (Vijaptimatrata, developed from She Lun and Ju She Schools), and Zhen Yen School (which was transmitted from India).

The Lu Zong or Vinaya School was founded by the famous monk Tao Hsuan (Dao Xuan, 596-667), and is based on the strict vinaya or monastery code developed by the Buddha. There are about 250 rules for monks, and 350 for nuns. (The actual numbers may vary among different schools.)

This vinaya code is also followed by Mahayana monks, who, nevertheless, made some minor modifications like taking another meal in the evening beside the only one in the morning, and growing their own food instead of begging from the public. The Buddha did say that changes could be made to minor rules according to the needs of the situation.

Major rules of course have to be obeyed strictly. The most important are the following four Parajika Rules, failing which the offender would be expelled from the monastic order: no sexual intercourse (even with an animal, and even if it is asked), no stealing, no killing of a human, and no false claim to ability not really possessed.

Other rules forbid a monk to be alone with a woman in a secluded place, to have more material possessions than are permitted, or to behave in any unbecoming manner in public or in private. Lesser rules forbid a monk to wear make-up, to sleep on a luxurious bed, and to be indulged in public entertainment. It is worthwhile to note that the aim of the rules is not to restrict the monks' freedom but to help them in their spiritual cultivation.

If you wish to practice Buddhism, do not be flabbergasted by these strict rules, for they apply to monks only and not to lay followers. This, of course, does not imply double standard of discipline; unlike lay persons, monks have renounced all worldly matters for spiritual development. So if you meet any monks who indulge in sex, possess flashy cars or hoard gold, you have good reasons to suspect.

There is no excuse for a monk to have sexual activity; the Buddha made it very clear that sexual abstinence is the foremost vinaya rule. Why is abstinence from sex so important in the monastic order? Certainly not because of any misguided connotation that sex is "bad", but because it is the most difficult desire to be subdued, and as desire will generate karmic effect (in the form of mental vibrations) leading to rebirth, the monk will be unable to break off from his samsaric cycle to achieve nirvana.

Readers who wish to know why the world is neither false nor real, but relative would be interested in the San Lun or Three Treatises School, which is based on two treatises of Nagarjuna, *Madhyamika-karika* (Treatise on the Mean) and *Dvadasa-dvara* (Twelve Gates), and *Sata Sastra* (Treatise on Hundred Verses), a treatise of his disciple, Aryadeva.

These three treatises were translated by the great Kumarajiva from Sanskrit into Chinese about 400 CE, marking the beginning of this school in China. Of his numerous disciples, Seng Zhao (374-414) was instrumental in formulating the doctrines.

The main philosophy of this school is that the nihilistic view of reality, i.e. viewing reality as absolute nothingness, and the objective view of reality, i.e. thinking that the external world is real, are both perverse; ultimate reality is the mean between these two extremes, and can only be comprehended relatively.

In other words, the external world, though not *ultimately* real, is *relatively* real, and is necessary for our worldly existence as well as for achieving actualization of ultimate reality or nirvana.

Heaven, Zen and the Lotus

If you want to be assured of going to heaven, you may like to find out about the Jing Tu or Pure Land School, which is the most popular school of Buddhism today. The Jing Tu School is based on the *Amitabha Sutra, Amitayus Sutra* and *Meditation on Amitayus Sutra*, and its main cultivation method is reciting the name of Amitabha Buddha. It is therefore also called the Amitabha School.

It is estimated that in Japan alone, where the Pure Land School is known as the Jodo School from which is branched out the Shin School and the Ji School, more than half her population are followers. Its popularity amongst Chinese Buddhists in China and elsewhere is reflected in their custom of their saying

"Ami-Tuo-Fo" when others would say "how are you", "thank you" or "God bless you".

"Ami-Tuo-Fo" means Amitabha Buddha, who is another Buddha different from Gautama Buddha, and who has vowed that whoever follows his teaching sincerely will be reborn in Sukhavati or the Western Paradise billions of light-years from our world.

Some readers may think this promise by Amitabha Buddha too good or too ludicrous, but its philosophy can be explained "scientifically" and its validity substantiated by some of the best minds in human history. It is too complex to go into details here, but it may suffice to say that since all phenomenal worlds, including heavens and hells, are in reality a creation of mind, the methodological and devoted cultivation of the Pure Land School subtly prepares the devotees to experience what their minds create.

Do not be grossly mistakenly that this Western Paradise is only imaginary; it is as real to the devotees as the physical world is now real to you. After all, your so-called external world is also a creation of your mind — a fundamental Buddhist teaching, interestingly, being seriously investigated and confirmed by the latest science.

Zen Buddhism, the school of Buddhism practiced in the Shaolin Monastery, and is probably the next most popular Buddhist school after the Pure Land School, is sometimes described as the cultivation method meant for the best minds. For those who are ready, it is the fastest method because it points directly at Buddha nature, attaining enlightenment in an instant.

This means that instead of emphasizing the study of scriptures as in Theravada Buddhism, or investigating into whether ultimate reality is "empty", "real" or "relative", or whether it is mutually arising or merely ideation as in other Mahayana schools, Zen practitioners seek to perceive ultimate reality directly.

This does not mean that Zen Buddhism pays no attention to scripture study or investigation into reality; but it means that Zen practitioners do not want to be over involved in such activities that they mistake scripture study or meditative investigation as direct experience of ultimate reality.

In Zen terms, they do not want to mistake the finger that points to the moon, as the moon itself. The paramount way to experience cosmic reality is through meditation. Throughout the centuries Zen masters have employed extraordinary methods to test and sometimes to stimulate such a direct cosmic experience, and these occasions have been recorded as *gong-ans*, or *koans* in Japanese. The philosophy and practice of Zen will be explained in more detail in the next two chapters.

The Tian Tai School, named after the Tian Tai Mountain in China, was founded by the great monk Zhi Yi (538-597), whose childhood was filled with miraculous events. For example, at birth a celestial light illuminated the whole sky, and at seven he could recite a whole sutra after listening to it once.

Zhi Yi's greatest contribution was his classification and systematization of the tremendous amount of the Buddha's teaching which sometimes appear contradictory to uninformed people, into "Five Periods and Eight Doctrines" as follows.

Five Chronological Periods:
1. Avatamsaka (Flower Adornment) Period — first seven days, emphasis on cosmic reality.
2. Agama (Transmission) Period — first ten years, emphasis on moral purity and elimination of suffering.
3. The Vaipulya (Development) Period — next eight years, emphasis on compassion and the development of the Bodhisattva doctrine.
4. The Prajna (Wisdom) Period — next twenty years, emphasis on emptiness.
5. The Pundarika (Lotus) Period — last seven years, emphasis on attaining Buddhahood.

The Buddha's teachings are also classified into four groups according to methodological approach, and another four groups according to philosophical content, making eight doctrines together.

Four Methodological Approaches:
1. Instantaneous Approach — for the best minds, where enlightenment can be instantaneous, as in the Avatamsaka teaching and Zen.
2. Gradual Approach — the followers are led to progress from elementary to advanced levels, as in the Agama, Vaipulya and Wisdom teachings.
3. Mystical Approach — when the teaching is transmitted in a manner not easily explicable, as the transmission of Zen, or the teaching of mantras.
4. Indeterminate Approach — when many followers may listen to the Buddha at the same time, but interpret his teaching differently.

Four Philosophical Doctrines:
1. Pitaka Doctrine — the elementary teaching found in the Agama sutras, taught in Hinayana Buddhism.
2. Common Doctrine — the teaching common in Hinayana and Mahayana Buddhism.
3. Special Doctrine — taught to advanced followers like the Bodhisattvas.
4. Round Doctrine — the all-permeating, all-fulfilling, perfect doctrine for the attainment of Buddhahood, as found in the Lotus Sutra.

The Suddharma Pundarika Sutra, or the Lotus Sutra, is the most important in the Tian Tai School. Hence, the Tian Tai School is sometimes known in English as the Lotus School. In the Chinese language, however, the Lotus School refers to the Pure Land School, because devotees are reborn in Western Paradise through a lotus.

The basic philosophy of the Tian Tai School, considered by many as one of the finest Chinese contributions to Buddhism, is that all phenomena are devoid of real existence, and owe their appearances to the mind. This philosophy is poetically expressed as *yi nian san qian*, which means all the phenomenal worlds in the countless galaxies are due to a single thought.

It is indeed amazing that modern science comes to similar conclusion only now. More amazing is that Tian Tai adepts learnt about such wisdom not from speculation, but from direct experience through meditation. Their famous meditation, also developed by Zhi Yi, is called the "The Six Wondrous Gates", whereby the mind is first stilled, then used to investigate into what ultimate reality is.

Reality, Appearance and True Word

Many people have enjoyed William Blade's famous lines:

To see a world in a grain of sand
And a heaven in a wild flower.
Hold infinity in the palm of your hand
And eternity in an hour.

But not may people can understand how one can see a world in a grain of sand, or hold eternity in an hour. As a student of literature I used to interpret this beautiful poem figuratively or symbolically, but now after my study of Zen I believe that the poet is describing his mystical experience literally.

Hua Yen philosophy explains why a Bodhisattva can see a whole cosmos at the tip of his hair. This may be appreciated at two levels. At the phenomenal level, the tip of the hair, while minute at our human scale, can actually be a cosmos to even smaller beings at the subatomic scale.

At the transcendental level, the hair tip is the whole cosmos, because there is in reality no boundary separating the hair from anything else. Similarly Hua Yen philosophy explains that time is only a human construct: in ultimate reality an hour is eternity.

The Hua Yen School, founded by Du Shun (557-640), is based on the Hua Yen or Avatamsaka Sutra, meaning Flower Adornment Sutra, which is an expression of the enlightenment experience of the Buddha himself.

Within the first week of his enlightenment and still sitting in his meditation position, the Buddha gave a majestic sermon on cosmic reality to heavenly beings who had gathered around him, but the teaching was too profound even for the gods to understand.

The Buddha explains that an enlightened being realizes that his so-called individual self is actually the vast, unlimited universe, where there is no duality between the knower and the known.

This transcendental cosmic reality may also manifest as countless phenomena, which are illusory and relative, brought about by a matrix of causes and conditions. Modern science calls the transcendental and the phenomenal dimensions the implicate and the explicate orders respectively.

Ordinary persons, who are deluded by their gross senses, see phenomena as separated and differentiated; in reality phenomena are only appearances, brought about by *dharmas* which are independently arising and mutually penetrating.

This concept becomes meaningful to us only after modern science has explained that phenomena are made up of subatomic particles that are constantly arising and penetrating. But all these are a dream; in the realm of enlightenment, everything is eternally tranquil; all phenomena, the mind and the Buddha are not three entities but one undifferentiated whole.

If the Ultimate Truth, called by various names like the Tathagata, Brahman, Cosmos, God and Allah, is undifferentiated and eternally tranquil, why do we in our ordinary consciousness perceive this Spiritual Body of the Supreme Reality as separated and differentiated entities? In scientific terms, if the universe is ultimately an unbroken spread of energy, if an elementary particle actually has no defined boundary, why do we see a particular collection of particles as a tree or an elephant, whereas a living cell in the tree or elephant may see the same collection as its own universe? Of all the Buddhist schools, the Fa Xiang School probably explains this phenomenon most thoroughly.

The Fa Xiang or Mere Ideation School, founded in China by the great monk of the Tang Dynasty, Xuan Zang (Hsuan Tsang, 596-664), and his disciple Kui Ji (632-682), was a continuation of the Yogacara School of Asanga and Vasubandhu in India. When Xuan Zang returned from India after his famous pilgrimage of sixteen years, he stayed for some time at the Shaolin Monastery to translate into Chinese the Sanskrit works he had brought back.

The basic Fa Xiang philosophy is that the world is ideation only, which means the external world does not exist independently by itself, but the internal ideation presents an appearance of it as an external world. This Buddhist concept is now expressed by scientists as the multi-dimensional hologram.

The mind, which is the most important principle in the Fa Xiang School, is classified into the following eight kinds of consciousness: eye-consciousness, ear-consciousness, nose-consciousness, tongue-consciousness, body-consciousness, mano-consciousness or sense-center, manas-consciousness or thought-center, and alaya-consciousness or storage-center.

What a human sees as an elephant, a bacterium may see as a universe, whereas a fairy may see nothing. This is because, among other factors, a human, a bacterium and a fairy possess different alaya-consciousness, which Jungian psychologists would call collective mind.

Modern scientists who are puzzled why you, they and I see a table as a table, and not as a cow or a chair, although that table is actually a creation of our individual minds, would be glad to learn that our minds, though different, share the same alaya-consciousness common to humans.

Zhen Yen or Mantra means "True Word". The Zhen Yen School was transmitted to China from India by Subhakarasinha (637-735), Vajrabodhi (663-723) and Amoghavajra (705-774). It is representative of the third and final (until now) developmental stage of Buddhism, and is known as Mantrayana, Tantrayana or Vajrayana; the earlier two developmental stages being Hinayana and Mahayana.

Thus, the Mantra School is also called the Tantra School, or Mi Zong in Chinese, meaning the Secret School. Vajrayana Buddhism is now widely practiced in Tibet and Mongolia.

There are three typical differences between Hinayana or Theravada and Mahayana on one hand, and Vajrayana on the other. Even the highest Theravada and Mahayana teachings are public properties, but Vajrayana is taught only to initiated students.

Theravada and Mahayana monks are strictly celibate, and their lay followers are forbidden to have immoral sexual activities, whereas some Vajrayana sects use sex as a means of spiritual cultivation. Even Buddhas and Bodhisattvas are supplied with female consorts!

Thirdly, Theravadins and Mahayanists regard Gautama Buddha, or Sakyamuni Buddha as he is more widely known in Mahayana, as their paramount teacher, whereas Vajrayanists place more importance on Vairocana Buddha, who is regarded as the Spiritual Body of Gautama.

Besides mantras, mudras and mandalas are extensively employed in the Zhen Yen School. A mudra is a particular way of holding the fingers during meditation; a mandala is a symbolic diagram consisting mainly of circles, squares and triangles representing various cosmic spheres where Buddhas and Bodhisattvas reside.

A mantra, representing the true words of the Buddha's Spiritual Body, is a mystical combination of sounds, usually in a phrase and often with supernatural effects. A long mantra, running to many sentences, is called a dharani.

Mantras are employed for entering into meditation, praising Buddhas, Bodhisattvas or other deities, protection against evil forces, exorcism, escaping from calamities, identification with a particular Bodhisattva, developing psychic powers, and other similar uses.

Mantras are also used in Theravada and Mahayana Buddhism, though its use is not as extensive as in Vajrayana. Mantras are found in other religions like Taoism, Hinduism and Jainism too. The following is an example of a Buddhist mantra for soothing local deities:

Namo saman tuo mutuonam Om
Tiwai tiwai saboha

While mantras are usually in Sanskrit, the following praise in Chinese to the Buddha and Bodhisattvas at the gathering of the wisdom sutras, chanted daily in the Shaolin Monastery before the recitation of the Heart Sutra, is regarded by many as a mantra:

Namo ban ruo hui shang fo pu sa

Hence, Shaolin monks and secular disciples not only practice kungfu and chi kung, appreciate poetry and chant mantras, but have access to Buddhist wisdom that only now the latest sciences are beginning to study.

Yet, the rarest opportunity is to have not just a deep understanding of profound philosophy but a direct experience of the greatest achievement any being can ever attain. This will be explained in the next chapter.

26
The Beauty And Profundity Of Zen

(Some Philosophical Considerations for Zen Training)

This cosmic glimpse is always inspiring and exhilarating, where the adept directly experiences the beauty, grandeur and magnificence of transcendental reality, where he realizes for himself that what masters have said like transcending space and time, breaking down the illusory barrier between the knower and the known, is true.

What is Zen

"What is Zen?"

"A brick."

"What is Tao?"

"A piece of wood."

The gong-an above is a celebrated conversation between a Zen monk and Shi Tou (700-790), a great Zen master of the Tang Dynasty, recorded as a *gong-an* (or *koan* in Japanese) for posterity. Most people have difficulty understanding a gong-an because of at least the following two reasons. One, they do not know the purpose of a gong-an; and two, they do not know that Zen has a few related meanings.

A gong-an is a Zen story that actually took place (and recorded by specially assigned monks) whereby a Zen master used often-extraordinary verbal or non-verbal means to awaken his student spiritually, or to test if he had such an awakening, known as *wu*, or *satori* in Japanese. Hence, in the above gong-an, it was not Shi Tou's intention to explain what Zen was; his purpose was to awaken the monk to Zen, sometimes called Tao.

"Zen" is the Japanese word for the Chinese word "Chan", which in turn is derived from the Sanskrit word "Dhyana". At its lowest or basic level, Zen means meditation. It is not restricted to Buddhist meditation: thus yogis, who may be Hindu or of other religions, practice Dhyana too; Taoists and Confucians also practice Chan.

The meaning of Zen at the intermediate level is a glimpse of cosmic reality. This cosmic glimpse is always inspiring and exhilarating, where the adept directly experiences the beauty, grandeur and magnificence of transcendental reality, where he realizes for himself that what masters have said like transcending space and time, breaking down the illusory barrier between the knower and the known, is true. This is *wu*, an experience that he can never forget, an awakening that will transform his life from the physical to the divine.

The supreme meaning of Zen is Ultimate Reality itself, called variously by different peoples as the Buddha, Tathagata, Cosmos, Brahman, Allah or God, or by mundane names as *sunyata*, or void, and energy field. Attaining Zen at this supreme level is the fulfillment of all religions, and is known as nirvana or enlightenment in Buddhism. It can be attained here and now.

Zen is sometimes used as a short form for Zen Buddhism, that school of Mahayana Buddhism with special emphasis on attaining enlightenment instantaneously using meditation as the paramount approach.

Zen was transmitted by Bodhidharma in 527 CE from India to China, where Zen Buddhism, or Chan Buddhism as it is known in Chinese, originated as an institutionalized teaching at the Shaolin Monastery. It reached its golden age in China during the Tang Dynasty from the 7th to the 10th centuries, and spread to Japan during the Song Dynasty in the 13th century.

In the gong-an above, how could Shi Tou help to awaken the monk by telling him that Zen was a brick, or Tao a piece of wood? It should be remembered that this gong-an was not an isolated occurrence; the monk stayed in the monastery with the master, and had been undergoing Zen training, especially meditation, for many years.

In this encounter, the master hoped to use a verbal means to achieve a non-verbal effect. In other words, instead of giving an intellectual answer, which would set the monk thinking, Shi Tou gave a seemingly illogical answer which, he hoped, would stop the monk's thought, jerking him into an awakening.

Should the monk be awakened and has a glimpse of ultimate reality, he would, in his wonderment, discover that Zen was really a brick and Tao a piece of wood, because in ultimate reality there is no separateness and no differentiation.

Chinese Invention and Taoist Origin?

Some scholars have said that Zen was a Chinese invention; others that it was developed from Taoism! Both these statements are rejected by virtually all Chinese Zen masters, and it is not difficult to see why, if we study its history, philosophy and practice from the Zen perspective, and not from the perspective of scholars, who are mainly Confucianist in attitude.

Practically all Chinese Zen masters traced their lineage to Bodhidharma, who was the twenty-eighth Patriarch in India and became the First Patriarch in

China. The Buddha transmitted Zen directly to Mahakasyapa, the Indian First Patriarch, who in turn transmitted "the marvelous mind of enlightenment" through twenty six Indian patriarchs — including Asvaghosha (11th Patriarch), Nagarjuna (13th Patriarch) and Vasubandhu (20th Patriarch) — to Bodhidharma.

The evidence of Bodhidharma teaching Zen in the Shaolin Monastery is so overwhelming that unless scholars are ignorant of the evidence, it is incredible how they could say Bodhidharma was only a myth. Temple records, imperial histories, official diaries, personal writings and other documents clearly show Bodhidharma's activities in China. The cave where Bodhidharma meditated for nine years, the pavilion where he transmitted Zen to the Second Patriarch, and the First Patriarch Temple built in his honor are still found in the Shaolin Monastery today.

To say that Zen Buddhism developed from Taoism is equally untenable. This mistake probably started when some scholars, who were expert in Chinese literature and philosophy but knew little about Zen, speculated that the great monk Tao An (313-385) and his distinguished disciple Hui Yuan (344-416) initiated Chan (Zen) Buddhism, because they practiced meditation, which in Chinese is often written as "Chan".

What these scholars might not realize is that here the name "Tao" and the term "Chan" are not related to Taoism and Chan Buddhism respectively; just as when the monk asked "What is Tao" in the quotation at the head of this chapter, the word "Tao" means the Ultimate Reality or enlightenment, and does not refer to Taoism.

If these scholars had investigated deeper, they would have found that the "Chan" or meditation Tao An and Hui Yuan practiced was Anapanasati (please see the next chapter), the meditation of the Sarvastivada School, which is similar to Theravada meditation practiced today, but different from Zen meditation.

More importantly, although both Tao An and Hui Yuan, like other great monks, were familiar with Confucianism as well as Taoism, there was little Taoist (or Confucian) philosophy or practice in the Buddhism they preached.

Tao An, for example, was dissatisfied with the method of early translators using Taoist terms for Buddhist concepts; Hui Yuan said that Buddhist thought was far ahead and more profound than that of Confucianism and Taoism. There is also no records of any Zen Buddhism in China in the interim hundred years between them and the arrival of Bodhidharma.

In the development of Zen Buddhism in China, not a single one of the six Chinese Patriarchs had any significant Taoist influence. All the first three Patriarchs — Bodhidharma, Hui Ke and Seng Can — taught at the Shaolin Monastery; the other three — Dao Xin, Hong Jen and Hui Neng — taught at the Dongshan Temple and the Bao Lin Temple, which were typically Buddhist temples directly related to Shaolin.

Zen masters talk about no mind, Buddha-nature, Bodhisattvas and return to society to help others — all these are characteristically different from the Taoists' yin-yang, cosmos, immortals and retreat to mountains to avoid worldly affairs.

Zen monks shave their head bald, abstain from meat and wine, and practice celibacy strictly; whereas Taoist priests value their typical head-buns, often drink wine and play chess in merriment, and are permitted to have wives and children.

Zen monks refer to the Heart Sutra, the Diamond Sutra and other Buddhist scriptures, which are distinctly different from the Tao Te Ching, the Chuang Tzu and other Taoist texts in both style and substance.

The typical meditation method of Zen practitioners is to keep the mind void, with the mind abiding at nothing. This is characteristically different from the typical Taoist method of meditation where visualization is used extensively.

Meditation techniques frequently employed by Taoist adepts, like nurturing vital energy into "divine foetus", and visualizing specific deities residing at particular energy fields inside their body, are considered "perverse" by Zen masters as these techniques cause thoughts to arise, therefore conflicting with the Zen technique of aiming for the state of non-thought.

Hence, whether it is from the perspective of history, canonical works, daily mode of living, philosophy or spiritual cultivation, Zen and Taoism are distinctively different. Anyone who has actually gone through either Zen or Taoist training, instead of merely reading from some second-hand material, will find it hard to see how Zen Buddhism could have developed from Taoism. In this respect I am lucky to have some first hand experience: my master, Sifu Ho Fatt Nam, was well trained in Taoism before he started cultivating Zen.

Main Doctrines of Zen Buddhism

Not recorded in language and words,
Transmission beyond the tradition,
Directly pointing at the mind.
Entering Buddhahood in an instant.

The above lines originally spoken by the Buddha to Mahakasyapa when the World-Honored One transmitted Zen to the Indian First Patriarch, and later propagated by Bodhisattva, summarize the main features of Zen Buddhism. They also show the principal doctrines in Zen Buddhism, illustrating how different they are from Taoism.

The first doctrine, "Not recorded in language and words", indicates that in Zen Buddhism the essential teaching is passed on from heart to heart, or from the mind of the master directly to the mind of his disciple, and not in the form of learning from written records of past masters.

In Buddhist terminology, it is the direct transmission of "cosmic wisdom" from master to disciple, without depending on "language wisdom". This means the disciple has a direct experience of cosmic reality as a result of the master's transmission, and not as the result of his description in words. This is different from Taoist instruction which often depends on words, written or spoken.

Indeed, all advanced Shaolin arts are transmitted from heart to heart. For example, when I teach Shaolin Cosmos Breathing to a student, I personally show him the techniques and guide him in his practice, often channeling my vital energy into him to stimulate his own energy flow.

Thus, his cosmic chi flow has some of my chi, passed on to him during training. In this way, I transmitted, not merely taught, Shaolin Cosmos Chi Kung to him. Had I written or tape-recorded the same teaching instructions in words and he followed the written or spoken instructions exactly, instead of learning from me directly the result would be very different.

"Transmission beyond the tradition" means that the Zen teaching was taught in a way different from the traditional way of other Buddhist schools. For example the Buddha transmitted Zen, or enlightenment, to Mahakasyapa by means of a golden kumbhala flower without uttering a word.

This was different from his normal way of preaching to his disciples. Mahakasyapa transmitted Zen to Ananda when he told Ananda to take down the banner hanging at their temple. This sudden order, which seemed unrelated to what they were doing then, jolted Ananda's mind, resulting in his enlightenment instantly.

Such transmission beyond the tradition is unique in Zen; it is not found in Taoism or any other systems of spiritual cultivation. This is another reason why I say that anyone who has practiced Zen will find it difficult to see how Zen could have developed from Taoism.

The third doctrine, "Directly pointing at the mind", shows that Zen is practical and direct. When asked what Zen or Tao was, instead of giving a lengthy, philosophical discussion or a profound answer clothed in symbolic language as many Taoist masters would do, the Zen master Shi Tou simply said it was a brick or a piece of wood! Superficially the reply appeared ridiculous, but actually it was an astonishingly practical and direct way to help the seeker experience Zen or Tao.

A Taoist master would never have replied in this way: in the long history of Taoism, not a single Taoist worth his name had said Tao was a toad, a lump of clay or something as "outlandish" as a Zen master would say.

Perhaps the furthest any Taoist master had ventured was that romantic and lovable Chuang Tzu (4th century BCE) who said, in his striking rhetoric to show Tao is everywhere, that it is found in an ant, a weed, broken pieces of pottery, and a heap of dung!

It illustrates a crucial difference between Taoist and Zen teachings. Chuang Tzu and other Taoist masters describe Tao; from them we get an intellectual description. Shi Tou and other Zen masters direct us to Tao; if we are ready, we get an intuitive experience.

A typical answer to the question "What is Tao?" is something like the following poetic lines from the great Taoist master of the Song Dynasty, Zhang Bo Duan (984-1082), who explained what modern science would describe as the creation of matter from neutrons, protons and electrons:

Tao from the void is born an energy whole
From energy whole yin and yang unfold
Yin and yang combine to become three rings
Three rings regenerate to form myriad things

"Entering Buddhahood in an instant" illustrates a characteristic feature of Zen Buddhism, which expounds that every person has Buddha-nature. Buddhist masters, perhaps more in Zen Buddhism than in any other schools, teach that everyone is originally enlightened, i.e. everyone is originally the Eternal Buddha!

However due to ignorance he is deluded into thinking of himself as an individual self imprisoned in his body, and also thinking of countless phenomena as reality when these phenomena are actually appearances brought about by various causes and conditions.

This, again, is a crucial philosophical difference between Zen and Taoism as well as all other great religions. Except their greatest masters whose realization that at the highest spiritual attainment they and the cosmos (also called God by some religions) are one is similar to the Buddhist enlightenment.

As discussed in Chapter 23, Taoists and aspirants of other religions in general aim to liberate their imprisoned souls from their physical bodies so as to become immortals or go to heaven in their present life or the next. They also regard all phenomena in heaven as real.

In Zen and all other schools of Buddhism, becoming an immortal and going to heaven are only intermediate goals, and all phenomena whether on earth or in heavens and hells are illusory. The ultimate goal of Buddhism, especially Zen Buddhism, is to transcend the phenomenal and attain ultimate reality, i.e. nirvana.

When a Zen adept attains enlightenment, he realizes that selves and phenomena are illusions; in ultimate reality there is no separateness and no differentiation. His delusion is due to thoughts arising. The very moment he attains a state of non-thought or no mind in meditation, he regains his original enlightenment instantly, i.e. he enters Buddhahood in an instant.

The Zen school which considers this meditation of no mind as the direct approach to enlightenment is called Cao Dong (Chao Tsung) Zen, which later spread to Japan as Soto Zen, and which is a good contrast to Lin Ji (or Rinzai)

Zen which uses gong-ans (or koans) extensively as an aid to enlightenment. Although different schools of Zen had been practiced in the Shaolin Monastery, the most important is Cao Dong Zen.

Zen wisdom accepts and surpasses Taoist thought. The Taoist teaching of the mutual transformation of energy and matter, as suggested in the above quotation, is also taught in Buddhism, but while the Taoists, like modern scientists, regard it as an absolute truth, the Buddhists regard it as relative.

In other words, Taoists and scientists (perhaps with the exception of those who normally use relativity and quantum mechanics as their reference frames) regard "the interaction of three rings to form myriad things", or the interaction of neutrons, protons and electrons to form atoms, as ultimate reality, and the laws governing them as applicable everywhere in the universe.

Buddhists regard all this as "real" only relative to our present set of conditions, and to our local realm of existence. Should our conditions or locality be changed, the phenomena may appear differently.

If we had the wisdom-eye of a Bodhisattva, for example, we might see not just "three rings and myriad things", but much more, like what scientists refer to as "dark matter" which we (ordinary mortals) have never seen even with the most sophisticated scientific instruments, but which scientists believe constitutes 99 percent of our known universe.

If we happen to be in another galaxy, such as in Amitabha's Western Paradise, what we called neutrons, protons and electrons on our puny earth might not exist there, or even if they existed they might not form atoms.

Such Buddhist wisdom was, and has been, a crucial aspect of Zen philosophy — even when Zen Buddhism first started in China. Without such wisdom, gong-ans like Zen being a brick, or clapping with one hand would be meaningless.

It is therefore not logical to say that Zen Buddhism drew its philosophy from Taoism, which does not have the kind of cosmic wisdom characteristics of Zen. Indeed, many masters already well versed in Confucianism and Taoism changed to Buddhism because they found the Buddhist philosophy and goals amazingly more beautiful and profound.

The Easiest or the Most Difficult

Practicing Zen is the easiest approach to enlightenment, or the most difficult — depending on one's perspective and readiness. The whole discipline of Zen training can be put in one word — meditation.

All that is required in the training can be said in one sentence — sit comfortably in a lotus position, close your eyes gently and keep your mind blank! Isn't that easy? You do not have to know any doctrines, study scriptures, listen to sermons, say prayers, recite mantras, worship the Buddha, God or any Divinity, or worry about your soul or the after-life.

In theory, Zen is the easiest. If you are ready, and just do this correctly — sit comfortably in a lotus position, close your eyes and keep your mind blank — you will achieve enlightenment, i.e. the greatest achievement any being can achieve, in an instant!

But in actual practice, this approach may be the most difficult. It may sound odd, but sitting comfortably itself may not be easy! Some people cannot even sit comfortably on a chair; they feel restless after only a few minutes. Sitting in a lotus position, even if they are prepared to put up with some discomfort, is difficult for most untrained adults. Keeping the mind blank is the worst; some people have told me it was the most difficult thing they had ever attempted.

While Zen is easy for those who are ready, physically, emotionally, mentally and spiritually, it is the most difficult for the unready. That is why although many aspirants have practiced meditation, Buddhist or otherwise, for more than ten years, they achieve little effect.

How does one know whether he is ready? As a useful guide, if you are sick or have pain in your body, you are not ready physically. Good health is a prerequisite for spiritual development. For a person suffering from peptic ulcer or back ache, for example, long hours of meditation will not only be unlikely to help him progress spiritually but also may aggravate his illness or pain.

He should therefore overcome his illness and bodily pains before embarking on spiritual training. Shaolin Chi Kung is excellent for relieving illnesses and pains, and Shaolin Kungfu for providing radiant health and vitality.

A person is emotionally unready for spiritual training if he cannot relax or if lacks emotional stability. For example, if he is nervous, easily frightened, prone to anger, or worries unnecessarily, he should overcome his emotional problems before attempting Zen cultivation.

From my experiences with many of my students who have such emotional problems, conventional psychiatric treatments are not very helpful. They overcame emotional problems by practicing Shaolin Kungfu or Shaolin Chi Kung, which are also excellent for teaching people to relax at will.

If you have difficulties focusing your mind during meditation or in your daily activities, often find your mind wandering aimlessly, easily fatigued in mental work, or muddled in thinking, you are mentally not ready for spiritual training.

It should be known that Zen meditation demands much mental effort and energy; if the mind is weak, it is unsuitable for spiritual cultivation. Again, Shaolin Kungfu and Shaolin Chi Kung are very helpful for strengthening the mind. In the next chapter, we shall learn two meditation methods to help the mind to focus.

What is spiritual readiness? If a person has no urge to seek beyond his physical needs, to find out what his origin was and what his destiny will be, he is spiritually unready. Morality is the basic requirement for all spiritual training, and should be cultivated according to his own religious teaching.

In Buddhism the basic moral cultivation is to practice the five precepts of not killing, not stealing, not telling lies, not involving in licentious sex, and not taking intoxicating drinks.

Some readers, imbued with the western concept of "positive thinking", may complain that these moral rules are negative, emphasizing don'ts rather than dos. This attitude is an example of dualistic thinking, a mistaken rationalization that "don't kill" is the opposite of "save lives". These five precepts are the minimum requirements for the first of the threefold teaching of Buddhism:

Avoid all evil
Do good
Purify the mind

Logically, if one cannot even fulfill the most elementary requirement, i.e. avoiding all evil, it is premature to talk of doing good. Hence, from the Buddhist perspective, it is incongruous for a millionaire who earns his fortune through cheating (which is a form of "stealing" in the five precepts) to act like a charitable man.

Performing charity is one of the ways a Buddhist can do good. Charitable acts can be generalized into three classes. At the lowest level is the charity of giving material aids, like food and money, to the needy. The middle level of charity is giving service, like tending the sick and saving lives. The highest charity is in giving teachings, especially spiritual teachings, like distributing religious texts and reciting scriptures whereby lost souls who happen to be around may hear, learn and be saved.

The spiritual aspirant must clearly know the aim of his cultivation. If he is unclear of what he will achieve, when he eventually achieves, he is likely to waste much time. He should therefore be familiar with the teaching of the highest teachers of his chosen religion, or, if he professes not to have a religion, of his ideal philosophy of life.

In the Shaolin Monastery, most spiritual aspirants aim for the highest achievement, i.e. attaining nirvana or enlightenment. It is also called attaining Zen, Tao, Bodhi, Buddhahood, or seeing the original face. When this supreme goal is attained, the adept is no more his personal self, which actually is an illusion, but literally becomes the whole universe or the Eternal Buddha!

Others, who have taken the great compassionate Bodhisattva Vow, voluntarily postpone their own Buddhahood, so that they can come back to our world or to other worlds as highly spiritual beings to help others. They cultivate to become Bodhisattvas, in their present lives or subsequent ones.

Lesser minds aim to go to heaven. It is relatively easy to go to heaven. In the Buddhist teaching there are more than twenty heavens in our Saha world, which probably corresponds to our solar system, and literally billions of heavens in other stars and galaxies. Spiritually advanced cultivators can decide which heaven they wish to go to!

All these spiritual aims can be realized through Zen training. The basic meditation is quite similar, except that the vow the aspirants make and the particular way they direct their mind are quite different. Practical Zen training will be explained in the next chapter.

27
Methods Of
Zen Cultivation

(Sutras, Mantras and Meditation for Spiritual Training)

Acquiring blessings through reciting sutras to develop compassion is one way of spiritual training; acquiring merits through meditation to develop wisdom is another. Hence, reciting sutras and practicing meditation are the two essential daily tasks in all Zen monasteries.

Meditation of No Mind

When my master, Sifu Ho Fatt Nam, taught me Zen meditation he said, "Sit comfortably in a lotus position, close your eyes gently and keep your mind blank."

Its simplicity and directness, and with hindsight I would add effectiveness, caught me by surprise. I thought that the technique of Zen meditation would be very "deep" and complicated. Nevertheless, like a good student, I did what my teacher taught.

Because my legs were stiff, due to my early training of the horse-riding stance without performing the complementary leg stretching exercises, I could only manage a cross-legged sitting position. So I asked my teacher, "Can I use the cross-legged position instead, or even the simple sitting upright position on a stool?"

"No," my master replied, "you must use at least the single lotus position. Many people have achieved high levels, including psychic powers, using the cross-legged or even the simple sitting upright position, but if you aim for the highest you must use the double lotus, or at least the single lotus."

"But my legs are too stiff."

"Then practice leg stretching exercises," my master said.

I did that, for two years before my legs are flexible enough to attempt the single lotus position, Fig 27.1.

Fig 27.1 Single Lotus Position — Buddha Pose

I also asked my master, "Can I focus my mind at my abdomen, or at my third eye?"

"We do that in Taoist meditation, and also in Shaolin Kungfu and Chi Kung," my master explained. "Focusing the mind at the *dan tian* (the energy field at the abdomen) develops a tremendous amount of *jing chi* (vital energy). It is very good for kungfu. Some Zen practitioners also uses this method, and when this pearl of energy expands, fills the whole body and merges with the cosmos, enlightenment is attained. This is called silent-illuminating Zen. We look into this illuminating pearl silently. Then, when the time is ripe, this internal illumination merges with the external illumination of the cosmos, and nirvana is achieved.

"Focusing the mind at the *yin tang* (the third eye) or at the *bai hui* (the crown of the head) develops *shen chi* (spiritual energy). When the *yin tang* is opened, psychic powers are accomplished. When the *bai hui* is opened, the soul may be liberated from the body and becomes a heavenly saint. Taoists use this opening of the *bai hui*, known as *kai qiao*, to attain immortality."

"Achieving immortality! Isn't that wonderful?" I exclaimed.

"In Buddhism, attaining immortality is not the highest goal," my master explains. "To be a saint or an immortal in heaven is still existence in the phenomenal realm. The supreme aim of Zen is `to jump beyond the three realms', that is to transcend all phenomenal realms and realize the Ultimate Truth. This is attaining Buddhahood."

Much later I realized that this meditation of non-thought or no mind my master taught me was the same meditation taught by the Sixth Patriarch Hui Neng, which was transmitted down the generations by the First Patriarch Bodhidharma at the Shaolin Monastery!

Keeping thoughts away, or the state of non-thought, which is quite different from eliminating thoughts already in the mind, or the state of no-thought, is comparatively easy for me because I was adequately prepared after my years of kungfu and chi kung training where both one-pointed meditation and visualization are practiced.

This non-thought or no-mind meditation is known as Patriarch Zen. In *Tan Jing*, or Platform Sutra, one of the most important scriptures in Zen Buddhism, the Six Patriarch explained:

What is meant by *zuo chan* or sitting meditation? In our teaching, when there is no obstruction whatsoever — externally to all entities and space, internally no thoughts arise in the mind — that is *zuo* (sitting). Perceiving the original nature without any perturbation is *chan* (meditation). What is *chan ding* (dhyana-samadhi, or cosmic stillness)? Externally being free from all characteristics is *chan* (dhyana), and internally being un-perturbed is *ding* (samadhi).

In the above quotation, the Six Patriarch explains that in the Zen meditation taught by him, the meditator sits still without any external and internal interference.

Externally there is no obstruction, i.e. in his meditative state, he has transcended space: all external objects have ceased to have any reality to him (although other people in their ordinary consciousness still see him as an individual person differentiated from other objects).

Internally there is no thought in his mind, i.e. he has transcended time: his mind and the Universal Mind is the same infinity. This direct experience of ultimate reality, which is tranquil and undifferentiated, is Chan or Zen.

Praises and Vows in Spiritual Cultivation

For those who are ready, the meditation of no mind described above is sufficient for them to attainment a Zen awakening or even enlightenment in an instant. But it must be remembered that even if an aspirant is ready he still has to practice diligently for many years before that cosmic instant may happen.

For others who wish to have more preparation or some variety in their spiritual cultivation, the following methods, which are practiced in the Shaolin Monastery and other Zen monasteries, are helpful. Students need not follow the sequence listed below, and they may choose which ever methods they find suitable.

It is worth emphasizing that if they are not ready physically, emotional or mentally, they should practice Shaolin Kungfu and Shaolin Chi Kung or any other appropriate arts to equip themselves.

The information supplied in this book is sufficient for spiritual preparation, but of course it is recommendable to read more from authentic sources. It must be stressed again that morality is the prerequisite of all spiritual training.

An immoral person practicing methods meant for spiritual development, such as meditation and mantra recitation, may acquire some psychic abilities, but he will inevitably ruin himself. This is a cosmic truth.

It is helpful, but not essential, to place an image or any visual representation of a Buddha, Bodhisattva or Deity of your chosen religion on an altar for your daily "service" or devotion. Different cultures and religions perform religious services differently. The following is performed in Buddhism, as in Shaolin Monastery.

After you have cleansed yourself, offer a joss stick, flowers, water or a lighted candle to the Buddha or the Bodhisattva. If these external offerings are not available, just place your two palms together in prayer, and bow sincerely. Then sing or chant the praise to the Buddha or Bodhisattva three times. The following is the praise in Chinese to Sakyamuni Buddha, followed by its English translation:

Namo Ben Shi Shi Jia Mou Ni Fo

Homage to our teacher Sakyamuni Buddha

The praise to Avalokitesvara Bodhisattva or Guan Shi Yin Pu Sa (pronounced like "Kuan Shi Yin Bodh Satt") in Chinese, and its English translation are as follows:

Namo Da Bei Guan Shi Yin Pu Sa

Homage to the Great Compassionate
Guan Shi Yin Bodhisattva

You may chant the praises in English or in any language you wish.

After chanting the praise three times, prostrate once or thrice as follows. Start with palms together in prayer position, Fig 27.2. Kneel down, place both palms facing downward on the ground in front, gently knock your head on the ground, turn both palms to face skyward with the arms still on the ground, Fig 27.3, then stand up with palms in prayer position.

Fig 27.2 Palms in Prayer

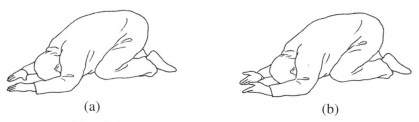

(a)   (b)

Fig 27.3 Prostrating to Buddha or Bodhisattva

Some people may feel uneasy prostrating to a Buddha, a Bodhisattva or to their teachers, thinking it is degrading. I had similar feelings before, but when I became more developed I realized that my earlier arrogance and egoism were due to my spiritual immaturity. Even emperors, generals and great monks prostrated to Buddhas, Bodhisattvas and their teachers, not out of compulsion but of gratitude and reverence.

It is illuminating to know that the purpose of prostration to Buddhas and Bodhisattvas is totally for the benefit of the devotees. It makes not the slightest difference to these enlightened beings whether any person prostrates to them; but it makes a great difference to the aspirant.

If he still harbors sense of ego and vanity, he is unlikely to progress much at the highest levels of spiritual training. Prostration is one of the most effective ways to help him overcome his vanity and ego.

The aspirant would have to modify his praise according to the deities he places on his altar for his devotion. If the aspirant does not have an altar or image of a Buddha or Bodhisattva, he can chant the appropriate praise towards the sky. If he does not have any particular Buddha or Bodhisattva in mind, he may chant the following praise to all Buddhas and Bodhisattvas:

Namo Shi Fang Fo Pu Sa

Homage to Buddhas and Bodhisattvas of ten directions

After paying the appropriate homage, the aspirant reconfirms his vow in front of the Buddha or Bodhisattva, said silently in his heart, spoken softly or aloud. He can compose his own vow; below are some examples.

The following vow, taught by the Six Patriarch himself, is made by many Zen cultivators:

Infinite sentient beings I vow to save
Infinite defilements I vow to abolish
The infinite dharma I vow to practice
The supreme Buddhahood I vow to accomplish

Those who are compassionate may take the Bodhisattva Vow, an example of which is given below:

All defilements I vow to terminate
The highest wisdom I vow to attain
To help all beings overcome suffering
The Bodhisattva way I return to maintain

The vow below is an example for those who wish to be reborn in heaven:

This marvelous teaching I vow to share
With all who wish to benefit from it
May we cultivate with unfailing heart
And be reborn in the land of bliss

Making a vow is important: it compels the aspirant to be seriously committed, and it gives him direction for his spiritual training.

The Heart Sutra of Transcendental Wisdom

After reconfirming his vow, the aspirant may chant or recite a sutra. He may stand, kneel, or sit in a lotus or cross-legged position in front of an altar or in any suitable place. If the sutra is long, he may recite a part of it and continue in another session.

The most popular sutra for recitation among Zen practitioners as well as followers of many other Buddhist schools is the "Great Heart Sutra of Transcendental Wisdom to Reach the Other Shore", usually shortened to the Heart Sutra.

It is an incredibly amazing masterpiece: consisting of only 260 words in Chinese, the Heart Sutra presents all the important doctrines of Buddhism! Understandably, in such an exceedingly concise form the Heart Sutra is incomprehensible to most people, including many devotees who recite it daily.

If you think it is about gods and morality, prayers and devotion, you will be most mistaken. The Heart Sutra explains what *sunyata* or the void is, and reveals wisdom that our scientists are investigating into, as in cosmology, explicate and implicate order, consciousness, relativity and quantum mechanics! The Heart Sutra translated into English is presented below. Do not worry if you find it difficult. Most people do.

Avalokitesvara Bodhisattva, coursing deeply through prajna-paramita, perceives the five skandhas are all empty, and overcomes all suffering and calamity.

Sariputra, form is no different from emptiness; emptiness is no different from form. Form is emptiness; emptiness is form. Feeling, thought, activity, consciousness are also thus.

Sariputra, all phenomena are emptied of characteristics: non-arising, non-ceasing; non-defiled, non-pure; non-adding, non-subtracting. Thus in emptiness, there is no form, no feeling, thought, activity, consciousness. There is no eye, ear, nose, tongue, body, and intellect consciousness. There is no form, sound, smell, taste, touch and phenomena. There is no realm of eye consciousness till no realm of intellect consciousness.

There is no ignorance and no termination of ignorance, till no age and death and no termination of age and death. There is no suffering, no cause, no extinction, and no path. There is no wisdom and no merits. Thus there is no attainment whatsoever. Due to prajna-paramita, Bodhisattvas have no obstruction of mind. Because there is no obstruction, there is no fear. Being far from delusion and dreams, perfect nirvana is attained.

Due to prajna-paramita, Buddhas of the past, present and future attain anuttara-samyak-sambodhi.

Thus, know that prajna-paramita is a great divine mantra, a great mantra of enlightenment, an unsurpassed mantra, a mantra that has no equal. It is able to eliminate all suffering. This is really true, without falsehood. If you recite the prajna-paramita mantra; say gate, gate, para gate, para sam-gate, bodhi svaha.

At the completion of a sutra recitation, it is usual to chant the name of the Buddha or Bodhisattva related to the sutra. The Heart Sutra is a description of the enlightenment experience of Avalokitesvara Bodhisattva, or Guan Shi Yin Pu Sa in Chinese. Hence, the following praise in Chinese is chanted thrice. The English version, which you may use in place of the Chinese, is also given below.

Namo Da Bei Guan Shi Yin Pu Sa

Homage to the Great Compassionate
Guan Shi Yin Pu Sa

After singing or chanting the praise three times, pay homage to the Buddha or Bodhisattva by prostration once or thrice.

Spiritual Development through Sutra Recitation

The inevitable question many people ask is why recite the Heart Sutra when its profound meaning is not understood. Different answers apply to different groups of reciters.

Monks in Zen monasteries recite the Heart Sutra because it is an essential part of their daily service. This in turn is because reciting the Heart Sutra has been a tradition passed down from the past, when reciting sutras, not reading them, was (and still is) the main way of preserving the Buddha's teaching.

As many monks were illiterate, only the elite had the opportunity to study the profound wisdom of the Heart Sutra. But all monks had a chance to listen to the explanation of the Heart Sutra and other sutras during daily sermons in their monasteries.

Similarly lay Buddhist followers recite the Heart Sutra because it is part of their daily service performed at home. It is meritorious to recite sutras, and many choose the Heart Sutra because it is short and popular.

For various reason which range from lack of good teachers or books to explain the sutra, to sheer laziness to find out more, most lay Buddhists do not understand the sutras they recite, especially when the language in the sutras was written fifteen centuries ago, and particularly the Heart Sutra expounding profound concepts in very concise language.

It is unbelievable but true that thousands of people are chanting sutras daily without understanding their meanings, just like thousands of people are performing kungfu without knowing their applications.

The gist of the Heart Sutra that form is emptiness, and emptiness is form, has been briefly explained in this book concerning *sunyata* or ultimate reality. If you wish to find out more about the Heart Sutra, which will be a very rewarding experience, please read my book *The Wisdom of the Heart Sutra*.

At the completion of the sutra recitation, the devotee transfers the blessings just gained through the recitation to others, who may be human or otherwise, still living or have departed from this world.

He may, for example, transfer the blessings to his spouse, his parents, his children, a friend who needs help, strangers he has never met, hungry ghosts wandering aimlessly around, or all sentient beings. This "transfer of blessings", carried out by Mahayanists virtually every time after have they recited a sutra is an example of the beautiful doctrine of "saving others" in Mahayana Buddhism, for the promotion of which the Shaolin Monastery was built.

The following is an example of "transfer of blessings", which can be said silently, softly or aloud:

May the merits accredited in this recitation
Be transferred to beings in all directions
And to my friends, parents and family
May they all be safe, peaceful and happy

How does one earn blessings by reciting a sutra? A sutra is the teaching of the Buddha, or sometimes of a Bodhisattva sanctioned by the Buddha as in the case of the Heart Sutra. When you chant or recite a sutra, you accomplish three meritorious acts.

One, you increase your own wisdom; even though you may not understand the sutra initially, the mental vibrations imprinted in your mind will always remain, and the wisdom will manifest when the time is ripe later in your life or future lives. Two, your recitation helps to preserve and transmit the sacred teaching for succeeding generations. Three, when you recite a sutra you act as a medium for the Buddha or Bodhisattva, so that other beings, like ghosts and gods who are around though you are unaware of them, may have a chance to benefit from the supreme teaching.

Some gods may attain enlightenment as a result of your sutra recitation! Giving spiritual knowledge is the highest form of charity — higher than building orphanages and saving lives. You can imagine the tremendous amount of blessings you acquire, and therefore the progress you make in your spiritual training, when you recite a sutra.

In the Shaolin spiritual training, which is based on Mahayana Buddhism, the aspirant is as much concerned with others' welfare as his own. His spiritual quest is not just personal salvation, but universal enlightenment.

In accordance with this doctrine, his spiritual training therefore involves the development of both compassion and wisdom. Acquiring blessings through reciting sutras to develop compassion is one way of spiritual training; acquiring merits through meditation to develop wisdom is another. Hence, reciting sutras and practicing meditation are the two essential daily tasks in all Zen monasteries.

Chanting Mantras as Spiritual Training

Instead of reciting a sutra some devotees may sing or chant the name of a Buddha or Bodhisattva continuously for tens, hundreds or even thousands of times, usually in a rhythmic or musical manner. For example, the name of the Bodhisattva of Great Compassion is frequently chanted:

*Namo Guan Shi Yin Pu Sa, Namo Guan Shi Yin
Pu Sa, Namo Guan Shi Yin Pu Sa, ...*

Homage to Avalokitesvara Bodhisattva, Homage to Avalokitesvara Bodhisattva, Homage to Avalokitesvara Bodhisattva, ...

The Buddha who is frequently chanted, especially by those who wish to gain rebirth in the Western Paradise, is Amitabha Buddha:

Namo Ami Tuo Fo, Namo Ami Tuo Fo, Namo Ami Tuo Fo, ...

Homage to Amitabha Buddha, Homage to Amitabha Buddha, Homage to Amitabha Buddha, ...

The chanting of a Buddha's or Bodhisattva's name, like the two examples above, is a mantra, although many people consider that a mantra should be worded in Sanskrit.

Chanting a mantra, like the name of a Buddha or Bodhisattva, is one way to protect ourselves from calamities and evil spirits. If you are worried about a natural disaster, a dreadful accident or some malevolent devils lurking around you, and you do not know what to do, you may attempt chanting a mantra.

If you think this is too ludicrous, you are, according to Shaolin philosophy, entitled to your opinion. However you would have denied yourself a spiritual method that might protect you, and at least give you some peace of mind.

How does a mantra work to give protection? There are three levels of operation. Firstly, a mantra is a powerful concentration of spiritual energy that has been conditioned by the mental vibrations of countless chantings. Next, there are many guardian deities around who had previously benefited from the Buddha or Bodhisattva, and who would protect the person chanting the Buddha's or Bodhisattva's mantra. Thirdly, chanting a mantra to call for help sends a signal to the Buddha or Bodhisattva who would respond in some marvelous ways.

But can spiritual energy change physical events like a landslide or a motor accident? These events are physical to us at our human level; at the level of highly developed spiritual beings, a landslide, a motor accident as well as malevolent devils are just patterns of dharmas or subatomic forces and particles, which can be manipulated by mind.

Nevertheless, it is usually easier and ethically more appropriate for the mystical operation of the mantra to get the chanter out of the way of a physical disaster, than to stop the disaster from happening. All these may sound strange to many people, but actually they are not more strange than some of our modern gadgets, like pressing a few keys to send a friend thousands of miles away a letter by fax.

A mantra can also be used to lead us into deep meditation. Sit in a lotus position, close your eyes gently, and continuously chant the name of a Buddha or Bodhisattva silently, softly or aloud. Put your mind into your chanting: feel every syllable of your chant, and hear every syllable in your mind. Initially practice for about five minutes per session, but gradually increase the time for as long as you feel comfortable. You must practice at least once a day. After a few months your mind will become one-pointed.

This mantra-chanting meditation is a very good way to train your mind. As you progress in this meditation, you will find that you can focus your mind easily. You will also find your thinking has become clearer, and you can concentrate on mental work for longer periods.

You will also progress spiritually — in ways that are easier felt than described. You may, for example, have no more fear for natural disasters or accidents, and you may even feel that malevolent devils now are afraid of you, although you have no intention at all to cause them any trouble. You certainly will have inner peace, and perhaps also experiences or abilities that previously you have never dreamt to be possible.

If you chant the name of Amitabha Buddha, such as *Namo Ami Tuo Fo*, or just *Ami Tuo Fo*, in your meditation, you practice what is known as "Zen - Pure Land Double Cultivation", or *chan jing shuang xiu* in Chinese. You may chant the Buddha's name in English, such as *Namo Amitabha Buddha*, or just *Amitabha Buddha*; or in any language. Chanting Amitabha's name is the principal method of cultivation in the Jing Tu or Pure Land School of Buddhism, and the aim is to be reborn in Amitabha's Western Paradise, which is also called the Pure Land.

The main aim in Zen Buddhism, however, is to attain enlightenment now and here, rather than to go to the Western Paradise in the after-life. But despite their seemingly opposing aims, Zen cultivation and Pure Land cultivation can be combined together rewardingly.

Pure Land practitioners use Zen or meditation to help them recite the Amitabha Buddha mantra, or to visualize the Pure Land with a one-pointed mind, as their method of winning rebirth in heaven. Zen practitioners use the Amitabha Buddha mantra to tame their mind so that they may later progress to no-mind meditation to attain nirvana in their present life.

Zen - Pure Land Double Cultivation practitioners combine both aims — to attain the Pure Land here and now instead of in their after-life. This can be interpreted in two ways: their meditation is so advanced that they experience the Western Paradise while their physical body is still on this earth; or they attain nirvana which is also called, figuratively, the Pure Land.

Meditation of One-Pointed Mind

Another apparently simple but efficacious method of meditation to attain a one-pointed mind involves focusing the mind on breathing. This method, known as *Anapanasati*, was taught by the Buddha himself, and is the chief meditation technique in Theravada Buddhism as well as widely practiced in many Mahayana schools.

In Zen Buddhism, it is called *Tathagata Zen*, but generally Zen practitioners use it as a supportive method to tame their mind, after which they progress to *Patriarch Zen* using the meditation of no mind.

The following is a brief description of this meditation of one-pointed mind. Sit in the single lotus or double lotus position. Close the eyes gently, or leave them half close gazing absentmindedly at the tip of your nose. You may use the "close eye" technique, or the "gazing at nose" technique, but not both at different times in the same meditation session.

As in all sitting meditation, your spine must be upright but relaxed, and your head tilted slightly. You can place your palms comfortably on your knees in what we call in Shaolin as the Lohan pose, Fig 27.4, or clasp your palms and rest them below your naval on your legs in the Buddha pose as in Fig 27.1 earlier.

Fig 27.4 Single Lotus Position — Lohan Pose

Keep your mind free from all thoughts, breathe naturally, then gently focus on your breathing. Be gently aware of your breathing out every time you breathe out, and be gently aware of your breathing in every time you breath in. It does not matter if your breathing is irregular, but it is important that your mind must be with your breathing all the time. After some time you will find that your mind and your energy, expressed here as your breath, have become one unity. As you progress you may become unaware of your body at all; you are just mind-energy.

In all meditation, you must not be disturbed during your practice. If you are deep in meditation, a sudden disturbance may cause your mind to scatter, which can be very uncomfortable and sometimes injurious. But there is a very simple way to prevent this. Should any disturbance occurs, immediately tell yourself that it will not harm you. Then, by a sheer but gentle act of will, keep your mind intact, and continue your meditation.

If your mind is scattered, your chi flow is usually also affected. Self-Manifested Chi Movement or selection from Eighteen Lohan Hands, followed by Standing Meditation (see Chapter 18) will help to remedy the deviation. When you feel better, practice mantra-chanting meditation or breath-focusing meditation to strengthen your mind before attempting any no-mind meditation.

In our Shaolin Wahnam School, we believe more in quality than in quantity. Thus, for beginners, we recommend that five minutes of meditation when the mind is well controlled, is better than thirty minutes when the mind runs wild like monkeys and horses. As you progress you can gradually increase your meditation time. If you can meditate well for fifteen minutes you would have achieved fairly high levels. Only later, after many years of diligent daily practice, or when you participate in a special meditation course taught by Zen masters, should you attempt meditating ten or more hours a day in an all-out effort to breakthrough the phenomenal realm to see *sunyata* or ultimate reality.

Zen or sitting meditation in a lotus position is the highest of the Shaolin arts. It should be practiced with the supervision of a master or at least a qualified instructor. However, if you cannot find a master or an instructor, and you are too eager to practice, you must proceed carefully and prudently, and you should not meditate for longer than five minutes at the beginning stage. Later as you progress and are more sure of yourself, you may very gradually increase your meditation time.

While Zen forms the core of Shaolin spiritual training, Shaolin is also rich in many other methods for spiritual development, like reciting sutras and chanting mantras. Some readers, especially those who practice kungfu or chi kung, may protest that all these sutra reciting and mantra chanting described in this chapter are not parts of the Shaolin arts.

Let them be assured that all Shaolin masters and disciples perform these sutra reciting, mantra chanting as well as prostration and Zen meditation every day at the Shaolin Monastery as an integral part of their spiritual training.

Indeed, as many readers may be surprised to find out, throughout the long history of the Shaolin Monastery most Shaolin monks spent more time reciting sutras and chanting mantras than practicing chi kung and kungfu.

28

In Search Of Shaolin Masters

(From Kungfu and Chi Kung to Zen)

*You will find that what you in your delusion called your own nature,
is actually the Buddha-nature, what you called your individual self
is actually the infinite, eternal Universal Mind!*

Kungfu for Demonstration and Fighting

Once a young man who was very keen in martial art witnessed an impressive demonstration of kungfu. He was amazed; he never thought any martial art could be so aesthetic to watch. The kungfu demonstration was strength, speed and beautiful forms in poetic motion.

"What's that?" he asked the demonstrator.

"It's Shaolin Kungfu."

"Can you teach me?"

"My Shaolin kungfu is nothing," said the demonstrators, who was around twenty years old, about the same age of the inquiring young man. "If you want to learn Shaolin Kungfu, I'll be glad to bring you to my instructor."

So they met the instructor, who was about thirty years of age. "Master," the young man asked politely, "can you please teach me Shaolin Kungfu? I saw the most beautiful martial art demonstration by your student, yet he said it was nothing."

"Although I am an instructor, I can't call myself a master. But you are quite right to say my student's art is nothing. Strictly speaking, his art is not Shaolin Kungfu; it is only flowery fists and embroidery kicks."

"I'm sorry, what's that?"

"It means a demonstrative art beautiful to look at, but useless for fighting," the instructor explained. "The basic purpose of kungfu is for fighting, not for pleasing spectators," he continued. "But if you want to learn Shaolin Kungfu, I'll recommend you to my teacher. He'll certainly do a better job."

"Why do you say he'll do a better job?" the young man was sharp to ask.

"I can only teach you fighting techniques; my teacher can teach you kungfu force. He always says that the essence of kungfu is developing force, not just learning techniques."

The instructor's teacher was about forty, yet he moved like a youth of twenty five though he was tough and massive. But the most remarkable thing about him are his hands, which are enormous and rough.

"Master," the young man asked, "how important is force training is Shaolin Kungfu?"

The Search for Kungfu Force

"Very important! There is a saying that if you only practice kungfu techniques without developing kungfu force, it will be futile even if you practice a whole life time," the master said. "Indeed, if you do not train force, you are not doing kungfu, any style of kungfu, not necessarily Shaolin."

"Can you please show me some kungfu force," the young man requested.

"I'll show you a type of force called Iron Shirt. Punch me."

The young man hesitated.

"Come on. Punch me," the master commanded. "Punch me hard, with all your might."

The young man punched the master.

"Come on, harder, harder, with all your might"

The young man punched with all his might, and almost dislocated his wrist. The master beamed with satisfaction. "Now I'll show you another kind of kungfu force, the famous Shaolin Iron Palm."

The master piled three bricks, one on top of another. With seemingly little effort he smashed the three bricks with a single stroke of his left palm.

The young man was spellbound. There was no trick, and the bricks were genuine. "I would not believe it if I have not seen it with my own eyes. The method to achieve this Iron Palm must be very difficult."

"The method is very simple," the master said casually, "it is the perseverance that is most difficult."

"I'm sorry I don't quite understand."

"You can learn the method in five minutes. Get a sandbag, and strike you palms on it for half an hour. If you do that every day for ten years, you'll be able to smash bricks as easily as I can."

"Ten years!"

"That's what I have done. But if you persevere even for a year, you would have achieved something. Yet, mine is only a rough art, as my teacher used to say. Wait till you have seen his Shaolin arts; he's a real master, whereas I'm only half a master."

"You can break bricks so easily, yet you call yourself half a master"

"My master told me I had accomplished too much in the hard force, but too little in the soft. Some people call me Iron Man, and they always do so with due respect. My master also calls me Iron Man, always with a twinkle in his eyes; he mocks me, but in good jest."

"Mock you? You mean he can break six bricks?"

"He may not be able to break one with his bare hand. Iron Palm is not his speciality. Once he told me, in his usual mocking way, that if he wanted to break ten bricks he used a hammer, not his palm'. He's a jovial person; I respect and love him."

"Can he fight?"

"Certainly! Nobody will call him a Shaolin master if he cannot fight. I'm no match for him, although he is much older than me."

"How can this old master be able to match your Iron Shirt and Iron Palm? If he strikes you, he breaks his wrist; if you strike him, you break his bones."

"Old master? He's not old, only about fifty. When he struck me the last time we sparred, I bent down with pain. Probably I shall break his bones if I strike him hard, i.e. without control. The trouble is I can't touch him; he's too agile."

"Did he strike you with a hammer?"

"No, with only one finger."

"One finger! Where did he strike you? Your eyes?"

"He will never strike me or anyone else in the eyes. Our Shaolin philosophy of compassion does not allow that. I'm sorry I can't tell you exactly where he struck me; that's our Shaolin secrets. He struck me at one of the "gates", which are actually points — points that can penetrate the Iron Shirt."

"His finger must be stronger than iron to penetrate the Iron Shirt."

"His finger that struck me is soft and gentle. Strictly speaking, it was not his finger that struck me; it was his internal force channelled through his finger."

"It must have taken you a long time to recover from that ... what'd you call that? Internal force touch?"

"We call that the art of One-Finger Zen. It took me less than five minutes to recover. My master opened the blocked vital point, channelled some of his chi, or vital energy, to stimulate my own chi to flow, and in less than five minutes I was back to normal. He's a chi kung master, and he used his powerful chi to cure me of the injury."

"What master?"

"Chi kung. The art of energy."

"The cure is so simple?"

"Simple, if you know how to release the internal energy blockage, and possess the internal force to do so. If you lack either the knowledge or the force, the patient will suffer for life, or may die after a short time."

"Simply incredible! But, may I meet your compassionate master?"

The Incredible Energy Flow

Although the compassionate master was fifty, he looked the same age as Iron Man.

"Master," the young man said, "can you show me the art of One-Finger Zen?"

"Yes. If you don't mind, I think you have some problem with your liver, and your eyesight is failing you, despite your young age."

"Fantastic! How do you know about my health problems; we have hardly met! I feel some occasional pain at my liver, though my doctors could not tell why. My vision sometimes gets blur; my eye specialist told me to get a pair of glasses, but wearing them has not helped."

"I can tell your problems from your face and your eyes. Your liver meridian is blocked, thus causing you pain occasionally. As the liver and the eyes are intimately connected, the energy blockage also causes your blur vision. Wearing glasses would not help because the site of the problem is not at the eyes, but at the liver meridian. Your doctors can't tell what's wrong with your liver because energy blockages and the meridian systems are not part of their medical paradigm."

"Can you help relieve me of these health problems?"

"I suppose so; I've helped many people with similar problems. Now you stand here. Close your eyes. That's right. Just relax. Don't think of anything."

With his eyes close, the young man did not know what the chi kung master was doing. But soon he felt as if a stream of warm water was flowing into him, then it branched into a few streams flowing all over his body. The streams of warm water moved his body! He tensed his muscles, preventing his body movement."

"Relax," he heard the master said kindly but firmly. "Don't resist your body movement. It's your own chi moving you. Follow the momentum, and enjoy the swaying movement."

He relaxed, as instructed by the Shaolin master. Soon his body started to sway, first gently, then quite noticeably. The movement was without his volition. He felt strange, but he enjoyed his swaying movement. He felt as if he was drifting in clouds.

After some time he heard the master's voice. "Now slowly get your movement to a gentle stop. Stay still for a while. Rub your palms together and use them to warm your eyes. Open your eyes. Walk about briskly."

The first impression the young man had when he opened his eyes was that the world actually appeared clearer and more beautiful. "Thank you for this wonderful experience. But can you show me your One-Finger Zen, the art that kills with a finger?'

"I've just done that. But I'm concerned with curing illness and saving lives, not injuring and killing. I've just used my One-Finger Zen to shoot some chi into you to clear the energy blockage in your liver meridian."

"It's fantastic. When I first saw Mr Iron Man smashing bricks with his palms I thought that was the most fantastic thing I have ever seen. But it was nothing compared to your One-Finger Zen shooting warm water into my body. The most fantastic, however, was my own swaying without my volition. I couldn't have believed it."

"It's a matter of perspective. It's unbelievable to you because you haven't seen or heard anything like it before, and it appears to be beyond reasons. But to me it's common; I do that everyday to dozens of patients, to help them be cured of so-called incurable diseases. But there are even more fantastic things in Shaolin."

"Oh yes, why did I move without my own volition? It was also a very pleasant experience."

"That's because your chi moved your body, and your self-manifested movement helped to clear energy blockage."

The Shaolin master then taught the young man some simple chi kung exercises. "If you practice these exercises for about fifteen minutes daily, your liver and eye problems should disappear in a week. Is that fantastic?"

"I'll always remember your compassion."

"Compassion is one part of the Shaolin teaching; the other part is wisdom," the master explained.

"Wisdom? Can you tell me more about wisdom?"

"For that you should see my master, the old Zen monk up the mountain."

The Search for Compassion

The young man climbed the mountain, with some difficulties, and finally found the old Zen monk in his little temple. He was indeed old, with long white beard, yet he had a child's complexion. The most noticeable feature about him, however, was the look of joy and serenity on his face.

The Zen monk was prostrating before an altar. This prostration was a big surprise to the young man, who thought to himself, "Here is the teacher of the most fantastic Shaolin master I have ever seen or imagined, yet he prostrated meekly like a child."

The old monk did not raise to his feet after his prostration, but knelt before the altar and started to chant. The young man could not understand the chanting but he felt an inexplicable yet unmistakable feeling of peace in the atmosphere. It was funny, he thought, but he even felt they were not alone in the temple! Afraid that he might disturb the great master in his chanting, the young man stood silently at the doorway, awed by the mystical surrounding which seemed to be charged with energy.

At last the chanting was over. The old Shaolin master prostrated thrice, after which he knelt again and recited what sounded like a short poem. The young man heard something like 'all beings be peaceful and happy'. Again the master prostrated thrice. Then he walked towards a nearby table, looked towards the young man and said, "Please come in and share some tea with me."

"How did he know I am here?" the young man thought to himself. "Perhaps he heard my footsteps; kungfu masters are very sharp."

"I sensed your energy," the monk said, as the young man walked nervously towards the master. "Please be seated and feel at home."

As the young man sat down, the fragrance of hot tea drifted into his nostrils. It must be very good tea, he thought.

"It's the best tea I have," the monk said. "I'm sorry to have kept you waiting, but I wish to complete my evening service."

"Your Venerable," the young man asked, "is that a Buddha on the altar?"

"She was a Buddha before, many aeons before our present Sakyamuni Buddha, but she comes back as a Bodhisattva. She is Guan Yin Pu Sa, the Bodhisattva of Great Compassion."

"Why don't you, your Venerable, have a Buddha at your altar?"

"The Buddha is everywhere; He is in the sky, in the tree, in you and me and in every minute dharma."

"What were you chanting just now?"

"The Amitabha Sutra, the sutra in which our Buddha, Sakyamuni Buddha, teaches sentient beings how to go to heaven."

"Why did the Bodhisattva need to listen to the sutra?"

"The chanting of the Amitabha Sutra just now was meant for other beings like ghosts and nature spirits. I chanted it in front of the Bodhisattva so that her divine presence can be an unfailing source of inspiration for all of us."

"Ghosts and spirits? Do you really believe in them?"

"When I was young I used to laugh at people who believed in ghosts and spirits, but now I have sufficient understanding and experience to justify my belief. But you must not believe in them just because some people mentioned their existence, otherwise your belief would degrade into superstition. You must always base your beliefs on understanding and experience."

"Are there any ghosts and nature spirits around here?"

"Not now, they have dispersed. But just now, many gathered around to listen to my chanting of the Amitabha Sutra."

The young man felt a shiver down his spine.

"You need not be afraid at all," the monk said assuredly. "They are quite harmless. In fact they are more afraid of humans, than humans of them. Our attitude towards them should be one of care and compassion. Because of our good karma, we have a very rare opportunity to be humans; we have many benefits which ghosts and nature spirits do not have.

For example, we have the tremendous blessing to understand cosmic reality from the Buddha's teaching, whereas they are generally lost. Reciting sutras so that they too can benefit from the Buddha's teaching is therefore a great service to do. And you do not have to worry about the intricacies of human language: these ghosts and spirits can pick out the meaning from your mental vibration."

The young man was touched. It dawned on him forcefully that the Shaolin teaching of compassion involved not only humans but also other beings, and that Shaolin masters did not merely talk about compassion but actually practiced it, like the chi kung master for humans, and this kindly old monk for ghosts and spirits.

The Search for Wisdom

The old Shaolin monk took out a scroll from his pocket and rolled it open on the table. It contained a poem written with a Chinese brush in bold Chinese characters. The young man did not pay attention to the meaning of the poem because he was attracted by the liveliness of the Chinese characters; they seemed to come alive, vibrating with energy.

"What beautiful, powerful calligraphy!" the young man thought to himself.

"I'm glad you like the calligraphy, but you should pay attention to the meaning," the Shaolin monk said kindly. "The calligraphy is mine, but the meaning, many times more beautiful than the calligraphy, is from the Venerable Bodhidharma, the First Patriarch of Shaolin." The young man read the poem aloud:

I had my mind when deluded in former days
Now I have no mind in ultimate reality
Without mind my mind still serves my ways
Using it in suchness as tranquil eternity

"I can't make any sense at all from this poem," the young man confessed.

"Not many can understand its profound wisdom. You have to find it yourself later on, not so much from intellectual study, but from Zen meditation. Nevertheless, the following few hints will be a helpful start. Once you have your mind, thoughts arise, which will tie you down to the phenomenal world. Having no mind means being free from the phenomenal dimension and actualizing ultimate reality. No mind is the same as All Mind, or Suchness, which is tranquil eternity. Although a Zen master has attained no mind, he still returns to society to help others, and therefore he also operates in the phenomenal world."

The young man was still puzzled.

"Keep this scroll as a present from me. You have come to ask for wisdom. This is my answer."

This was beyond the young man's expectation. Besides murmuring "thank you" a few times, more to himself than to the monk, he did know what else to say. Then, an unmanning feeling pervaded over him: the old Shaolin monk had been reading his mind!

"I don't mean to eavesdrop into your thoughts, or anybody's thoughts, but I can see your mind as easily as I see your face. In Buddhism, special extraordinary powers are classified into six groups, and telepathy is one of them."

"How did you develop your power of telepathy?"

"I didn't aim for it particularly; it came naturally with my Zen meditation? Different people may develop different powers, but these powers, though useful, are not essential for spiritual attainment."

"Are such powers a form of wisdom?"

"Of course not. Wisdom is necessary for spiritual development, these powers are not. Without wisdom, you cannot achieve nirvana."

Almost without knowing what he was doing, the young man intuitively knelt down before the Shaolin master, prostrated three times, then said.

"Your Venerable. I am dull and lost, and I have humbly come to seek guidance. Please have compassion on me; show me the way so that I too may have a chance to see the Buddha's wisdom."

"First of all you must know that the wisdom we are talking about is not the same as the ordinary wisdom people have in mind. That's why we call it higher wisdom or transcendental wisdom. It is *prajna* in Sanskrit, transcribed as *ban ruo* in Chinese. Ordinary wisdom, which includes all the knowledge gathered by scholars and scientists, is phenomenal wisdom, i.e. wisdom pertaining to the phenomenal world, which people because of ignorance, mistake as reality. Transcendental wisdom, on the other hand, is about ultimate reality."

"Your Venerable, what is the phenomenal world?"

The Search for Enlightenment

"The phenomenal word is the world we experience in our ordinary consciousness," the old master explained. "Phenomena include things and people we see that we think are ultimately real, but are actually a creation of the mind."

"Your Venerable, as I have said earlier, I am dull minded. I thought the chair I'm sitting on is real. You, your venerable, are certainly real."

"All phenomena, including the chair, you and me, are relative and illusory, not ultimately real!"

"What does that actually mean?" the young man asked in bewilderment.

"They are "real" relative to us. That is a chair to you, a chair to me, and to other people. But to an ant, it is not a chair; it may be a small hill. A sentient being from another realm of existence, such as a ghost, may not see you or me, just as people normally do not see ghosts. Now, this space in front is empty to us, but to devas or gods it is a solid mountain. They build their palaces in our air, which to them is a mountain. We are literally living inside their mountains just as hell beings are living inside our earth."

"I'm afraid I still cannot follow."

"It's not easy to understand higher wisdom. It needs a lot of Zen meditation before *prajna* manifests. But let me give you a simpler example. Look at those fish over there in the pond. To us they swim in the water. But to the fish the water is non-existence; they do not see water and they move about in it without obstruction. What happens if they get out of water into air? That of course is our way of looking at the phenomenon. To the fish the same phenomenon appears differently; to them it is getting into some solid material in which they couldn't move, something like a human getting into a rock."

"I have never perceived a fish in this way before! Come to think of it, a fish, with only its fish-intelligence, can never understand how we can move about freely in their `rock'. But I still cannot understand why we are not real. If I pinch myself, the pain assures me that I am real."

"That's true in our ordinary consciousness. But if you are awakened, what we call *wu* in Zen, you will find that your body which you think is solid and differentiates you from the so-call external surroundings, is actually not solid, and there is really no boundary between you and the so-called external surroundings! You will find that you are a collection of *dharmas*, or elementary particles, with a lot of `empty space' in between. These *dharmas* are never static: at one instance they are *dharmas*, at another instance they become *kriya*, or energy. There is also no line whereby you can say this is my "inside", and that is my "out-side". There is simply nowhere you can tell where your `body' begins or ends."

The Shaolin monk paused for a while to let the young man reflect on this profound wisdom.

"With due respect to you, Your Venerable, and to be honest myself, I must say I find it hard to accept that this is true."

"In Buddhism we never ask you to accept anything on faith alone. Even the Buddha did not do that. Out of great compassion, the Buddha shared his greatest achievement with others, but he never insisted that others must follow him, nor belittled other religions even if they differed substantially. He only showed the way, the way he himself had travelled, and he advised his followers to assess his teaching to the best of their understanding and experience."

The young man remained silent, gratefully silent.

"But what I have just told you is still not the highest attainment. In our Shaolin arts, a Zen awakening or *wu* is a confirmation and inspiration for even greater attainment to come. The highest attainment, the supreme aim of Zen, the apex of Shaolin training, is to attain *anuttara-samyak-sambodhi*, or the supreme perfect wisdom, where even *dharmas* and *kriya* disappear, and ultimate reality which is tranquil and undifferentiated is experienced. You will find that what you in your delusion called your own nature, is actually the Buddha-nature, what you called your individual self is actually the infinite, eternal Universal Mind! This is enlightenment or *jie*, the highest accomplishment any being anywhere can ever attained."

USEFUL ADDRESSES

MALAYSIA

Grandmaster Wong Kiew Kit,
81 Taman Intan B/5,
08000 Sungai Petani, Kedah, Malaysia.
Tel: (60-4) 422-2353
Fax: (60-4) 422-7812
E-mail: shaolin@pd.jaring.my
URL:http://shaolin-wahnam.tripod.com/
    index.html
    http://www.shaolin-wahnam.org

Master Ng Kowi Beng,
20, Lorong Murni 33,
Taman Desa Murni Sungai Dua,
13800 Butterworth, Pulau Pinang,
Malaysia.
Tel: (60-4) 356-3069
Fax: (60-4) 484-4617
E-mail : kowibeng@tm.net.my

Master Cheong Huat Seng,
22 Taman Mutiara,
08000 Sungai Petani, Kedah, Malaysia.
Tel: (60-4) 421-0634

Master Goh Kok Hin,
86 Jalan Sungai Emas,
08500 Kota Kuala Muda, Kedah,
Malaysia.
Tel: (60-4) 437-4301

Master Chim Chin Sin,
42 Taman Permai,
08100 Bedong, Kedah, Malaysia.
Tel: (60-4) 458-1729
Mobile Phone: (60) 012-552-6297

Master Morgan A/L Govindasamy,
3086 Lorong 21, Taman Ria,
08000 Sungai Petani, Kedah, Malaysia.
Tel: (60-4) 441-4198

Master Yong Peng Wah,
Shaolin Wahnam Chi Kung and Kung Fu,
181 Taman Kota Jaya,
34700 Simpang, Taiping, Perak, Malaysia.
Tel: (60-5) 847-1431

AUSTRALIA

Mr. George Howes,
33 Old Ferry Rd, Banora Point,
NSW 2486, Australia.
Tel: 00-61-7-55245751

AUSTRIA

Sylvester Lohninger,
Maitreya Institute,
Blättertal 9,
A-2770 Gutenstein.
Telephone: 0043-2634-7417
Fax: 0043-2634-74174
E-mail: sequoyah@nextra

BELGIUM

Dr. Daniel Widjaja,
Steenweg op Brussel 125,
1780 Wemmel, Belgium.
Tel: 00-32-2-4602977
Mobile Phone: 00-32-474-984739
Fax: 00-32-2-4602987
E-mails: dan widjaja@hotmail.com,
daniel.widjaja@worldonline.be

CANADA

Dr. Kay Lie,
E-mail: kayl@interlog.com

Mrs. Jean Lie,
Toronto, Ontario.
Telephone/Fax: (416) 979-0238
E-mail: kayl@interlog.com

Miss Emiko Hsuen,
67 Churchill Avenue, North York,
Ontario, M2N 1Y8, Canada.
Tel: 1-416-250-1812
Fax: 1 - 416- 221-5264
E-mail: emiko@attcanada.ca

Mr Neil Burden,
Vancouver, British Columbia.
Telephone/Fax: (250) 247-9968
E-mail: cosmicdragon108@hotmail.com

ENGLAND

Mr. Christopher Roy Leigh Jones,
9a Beach Street, Lytham, Lancashire,
FY8 5NS, United Kingdom.
Tel: 0044-1253-736278
E-mail: barbara.rawlinson@virgin.net

Mr. Dan Hartwright,
Rumpus Cottage, Church Place,
Pulborough, West Sussex RH20 1AF, UK.
Tel: 0044-7816-111007
E-mail: dhartWright@hotmail.com

GERMANY

Grandmaster Kai Uwe Jettkandt,
Ostendstr. 79,
60314 Frankfurt, Germany.
Tel: 49-69-90431678
E-mail: Kaijet@t-online.de

HOLLAND

Dr. Oetti Kwee Liang Hoo,
Tel: 31-10-5316416

IRELAND

Miss Joan Brown,
Mullin, Scatazlin, Castleisland, County,
Kerry, Ireland.
Tel: 353-66-7147545
Mobile Phone: 353-87-6668374
E-mail: djbrowne@gofree.indigo.ie

ITALY

Master Roberto Lamberti,
Hotel Punta Est Via Aurelia, 1
17024 Finale Ligure (SV), Italy.
Tel: ++39019600611
Mobile Phone: ++393393580663
E-mails: robertolamberti@libero.it

Master Attilio Podestà,
Via Aurelia 1,
17024 Finale Ligure (Savona), Italy.
Tel/Fax: +39 019 600 611
E-mail: attiliopodesta@libero.it
OR
Hotel Punta Est Via Aurelia 1,
17024 Finale Ligure (Savona), Italy.
E-mail: info@puntaest.com
Web-site: www.puntaest.com

Mr. Riccardo Puleo,
via don Gnocchi, 28,
20148 Milano, Italy.
Tel: 0039-02-4078250
E-mail: rpuleo@efficient-finance.com

LITHUANIA

Mr. Arunas Krisiunas,
Sauletekio al.53-9,
2040 Vilnius, Lithuania.
Tel: +3702-700-237
Mobile Phone: +370-9887353
E-mail: induva@iti.lt

PANAMA

Mr. Raúl A. López R.,
16, "B" st., Panama City,
Republic of Panama.
OR
P.O. Box 1433, Panama 9A-1433.
Tel: (507) 618-1836
E-mail: raullopez@cwpanama.net
taiko@hotmail.com

PORTUGAL

Dr Riccardo Salvatore,
Tel: 351-218478713

SCOTLAND

Mr. Darryl Collett,
c/o 19A London Street, Edinburgh,
EH3 6LY, United Kingdom.
Mobile phone: 0790-454-7538
E-mail: CollDod@aol.com

SPAIN

Master Laura Fernández,
C/ Madre Antonia de París, 2 esc. izq. 4° A,
Madrid - 28027 – Spain.
Tel: 34-91-6386270

Javier Galve,
Tai Chi Chuan and Chi Kung Instructor
of the Shaolin Wahnam Institute
C/Guadarrama 3-2°A-28011-Madrid,
Spain.
Phone: 34-91-4640578
Mobile Phone: 34-656669790
E-mail: shaolin@inicia.es

Master Adalia Iglesias,
calle Cometa, n° 3, atico,
08002 Barcelona, Spain.
Tel: 0034-93-3104956
E-mail: adalia@xenoid.com

Master Román Garcia Lampaya,
71, Av. Antonio Machad,
Santa Cruz del Valle,
05411 Avila, Spain.
Tel: 34-920-386717, 34-915-360702
Mobile Phone : 34-656-612608
E-mail: romangarcia@wanadoo.es

Master José Díaz Marqués,
C/. del Teatro, 13
41927 Mairena del Aljarafe / Sevilla,
Spain.
Tel: + 34-954-183-917
Mobile Phone: 34-656-756214
Fax: + 34-955-609-354
E-mail: transpersonal@infotelmultimedia.es

Dr. Inaki Rivero Urdiain,
Aguirre Miramon, 6 – 4° dch.,
20002 San Sebastian, Spain.
Tel: + 34-943-360213
Mobile Phone: 34-656-756214
E-mail: psiconet@euskalnet.net
Web-site: www.euskalnet.net/psicosalud

Master Douglas Wiesenthal,
C/ Almirante Cadarso 26, P-14
46005 Valencia, Spain
Tel/Fax: +34 96-320-8433
E-mail: dwiesenthal@yahoo.com

Master Trini
Ms Trinidad Parreno,
E-mail: trinipar@wanadoo.es

SOUTH AFRICA

Grandmaster Leslie James Reed,
312 Garensville, 285 Beach Road, Sea
Point,
Cape Town, 8000 South Africa.
Tel/Fax: 0927-21-4391373
E-mail: itswasa@mweb.co.za

SWITZERLAND

Mr. Andrew Barnett,
Bildweg 34, 7250 Klosters,
Switzerland.
Tel/Fax: +41-81-422-5235
Mobile Phone: +41-79-610-3781
E-mail: andrew.barnett@bluewin.ch

USA

Mr. Anthony Korahais,
546 W147th Street, Apt. 2-DR,
New York, New York, 10031, USA.
Tel: 917-270-4310, 212-854-0201
E-mails: anthony@korahais.com,
anthony@arch.columbia.edu

Mr. Eugene Siterman,
299 Carroll St., Brooklyn,
New York,11231.
Tel: 718-8555785
E-mail: qipaco@hotmail.com

INDEX